Key Concepts 1

Reading and Writing Across the Disciplines

First Edition

Barbara Smith-Palinkas

Kelly Croghan-Ford

HEINLE
CENGAGE Learning

Australia • Brazil • Japan • Korea • Mexico • Singapore • Spain • United Kingdom • United States

HEINLE
CENGAGE Learning

Key Concepts 1
Reading and Writing Across the Disciplines
Barbara Smith-Palinkas, Kelly Croghan-Ford

Publisher: Sherrise Roehr

Acquisitions Editor: Tom Jefferies

Associate Development Editor: Sarah Sandoski

Director of Global Marketing: Ian Martin

Director of US Marketing: Jim McDonough

Marketing Manager: Caitlin Driscoll

Senior Content Project Manager:
  Dawn Marie Elwell

Production Intern: Hannah Flaherty

Senior Print Buyer: Betsy Donaghey

Cover Designer: Lisa Mezikofsky

Compositor: Pre-PressPMG

Cover photo: © Shutterstock/Yurchyks

For product information and technology assistance, contact us at
Cengage Learning Customer & Sales Support, 1-800-354-9706
For permission to use material from this text or product,
submit all requests online at **cengage.com/permissions**
Further permissions questions can be emailed to
permissionrequest@cengage.com

Library of Congress Control Number: 2008937896

ISBN-13: 978-0-618-47461-5

ISBN-10: 0-618-47461-7

Heinle
25 Thomson Place
Boston, MA 02210
USA

Cengage Learning is a leading provider of customized learning solutions with office locations around the globe, including Singapore, the United Kingdom, Australia, Mexico, Brazil, and Japan. Locate your local office at:
international.cengage.com/region

Cengage Learning products are represented in Canada by Nelson Education, Ltd.

Visit Heinle online at **elt.heinle.com**

Visit our corporate website at **www.cengage.com**

Printed in Canada
1 2 3 4 5 6 7 8 9   13 12 11 10 09 08

Acknowledgments

We would like to express our gratitude to Tom Jefferies, Acquisitions Editor, and Sarah Sandoski, Associate Development Editor, at Cengage Learning, who provided support and guidance to us throughout the entire process.

We also wish to convey our thanks to Susan Maguire and Kathy Sands-Boehmer, from Houghton Mifflin, with whom we first worked to develop *Key Concepts*. It was their initial encouragement that kept this project alive.

We want to express our appreciation to our ESL colleagues who shared their expertise and ideas, and we are especially indebted to our colleague and good friend, Donna M. Tortorella, for her valuable and insightful comments on the book. Her e-mail responses were both thought-provoking and lightning quick.

We are grateful to the many students in the English for Academic Purposes Program at Hillsborough Community College, Ybor Campus, who provided us with "real-time" feedback as we developed and tested the contents of the book.

In addition, we thank the following reviewers of the entire *Key Concepts* series, whose comments and suggestions helped bring the books to their final form:

Carol Auerbach
Northern Virginia Community College

Anne Bachman
Clackamas Community College

Michael Berman
Montgomery College

Keri Bjorklund
Laramie Community College

Mary B. Caldwell
El Paso Community College

Richard Cervin
Sacramento City College

Gwendolyn Charvis
North Harris College

Maggie Discont
West Hills College

Cynthia Dunham-Gonzalez
Seminole Community College

Mark Ende
Onondaga Community College

Kathy Flynn
Glendale Community College

Beverly Gandall
Santa Ana College

Elizabeth Gilfillan
Houston Community College

Margo Harder
South Seattle Community College

Carolyn Ho
Cy Fair College

Michael Khirallah
Oakland Community College

Carole Marquis
Santa Fe Community College

Michelle Naumann

Esther Robbins
Prince George's Community College

Dan Smolens
Roxbury Community College

Shirley Terrell
Collin County Community College

Kent Trickel
Westchester Community College

Barbara Smith-Palinkas
Kelly Croghan-Ford

Contents

Key Concepts 1: Reading and Writing Across the Disciplines

Contents

CHAPTER 6 ● **From the Social Sciences: Philosophy   159**

Key Concepts 1 Skills Overview

In each Reading section, students practice surveying, predicting, summarizing, and the Academic Word List. In each Writing section, students revise, edit, and proofread their work.

	Reading	Writing	
Chapter	**Skills and Strategies**	**Skills and Strategies**	**The Process**

1	• stated/implied main idea: identify and locate
	• identifying text structure: definition
	• using context to guess meaning: definition
		• the grammar of gerunds
		• simple sentences: complete and incomplete sentences; compound subjects/verbs
		• fragments
			• structure of a paragraph
			• overview of process:
			  • brainstorming
			  • narrowing the topic and details
			  • choosing text structure
			  • topic sentence
			  • concluding sentence
			  • outlining
			• paragraph of definition

2	• types of supporting details • identifying text structure: classification and division • using context to guess meaning: examples	• the grammar of count and non-count nouns • compound sentences: using coordinating conjunctions	• paragraph format • major and minor support sentences • details from graphics • paragraph of classification or division
3	• making inferences and drawing conclusions: examples, facts/statistics, cause/effect, specific details or statements • identifying text structure: problem/solution • using context to guess meaning: inference	• the grammar of articles • compound sentences: using conjunctive adverbs and semicolons • punctuation: avoiding run-on sentences and comma splices	• conclusions • paragraph of problem/solution
4	• making inferences and drawing conclusions: assumptions, opinion, tone and bias • identifying text structure: comparison/contrast • using context to guess meaning: synonyms and antonyms	• the grammar of adjective clauses • complex sentences: using relative pronouns and adverbs	• identifying purpose • choosing tone • paragraph of comparison/contrast
5	• tools for interactive reading: highlighting, underlining, commenting • identifying text structure: process • using context to guess meaning: surrounding sentences	• the grammar of adverb clauses • complex sentences: using subordinating conjunctions	• unity and coherence • paragraph of process
6	• tools for interactive reading: paraphrasing, summarizing, outlining • identifying text structure: summary • using context to guess meaning: review of strategies	• the grammar of noun clauses • sentence review: simple, compound, complex sentences • avoiding plagiarism: using quotations and citing sources	• paragraph of summary

Introduction

The *Key Concepts* series takes a content-based approach to teaching students the academic skills they need to participate successfully in college or university classes in English. The series is designed for mid- and high-intermediate level students, and each level includes two books: *Listening, Note Taking, and Speaking* and *Reading and Writing.*

The books in the series may be used separately, each offering an integrated-skills approach to listening, note taking, and speaking or to reading and writing. Because the corresponding chapters at each level address the same academic disciplines, however, using both books in the level results in a fully-integrated four-skills approach to teaching academic English.

Key Concepts 1: Reading and Writing Across the Disciplines is the first of a two-volume series which focuses on the academic skills of reading and writing. The subject matter of the readings, along with the writing focus, centers on one of the following academic disciplines: college success, social science, business, history, biological science, and humanities. As students encounter recurring concepts and vocabulary, they build on their knowledge of academic subjects and use of academic language in English.

The chapters of *Key Concepts 1* include the topics from the following college disciplines:

- Social Sciences: Psychology

- Business: International Trade and Marketing

- Social Sciences: American Government

- Biological Sciences: Biology

- Social Sciences: Philosophy

In addition to presenting discipline-specific vocabulary from the readings, identified as Key Concept Words, each chapter of *Key Concepts* also introduces students to and offers practice with twenty vocabulary items from Averil Coxhead's Academic Word List. These words are the most frequently used vocabulary in college texts, and the words practiced in *Key Concepts* are taken directly from the chapter readings. In addition, vocabulary exercises in *Key Concepts* build the student's vocabulary by focusing on word forms and help the student discern differences in meaning by focusing on context and usage. A list of Glossed Words follows the concept words and assists students with comprehension of the material by defining words that are likely to be unfamiliar to them.

The content-based approach of *Key Concepts* promotes the integration of reading and writing skills, and each chapter helps students make the connection by drawing and/or reinforcing parallels between the two. The readings in each chapter mirror and serve as models for the methods of development students will use in their writing assignments and include, in *Key Concepts 1*, definition, classification/division, problem/solution, comparison/contrast, process, and summary.

Key Concepts simulates the university experience by offering intermediate-level students reading and writing activities with similar academic content. The experience of interacting with academic texts can provide students a better sense of what to expect in a college or university course. *Key Concepts* offers students this experience.

Text Organization

The first half of each chapter is devoted to reading skills. Students are introduced to the reading skills and strategies of surveying, predicting, and summarizing through presentation of an academic passage of approximately 500 words. Following the reading, students practice using words from the Academic Word List which are contained in the reading. Each chapter addresses identifying text structure and guessing meaning from context, as well. Each chapter also focuses on one of the following reading skills: main idea, details, inferences and conclusions, highlighting/underlining, and outlining/summarizing as study tools. Students are then given a second reading of approximately 600 words and are asked to practice reading skills "on their own."

The second half of each chapter is devoted to writing skills. The writing section opens with a short grammar focus on a structure common to the academic readings in the chapter. This is followed by a section on sentence essentials, focusing on sentence types (simple, compound, and complex). Chapter 1 presents an overview of the writing process, and each subsequent chapter mirrors the skills addressed in the reading section. Students are guided through the writing skills of brainstorming, narrowing the topic, writing a topic sentence, supplying details, writing a conclusion, and outlining before they are asked to write a paragraph "on their own." The reading passages in each chapter serve as models for the paragraph types students are asked to write and include definition, classification/division, problem/solution, comparison/contrast, process, and summary.

The appendices include a comprehensive list of words from the readings which appear on the Academic Word List; samples of different types of brainstorming; lists of conjunctions, transition words, and key words for specific text structures; additional writing topics; a glossary of reading and writing terms; and samples of MLA citations.

Contents of a Chapter

Reading 1: Skills and Strategies

Students are introduced to the first reading via two activities: Get Ready to Read, which activates their background knowledge about the topic, and Surveying and Predicting. After the reading, students do a Summarizing activity and Comprehension activity and are then introduced to ten words from the reading which appear on the Academic Word List. Students practice the vocabulary through different exercise types. Next, a reading strategy is introduced and practiced. The reading strategy is followed by an introduction to a specific text structure and the key words associated with it. Students then practice using the key words.

Reading 2: On Your Own

As with the first reading, students are introduced to the second reading via the Get Ready to Read and Surveying and Predicting activities. After the reading, they complete a Summarizing activity and Comprehension activity, followed by the introduction to a new set of ten words from the reading which appear on the Academic Word List. Students again practice the vocabulary through different exercise types. This is followed by a vocabulary exercise to practice guessing meaning from context.

Writing 1A: Skills and Strategies

Students are presented with a short introduction to the grammar of a structure found in the readings. After practice recognizing and/or using the structure, students work on Sentence Essentials. This section focuses on specific sentence types, sentence errors, or sentence punctuation.

Writing 1B: The Process

Students are introduced to the writing process via Get Ready to Write, which introduces an overview of the steps in the writing process in Chapter 1 and focuses on a specific writing skill in subsequent chapters. After practice with the specific skill, students are presented with How Did They Do That?, an interactive activity which requires them to follow the steps the writer took to develop a paragraph. The paragraph models the specific text structure introduced in the readings and practiced in the Reading 1: Skills and Strategies section in the first half of the chapter.

Writing 2: On Your Own

In this section, students are asked to write a paragraph using the text structure previously presented in Writing 1B: The Process. After writing their paragraphs, students use the checklist in the Revising activity to make changes and improvements in their writing. In the final activity, students use the Editing and Proofreading checklist to find and correct grammar, spelling, punctuation, or format errors in their writing.

Online Resources

Additional Web Activities for Students

The *Key Concepts* series offers additional materials for students and teachers that they can access online by logging into *http://elt.heinle.com/keyconceptsrw*.

Instructor Manual and Answer Keys

Students using the *Key Concepts* series can practice the Academic Word List vocabulary with flashcards. Web Quizzes test the students' comprehension of Readings 1 and 2, as well as their mastery of the writing skills addressed in that chapter.

Assessment

Answer Keys are available for every activity in the *Key Concepts* series. Teachers will also find chapter notes written by the authors that include brief guides to the activities in addition to summaries of each reading.

1 The Student Experience: Success in College

Most people agree that getting a college education pays off both literally and figuratively. For example, people with college degrees typically earn more than people without them. Getting a college degree often increases a person's feelings of self-satisfaction and self-confidence. Whether you are enrolled in a single class or a complete program, attending community college or university courses requires you to use the four basic skills of listening, speaking, reading, and writing. To succeed in school, you will also need good study skills and good time-management skills.

Look at the picture of the famous sculpture, *The Thinker,* by the French sculptor Rodin. Discuss the following questions with a partner or in a small group.

- What is your definition of *thinking*?
- Is all thinking the same? Why or why not?

This chapter will help you understand some **key concepts** for success in college, such as:

- using critical thinking skills
- developing critical reading skills
- recognizing patterns used in writing

Get Ready to Read

Agree or Disagree

Read the following statements and decide whether you agree or disagree. Circle your choice. Discuss your answers and your reasons for them with a partner.

1. Thinking is a learned mental process.	AGREE	DISAGREE
2. Daydreaming is a form of thinking.	AGREE	DISAGREE
3. People who know a lot of facts are good thinkers.	AGREE	DISAGREE
4. Good thinkers are highly educated people.	AGREE	DISAGREE
5. People must be good thinkers to be good problem-solvers.	AGREE	DISAGREE

Surveying and Predicting

Survey: to look at the parts of a text to get an idea of the topic

Predict: to guess what information will be presented about a topic

Reading is an active, not passive, process. In fact, good readers interact with the text the entire time they are reading. Before they begin reading, good readers survey the text. Surveying means looking at parts of the text in order to get an idea of the topic or subject of the text. Surveying involves a number of steps. After they survey a passage, good readers try to predict what information they are going to receive. They continue to predict while they read the passage. They ask themselves questions about the reading and, as they read, they look for the answers to their questions.

Survey and Predict

A. Follow the steps below to survey Reading 1 on pages 3-4.

1. Read the title. Write it here. _____

2. Read the first paragraph. Write one or two words which tell the topic or what the paragraph is about. _____

3. Read the headings, the titles of the sections in the reading. Write them here.

   _____

4. Look for any graphic or visual aids in the reading. Graphic aids are charts, graphs, pictures, maps, diagrams, etc. Describe them here. _____

   _____

5. Look for key (important) terms related to the topic. They are usually in bold. List them here. _____

   _____

6. Read the last paragraph. It is a summary of the entire reading.

B. Share your survey answers with a partner and discuss what you think the reading will be about. Then circle the number of the statement below which matches your prediction.

1. The passage will define thinking and explain when you use different kinds of thinking.

2. The passage will define thinking and explain why it is important to think critically.

3. The passage will define thinking and explain how your brain thinks.

C. Now read the passage to see if your prediction is correct. Try to read as quickly as you can. Do not stop to look up words in your dictionary.

Reading 1

What Is Thinking?

Thinking is a purposeful mental activity. You control it, not vice versa. Generally, thinking is a **conscious** activity. This means you are awake and aware of your thinking. However, the **unconscious** mind can continue working on a problem, for example, while you sleep.

Thinking is sometimes regarded as two harmonious processes. One process is the production of ideas. This is **creative thinking**. When you think creatively, your focus is wide, and you look at many possibilities. The other process is the evaluation of ideas. This is **critical thinking**. When you think critically, your focus is narrow. You sort out the ideas you have generated and identify the most logical ones.

For example, imagine you are going to the airport. You picture yourself ready for a cruise in the Caribbean. Your pockets are stuffed with money. Is this mental process thinking? Now imagine you are discussing politics with friends. When they ask which candidate you support, you say you will vote for the one who comes from your state. Is your choice based on thinking? Imagining yourself on a Caribbean cruise is not thinking. It is daydreaming. On the other hand, the discussion of politics may or may not involve thinking. Your support for a candidate may be based on issues you have evaluated. It may also just be based on something you have heard someone else say.

> Creative Thinking
> is
> producing ideas.
>
> Evaluating ideas
> is
> Critical Thinking.

What is involved

Both creative and critical thinking are natural activities for human beings. However, it is difficult to do them well without training and diligent practice. In fact, shallow and illogical thinking is very common. Much of our education was based on the idea that thinking can't be taught or that some subjects teach thinking automatically. Modern research proves that both ideas are wrong. Thinking can be taught to all students. No course automatically teaches thinking. Students can get regular practice in producing and evaluating ideas when teachers make thinking skills a specific goal. Around the world, authorities are encouraging schools to make critical thinking a priority.

Importance of thinking critically

Good thinking skills are necessary for academic success. Professors do not want students simply to repeat information they have learned in lectures and readings. Successful students will analyze facts and opinions. They will synthesize information from different resources, such as books and journals, and will apply their knowledge to assignments. Students who have poor thinking skills will have difficulty making conclusions after conducting research. It will also be difficult for them to create ideas or solve problems.

Success in work also depends on thinking skills. People who want to succeed must be able to apply what they know to the challenges of their jobs. Employers are looking for problem solvers and decision makers, not walking encyclopedias.

Critical thinking is appropriate whenever someone makes a statement or claim that is open to question. Such statements are made daily in every field of study and work. Using creative thinking to produce ideas and critical thinking to evaluate them will allow you to find the most logical solutions to problems.

Key Concept Words

conscious – (adj.) having an awareness of one's environment, sensations, and thoughts

creative thinking – (n.) the production of ideas

critical thinking – (n.) the evaluation of ideas

unconscious – (adj.) lack of awareness of one's environment, sensations, and thoughts

Glossed Words

claim – (n.) a statement of something as fact; **daydreaming** – (n.) imagining things one wishes would come true; **diligent** – (adj.) marked by dedicated and persistent effort; **harmonious** – (adj.) having elements that are pleasingly or appropriately combined

Summarizing

Summarize: to briefly state the main points of a text

Good readers summarize what they are reading while they are reading. They make notes of important ideas in the margin of the text to help them remember the key points. At the end of each section they repeat to themselves, in their own words, what they have just read. They connect the ideas in each section so that when they have finished reading, they are able to summarize what the entire text or passage was about. Summarizing takes practice, but it is a skill that will help you review for exams quickly and efficiently.

 ACTIVITY **3**

Share What You Read

A. Use two or three sentences to tell your partner what you thought the reading was about. Then listen to your partner's sentences. Next, read the following statements and circle the number of the statement that best summarizes the reading.

1. Critical thinking is important if you want to succeed in your job.

2. Critical thinking is a learned skill that helps people perform better in their jobs, education, and daily lives.

3. Much unpleasantness and disappointment can be avoided by testing ideas for reasonableness before accepting them.

B. Did you choose statement 2? If you chose a different answer, go back and review your survey answers. Try to determine why they lead to summary statement 2.

ACTIVITY 4   ***Check Your Comprehension***

Read each statement below and circle the letter of the word or phrase that best completes it. Then share your answers with a partner. The first one has been done for you.

1. Thinking is a(n) _____ mental activity.
   a. natural
   b. unconscious
   c. purposeful *(circled)*

2. Evaluation of ideas is an important part of _____.
   a. critical thinking
   b. creative thinking
   c. ruminating

3. Research has proven that _____.
   a. thinking cannot be taught
   b. some subjects teach thinking automatically
   c. thinking can be taught with any subject

4. Employers are looking for people who _____.
   a. have a large body of information in their field
   b. can apply their knowledge to challenges
   c. are walking encyclopedias

5. _____ is not an example of thinking.
   a. Daydreaming about a vacation
   b. Synthesizing information from a lecture
   c. Finding a logical solution to a problem

6. Creative thinking requires _____.
   a. narrowing your focus
   b. evaluating your ideas
   c. looking at many possibilities

Academic Word List

In *Key Concepts,* you will practice many vocabulary words from the Academic Word List, which contains the most frequently used vocabulary words found in college-level textbooks. You may already be familiar with some of the vocabulary words.

ACTIVITY 5   ***Scan and Define***

> **Scan:** to find specific information in a text by reading quickly

A. Look at the ten words listed below. Scan Reading 1 and underline the words from the list. Write the definitions for the words you know. Do not use a dictionary. The first one has been done for you.

1. appropriate _correct or proper for a situation_
2. authority _____
3. aware _____
4. critical _____
5. focus (n.) _____
6. illogical _____
7. involve _____
8. priority _____
9. process (n.) _____
10. research (n.) _____

B. Share your definitions with a partner and then with the rest of your classmates. As a group, try to complete the definitions for all ten words. Use a dictionary to check the definitions if you are unsure about them. Then complete the vocabulary activity.

Vocabulary Challenge

A. Circle the word that is closest in meaning to the boldfaced word. The first one has been done for you.

1. **aware**	(conscious)	purposeful	unconscious
2. **critical**	intelligent	amusing	analytical
3. **research**	evaluation	investigation	identification
4. **authority**	felon	psychologist	expert
5. **priority**	objective	conclusion	process
6. **focus**	attention	imagination	curiosity
7. **illogical**	slow-witted	unlucky	irrational
8. **involve**	include	revolve	expect
9. **appropriate**	meaningful	special	correct
10. **process**	event	procedure	parade

B. Complete the sentences using the boldfaced words in Part A. Make sure you use the correct form of the word. Some words may be used more than once. The first one has been done for you.

1. Sometimes the easiest solution is not the most ___appropriate___ one.

2. Maintaining your _____ is very important in completing a project in school, at work, or in daily life.

3. Your unconscious mind can work on problems, but most thinking takes place when you are awake and _____.

4. New _____ is telling us how teachers can make students better thinkers.

5. Widening and narrowing your focus are parts of the thinking _____.

6. Using critical thinking will help you avoid making _____ decisions.

7. According to _____, it is possible to learn how to be a critical thinker, even if you are not a gifted student.

8. Success as a student _____ diligent practice and studying.

9. Teachers around the world are now making critical thinking skills a(n) _____ in their lessons.

10. You will spend your money more wisely if you make a(n) _____ evaluation of advertisers' claims.

C. Using your dictionary, work with a partner to find the missing word forms and complete the chart. If no form exists, draw a line in the space. The first one has been done for you.

Noun	Verb	Adjective	Adverb
1. process	process	processed	---------
2.		aware	
3. focus			
4.		critical	
5. research			
6. priority			
7.	authorize		
8.		illogical	
9.	involve		
10.		appropriate	

The Stated Main Idea

> **Main idea:** the most important idea the writer wants the reader to know

The *main idea* of a paragraph or a longer passage of text is what the author wants the reader to know about the topic. The title of a text or passage is often a clue to the topic and thus to the main idea. The main idea can be stated or unstated. In most academic texts, the main idea is stated.

In a longer passage of text, each paragraph has a main idea. A longer text also has a *thesis statement*. The thesis statement contains the topic or subject of the complete passage and is often a general statement which is supported by the main idea and details in each paragraph of the text.

In a paragraph, the sentence which contains the topic and the main idea is called a *topic sentence*. The topic sentence is often the first sentence in the paragraph, but it can also be in the middle or at the end of the paragraph.

A. Below is the first paragraph from Reading 1. The topic of the paragraph is *thinking*. Underline the main idea in the topic sentence, the sentence that states what the author wants the reader to know about the topic of *thinking*.

Thinking is a purposeful mental activity. You control it, not vice versa. Generally, thinking is a conscious activity. This means you are awake and aware of your thinking. However, the unconscious mind can continue working on a problem, for example, while you sleep.

B. Below is another paragraph from the same reading. The topic of the paragraph is *thinking skills*. Underline the main idea in the topic sentence, the sentence that states what the author wants the reader to know about the topic.

Good thinking skills are necessary for academic success. Professors do not want students to simply repeat information they have learned in lectures and readings. Successful students will analyze facts and expert opinions. They will synthesize information from different resources and apply their knowledge to assignments. Students who have poor thinking skills will have difficulty making conclusions after conducting research. It will also be difficult for them to create ideas or solve problems.

C. Find the main idea in two additional paragraphs from the reading. Share them with a partner.

The Implied Main Idea

> **Main idea:** can be stated (written) or implied (suggested)

Sometimes the writer does not directly state the main idea in one topic sentence; it is *implied*. The writer implies the main idea through the details in the sentences. If you are unable to find one sentence that states the topic and what the writer wants you to know about it, you will have to state the main idea in your own words. Follow these steps:

- ask yourself what the topic of the passage is
- study the details in the passage
- ask yourself what the details say about the topic
- using your own words, put the answers to those two questions in a sentence

That sentence is the implied main idea of the text or passage. Use the title of the passage to help you identify the topic and main idea. Use any headings and subheadings to help you formulate the main idea as well.
Example:

Sign on the Dotted Line

Don't just take the salesperson's word for it. Read a purchase agreement before you sign it. Find out whether you can change your mind and cancel the agreement without a financial penalty. Before you sign a loan agreement, read it over carefully. Are there penalties for paying the loan back early? Does the interest rate stay the same, or can it change? Read a lease before signing your name. Does it state specific costs you must pay for taking care of the property? Is the lease automatically renewed each year?

1. What is the topic of the passage? _signing agreements, loans, and leases_
2. What do the details say about the topic? _Read everything before signing anything._
3. What is the implied main idea? _Reading carefully might save you money and_ _prevent problems._

ACTIVITY 8

Find the Implied Main Idea

Read the paragraphs below. For each, circle the word or phrase that best expresses the topic of the paragraph. Determine what each detail says about or contributes to the topic. Then write a sentence that expresses the implied main idea.

Online Shopping

Every day, people shop online. They may purchase items they can't find in stores, or they may save time by shopping online. Unfortunately, some shoppers end up paying more than just the price of their purchase. If a site does not display "https" or a lock icon on the page that asks for payment information, it is not a secure site. If personal financial information is requested, determine how that information will be used. Read the site's privacy policy. Paying by credit card is the safest way to shop online. If the merchandise is never received, yet a charge for it appears on a credit card statement, the charge can be disputed. Keep a record of the order and confirmation number in case there is a problem with the order. By law, online businesses must fill an order within 30 days or notify the purchaser of any delay.

Implied main idea: _____

_____

Using Critical Thinking Skills

College and university students use critical thinking skills when they weigh the pros and cons of an argument presented in an essay, or when they research information to support their own ideas in a paper or essay. Consumers use critical thinking skills when they compare prices and qualities of various products before making a purchase decision. Employees use critical thinking skills to solve problems they encounter in their work, whether it is how to improve the quality of a product or how to reduce costs.

Implied main idea: _____

_____

Identifying Text Structure—*Definition*

Text structure: the pattern a writer uses to present ideas

Writers organize and present their ideas according to patterns of thinking. Recognizing the pattern or text structure of a reading helps you understand the writer's thoughts, and thus helps you read more efficiently and effectively. Often, the main idea and topic sentence offer clues to the text structure of a passage.

Common patterns of thinking include analysis, classification, definition, compare/contrast, process, and problem/solution. Although writers may combine different patterns, they typically use one overall organizational pattern that fits the kind of information being presented.

In Activity 7, you identified the main ideas underlined here in two paragraphs from Reading 1:

Thinking is <u>a purposeful mental activity.</u> You control it, not vice versa. Generally, thinking is a conscious activity. This means you are awake and aware of your thinking. However, the unconscious mind can continue working on a problem, for example, while you sleep.

Good thinking skills <u>are necessary for academic success.</u> Professors do not want students simply to repeat information they have learned in lectures and readings. Successful students will analyze facts and opinions. They will synthesize information from different resources and apply their knowledge to assignments. Students who have poor thinking skills will have difficulty making conclusions after conducting research. It will also be difficult for them to create ideas or solve problems.

In the first paragraph, the main idea defines a term or concept: *thinking*. After providing a definition of the term *thinking,* the writer uses the remainder of the reading to explain the term by giving examples and listing characteristics or traits.

In the second paragraph, the writer gives examples of skills necessary for academic success; these examples explain the importance of *good thinking skills*.

Examples and lists of characteristics are commonly used in a *paragraph of definition.* The text structure of *definition* can also be identified through key words and sometimes through punctuation.

Key Words—*Definition*

Good readers recognize the key words that are used with different patterns of text structure. Recognizing the key words improves the reader's speed and increases comprehension of the material. Key words associated with the pattern of definition include:

is/are	means
is/are defined as	refers to
for example	such as
to illustrate	can be seen as

 ACTIVITY 9

Use Key Words

A. Study the first three examples which use key words associated with the pattern of definition. Then fill in the blank with the appropriate key words for sentences 4–6. Be sure to use the correct form. Underline the word or words being defined.

1. <u>Reading</u> ___*refers to*___ the process of looking at and taking in the meaning of written characters, words, or sentences.

2. <u>Thinking</u> ___*is*___ a purposeful mental activity.

3. <u>Evidence</u> ___*such as*___ facts, statistics, and expert testimony can all be used to support the main idea of a passage.

4. Graphic or visual aids _____ any charts, graphs, pictures, maps, or diagrams which explain or support the written text.

5. Students may perform poorly in a class, _____ getting low scores, just because they don't like the professor.

6. The unconscious mind can continue working on a problem after conscious activity stops, _____, while you sleep.

B. Go back to Reading 1, and find sentences with examples of key words which show the pattern of definition. On the lines below, write the sentences and underline the key words and the word or words they define.

1. _____

2. _____

3. _____

Punctuation—*Definition*

Punctuation is also a key to recognizing the pattern of definition. The term or the concept is often set off by commas, but may also be set off by a colon, parentheses, or dashes. Sometimes the definition is set off by punctuation. Study the examples below.

One process is the production of ideas**, creative thinking,** which involves widening your focus and looking at many possibilities. (term set off by commas)

Imagining yourself on a Caribbean cruise is simply **daydreaming**: following the drift of fantasies. (term set off by a colon)

The other process is the evaluation of ideas **(critical thinking),** in which you look at all of the ideas you've generated and identify the most reasonable ones. (term set off by parentheses)

Read the *headings*—the titles of the sections—in the passage before you begin reading the text. (definition set off by dashes)

Use Punctuation

Circle the correct punctuation to set off the term or definition in each sentence and insert it in the sentence. Then write the term and its definition on the line. The first one has been done for you.

1. Some authorities believe **neuroses,** (, :) or mental disorders **,** stem from shallow, illogical thinking. *neuroses are mental disorders* _____

2. **Retaining** (( ) — —) remembering what you have read is enhanced by summarizing what you have read. _____

3. Not all students practice **critical reading** (: ( )) a skill that needs to be taught explicitly and exercised regularly. _____

4. Identifying what the author wants you to know about the topic (: — —) **the main idea** is key to understanding a text or passage. _____

5. Employers want **critical thinkers** (, , :) problem solvers and decision makers not walking encyclopedias. _____

6. Reading for **pleasure** (— — , ,) enjoyment requires less concentration than reading to learn. _____

In the first section of this chapter, you were introduced to surveying, predicting, summarizing, finding the main idea, and identifying text structure. You practiced those skills and strategies with Reading 1. In this section you will practice these same skills with a new reading.

Get Ready to Read

Agree or Disagree

Read the following statements and decide whether you agree or disagree. Circle your choice. Discuss your answers and your reasons for them with a partner.

1. Readers must accept all of a writer's ideas.	AGREE	DISAGREE
2. Critical reading is needed only for college.	AGREE	DISAGREE
3. Facts and statistics serve as support for main ideas.	AGREE	DISAGREE
4. Critical readers analyze text and ideas.	AGREE	DISAGREE
5. Readers use critical thinking skills.	AGREE	DISAGREE

Surveying and Predicting

Survey and Predict

A. Survey Reading 2 and predict what information you will find.

1. Read the title. Write it here. _____

2. Read the first paragraph. Write one or two words which tell the topic, or what the paragraph is about. _____

3. Find the sentence which states the topic and explains the main idea. Write the sentence here. _____

   _____

4. Read the headings, the titles of the sections in the reading. Write them here.

   _____

5. Look for key (important) terms. They are usually in bold. List them here.

   _____

   _____

6. Read the last paragraph. It is a summary of the entire reading.

B. Share your survey answers with a partner and discuss what you think the reading will be about. Then circle the number of the statement below which matches your prediction.

1. The passage will describe critical reading and what critical readers do.

2. The passage will explain critical reading and when critical readers use it.

3. The passage will list the reasons critical reading is important and when critical reading is used.

C. Now read the passage to see if your prediction is correct. Try to read as quickly as you can. Do not stop to look up words in your dictionary.

Reading 2

What Is Critical Reading?

Critical reading does not mean criticizing or finding mistakes in a text or an article. Critical reading means noticing techniques that writers use to convince readers to accept ideas or information. Readers who recognize these techniques can evaluate a reading selection more easily. Critical reading is a skill used in everyday life. For example, in college, choosing an answer on a multiple choice test requires critical reading skills. Purchasing a product online is another example of a task that requires critical reading skills.

Critical readers

Critical readers do not automatically believe that everything they read is true. They ask themselves questions about the text. For example, they might ask if the author is well-known. They might ask if the author is an expert on the subject. They also ask what the author's purpose is for writing. Is it to present facts or statistics, or is it to persuade or convince the reader to believe something? In addition, critical readers are aware of the author's approach. Is the information presented in an objective or neutral way? Does the writer reveal a subjective (positive or negative) attitude toward the subject?

Identifying and evaluating the main idea

Critical reading means analyzing ideas and then deciding whether to accept them, reject them, or think about them further. In order to analyze ideas, good readers first identify the main idea. Finding the main idea is key to understanding the writer's argument. Good readers skim the reading and find the main idea before reading the entire article. This results in faster and more effective reading.

Critical readers also evaluate the main idea. They do this by asking questions. Does the main idea seem important? Does it seem logical? Does it allow for other viewpoints? Does the author insist that this viewpoint is the only valid one? If the main idea doesn't seem important or logical, critical readers pay close attention to the details the author uses to support it.

Examining support for the main idea

Paying close attention to the details means examining the evidence the author uses to support the main idea. Evidence may include facts, statistics, examples, experience, and opinions. The critical reader asks two key questions. The first is, "Is the evidence adequate?" The reader decides whether the author has provided enough support for the main idea. One or two examples are usually not enough to support a viewpoint. If the support is inadequate, the critical reader will not accept the author's opinion as true.

The second key question is, "Does the evidence seem accurate?" The reader considers the source of the information. The reader also considers the methods that were used to collect the facts. If the source is questionable, the support may also be questionable. If the method is unreliable, the facts may be unreliable as well.

Analyzing the presentation of evidence

Critical reading also requires the reader to recognize errors in the author's thinking. Errors weaken the author's support and, thus, the author's ideas. For example, the author may use **circular reasoning**. This is simply repeating the main idea in different words without adding any reasons or evidence to support the idea. The author may also try to distract the reader with a **red herring**. A *red herring* is an idea or statement that distracts or leads the reader away from the issue. Finally, the author may make a **hasty generalization**. This means the author bases a conclusion on very little evidence or support.

Putting it all together

Critical readers understand both *what* a text says and *how* it says it. Critical reading, then, means three things. It means recognizing the techniques authors use to convince the reader to accept the ideas as presented. It means evaluating the text in light of these techniques. It also means deciding whether to accept or reject the text, or to gather more information before making a decision.

Key Concept Words

circular reasoning – (n.) repetition of the same idea using different words
critical reading – (n.) analytical reading which leads to making a decision
hasty generalization – (n.) a rapidly drawn, often inaccurate, conclusion
red herring – (n.) something used as a distraction

Glossed Words

distract – (v.) draw attention away from something; **evidence** – (n.) something helpful in coming to a conclusion; **in light of** – (idiom) in consideration of; **text** – (n.) main part of a written work; **viewpoint** – (n.) an attitude or opinion

Summarizing

Share What You Read

A. Use two or three sentences to tell your partner what you thought the reading was about. Then listen to your partner's sentences. Next, read the following statements and circle the number of the statement that best summarizes the reading.

1. Critical reading is important for determining whether the evidence is adequate and accurate when looking at facts, statistics, and opinions.

2. Critical reading means understanding the author's argument, evaluating the support, and making a decision about the information.

3. Critical reading means reading to determine what is wrong with a text that tries to persuade or convince the reader to accept a viewpoint.

B. Did you choose statement 2? If you chose a different answer, go back and review your survey answers. Try to determine why they lead to summary statement 2.

Check Your Comprehension

Read each statement and circle *T* if it is true or *F* if it is false. Change a false statement to make it true. The first one has been done for you.

1. T / (F)   Critical reading ~~means~~ looking for mistakes in the author's text. *(does not mean)*

2. T / F   Personal experience is not an example of supporting evidence.

3. T / F   Finding the main idea before reading the text contributes to more effective reading.

4. T / F   Critical readers ask themselves questions about the text while they are reading.

5. T / F   Critical readers do not evaluate the source of a writer's information.

6. T / F   A hasty generalization weakens the author's support for the main idea.

7. T / F   Critical readers assume the author's support is both adequate and accurate.

8. T / F   Answering a test question does not require critical reading.

9. T / F   Circular reasoning means restating the main idea in different words.

10. T / F   Details, or evidence, must support the main idea.

● Academic Word List

Scan and Define

A. Look at the ten words listed below. Scan the reading and underline the words from the list. Write the definitions for the words you know. Do not use a dictionary. The first one has been done for you.

1. adequate _enough, sufficient_____

2. author (n.)_____

3. convince _____

4. expert (n.) _____

5. issue (n.) _____

6. methods _____

7. reject (v.) _____

8. reveal_____

9. source _____

10. valid _____

B. Share your definitions with a partner and then with the rest of your classmates. As a group, try to complete the definitions for all ten words. Use a dictionary to check the definitions if you are unsure about them. Then complete the vocabulary activity.

ACTIVITY 16

Vocabulary Challenge

A. Match the vocabulary word with its synonym. The first one has been done for you.

1. __*e*__ author
2. _____ method
3. _____ convince
4. _____ adequate
5. _____ expert
6. _____ reject

   a. persuade
   b. authority
   c. supportive
   d. refuse
   e. writer
   f. enough
   g. system

B. Use the vocabulary words in the first column above to complete the sentences. The first one has been done for you.

1. Writers need to ____*convince*____ the reader to accept their viewpoints.

2. Presenting information from a(n) _____ strengthens a writer's argument.

3. It is the responsibility of the _____ to provide sufficient support for the main idea.

4. The _____ used to collect data or facts must be reliable.

5. Critical readers will _____ a text if the evidence does not support the main idea.

6. Without _____ support, a writer cannot convince the reader to accept his or her viewpoint.

C. Read the definitions of the words below. Then decide which meaning is the one used in the sentence. Put the definition number next to the sentence.

1. **issue** *noun* **1.** something put into circulation; **2.** a subject being discussed

_____ Writers may make statements that distract their readers from the **issue.**

2. **reveal** *verb* **1.** to tell or disclose a secret; **2.** to show or display something

_____ Does the author **reveal** a subjective attitude toward the subject?

3. **source** *noun* **1.** a point of origin; **2.** the beginning of a stream or river; **3.** a person or thing that supplies information

_____ If the **source** of the facts is questionable, so are the facts.

4. **valid** *adjective* **1.** logical or convincing; **2.** legal

_____ Does the author allow for other viewpoints or insist that this is the only viewpoint that is **valid?**

Using Context to Guess Meaning—*Definition*

When you read, you may come across a word which is new to you. When this happens, you can stop and look the word up in the dictionary, skip over the word, or guess its meaning. If you stop reading to look up every unfamiliar word you come across, you will lose your concentration. If you skip over the word, it will probably not affect your comprehension unless the word is used multiple times; that indicates it is a key word and you need to know its meaning. Your third choice is to guess the meaning of the word. Guessing the meaning of a word is sometimes difficult, but there are some strategies you can learn to use.

Read the sentence and explanation below to see how punctuation and/or key words help define the term *circular reasoning*.

The author may use circular reasoning, which is simply repeating the main idea in different words, without adding any reason or evidence to support the idea.

After the term *circular reasoning*, there is a comma. The comma is followed by key words (*which is*) which introduce the definition of the term. Thus, *circular reasoning* means *repeating the main idea in different words*. The meaning of a word can be set off by commas, colons, parentheses, or dashes. Common key words include the verb *to be, means, or, refers to, such as,* and *can be seen as.*

Recognize Clues to Meaning

Read the sentences below and identify the signal (key word and/or punctuation) which defines the term(s) in bold. The first one has been done for you.

1. Does the writer present the information in an **objective**, or neutral, way?

    Signal: *commas set off "or neutral"*

2. Does the writer reveal a **subjective** (positive or negative) attitude toward the subject?

    Signal: _____

3. The **red herring**, an idea or statement that distracts or leads the reader away from the issue, is another example of an error in reasoning.

    Signal: _____

4. The author may make a **hasty generalization**, which means basing a conclusion on very little evidence.

    Signal: _____

5. **Evidence** such as facts and personal experience are used to support the main idea.

    Signal: _____

Guess Meaning from Context

Identify the context clues, either key words or punctuation, which define the boldfaced words. Then define the words. The first one has been done for you.

1. Providing sufficient support for the main idea is the responsibility of the **author**, or writer, of a text.

   Clue: <u>commas</u>   Definition: <u>author means writer</u>

2. **Adequate** support means enough support through examples, statistics, and facts to convince a reader to accept an idea.

   Clue: _____   Definition: _____

3. A person who has acquired knowledge about a subject over a period of many years of study and research can be seen as an **expert.**

   Clue: _____   Definition: _____

4. A good writer uses facts and statistics as a **source,** or origin, of evidence.

   Clue: _____   Definition: _____

5. The reader looks for **validity**: the logical reasoning of a writer's argument.

   Clue: _____   Definition: _____

6. Support for the main idea is weakened by using **methods,** procedures followed to collect information, which are questionable.

   Clue: _____   Definition: _____

7. **Issue** refers to the subject being discussed or written about.

   Clue: _____   Definition: _____

8. One way writers **reveal**—make known—their attitudes toward a subject is through their choice of words.

   Clue: _____   Definition: _____

9. Critical readers who **reject**—refuse to accept—weak arguments are better students, better employees, and better consumers.

   Clue: _____   Definition: _____

10. A well-supported viewpoint **convinces,** or persuades, the reader to accept the writer's main idea.

    Clue: _____   Definition: _____

In this section, you will learn some skills and strategies associated with the writing process. This section addresses gerunds, a grammatical structure used in the readings, and writing complete simple sentences. You will practice different steps in the writing process and will write a paragraph of definition.

The Grammar of Gerunds

A gerund is a verb ending in -ing that functions as a noun.

Subject	Verb	Object/Complement
Reading	is	a skill needed to do well in college.
I	have always enjoyed	*reading* mysteries.
I	have always looked forward to	*taking* college courses.
Many students	complain	about *having* homework.

Don't confuse gerunds with verbs or participial adjectives.

Subject	Verb	Object/Complement
She	*is reading*	her biology textbook.
I	need	some *reading material* for the trip.

Some verbs commonly followed by gerunds include *appreciate, consider, enjoy, prefer,* and *recommend.*

ACTIVITY **19**

Use Gerunds in Sentences

A. Write two sentences for each of the gerunds listed below. Use the gerund as the subject in one sentence and as an object in the other. Share your sentences with a classmate when you have finished. Your sentences can be about any topic.

Examples: *Writing* paragraphs in English takes lots of practice.
         Some students enjoy *writing* in another language.

1. learning

    a. _____

    b. _____

2. recognizing

    a. _____

    b. _____

3. asking

    a. _____

    b. _____

4. presenting

    a. _____

    b. _____

B. Read the paragraph below and circle the six errors the writer made using gerunds. Correct the errors. The first one has been done for you.

Writing Ritual

Writing
(Write) in my journal has become a favorite early-morning ritual. Most days, I get up before the sun comes up and first make a pot of fresh coffee. With a mug of steaming coffee in one hand and my journal in the other, I head for the porch. I sit on the front porch swing and sip hot coffee from my mug. Sitting there and think about what I want to writing is the best part of my ritual. I enjoy watch the sun rise slowly in the sky, and I take advantage of use the morning stillness to organize my thoughts. I spend a few minutes writing those thoughts down and then go back inside the house and get ready for work. I look forward to do the same thing the next morning.

Sentence Essentials

Complete and Incomplete Sentences

Writers communicate their ideas in complete, well-thought-out sentences. Sentences are constructed from clauses: groups of words containing a subject and a verb. An independent clause contains a complete idea and can stand alone as a sentence. Sentences that contain one independent clause are called *simple sentences*.

Examples of complete sentences / independent clauses:
<u>Critical reading</u> <u>involves</u> critical thinking.
     Subject   Verb   (complement)
<u>Students</u> <u>need to read</u> critically in college.
  Subject   Verb   (complement)

Examples of incomplete sentences:
<u>Critical reading</u> <u>involves</u> (idea is not complete)
     Subject   Verb
<u>Taking the time to find a main idea</u> (no verb)
          Subject

Complete the Sentences

A. Complete the sentences by connecting the words on the left with the phrases on the right. Put the letter of the correct phrase in the blank. The first one has been done for you.

1. ___*e*___ Details   a. is the first step in critical reading.

2. _____ The author   b. contain the main idea.

3. _____ Understanding a passage   c. is an expert in the field.

4. _____ Topic sentences   d. requires careful reading.

5. _____ Identifying the main idea   e. support the main idea.

B. Read each statement below. If the statement is a complete sentence, put *C* in the blank. If the statement is an incomplete sentence, put *I* in the blank and rewrite the sentence to make it complete. The first one has been done for you.

___I___ 1. Scanning the reading. *Scanning the reading is an important step.*

_____ 2. Research requires time and effort. _____

_____ 3. Thinking involves. _____

_____ 4. Widening your focus is creative thinking. _____

_____ 5. What methods were used to collect the facts? _____

_____ 6. Some ideas in writing. _____

Sentences with Compound Subjects or Verbs

A simple sentence can have more than one subject or verb. Although it may have two subjects or two verbs, a sentence with only one clause is still a *simple sentence*. Study the examples below.

Compound subject:
<u>Reading and writing</u> <u>share</u> common traits.
     Subject   Verb

Compound verb:
<u>Good writers</u> <u>organize</u> their thoughts and <u>plan</u> their writing carefully.
  Subject   Verb   Verb

Compound subject and verb:
<u>Critical thinkers and critical readers</u> <u>analyze</u> evidence and <u>recognize</u> errors in ideas.
       Subject   Verb   Verb

Write Sentences with Compound Subjects and Verbs

A. Read the following sentences. Underline the subjects and circle the verbs. The first one has been done for you.

1. <u>Employers</u> (appreciate) and (reward) creative and critical thinkers.

2. Readers and writers need to understand the main idea of a passage.

3. Good students read their textbooks carefully and take good notes in their college classes.

4. Compound subjects and verbs add variety to sentence structure.

B. Write three simple sentences: one with a compound subject, one with a compound verb, and one with a compound subject and compound verb. Your sentences can be about any topic.

1. _____

2. _____

3. _____

Problems with Fragments

A very common problem writers have is writing incomplete sentences. Incomplete sentences are called *fragments.* They can be corrected by:

- inserting a subject
- inserting a verb
- adding a complement (an object) to complete the thought

Examples:

Organized the details according to their importance. (subject missing)
<u>This author</u> organized the details according to their importance.

Using this outline format. (verb missing)
Using this outline format <u>works</u>.

Critical readers do not automatically accept. (complement needed)
Critical readers do not automatically accept <u>written arguments.</u>

Correct the Fragments

A. Correct the fragments below. There may be more than one way to correct some of the writing errors. The first one has been done for you.

1. Reading a textbook and taking notes. <u>*Reading a textbook and taking notes are parts of college life.*</u>

2. Ruminations about winning the lottery. _____

_____

3. Critically examine what they read and hear before spending money. _____

_____

4. Students with poor thinking skills. _____

_____

5. Critical readers first ask themselves. _____

_____

6. Writers should find. _____

_____

7. Checked for the flow of ideas. _____

_____

8. Research needs to support. _____

_____

9. Is an important one in the writing process. _____

_____

B. Read the paragraph below and circle the four fragment errors. Then correct the fragments. There may be more than one way to correct some of the writing errors. The first error has been circled for you.

Reading for Fun

(Reading for fun or pleasure.) It has many benefits. Reading improves your vocabulary, and it will also increase your awareness of grammar. Vocabulary and grammar are also important elements of writing. Reading will ultimately help. You improve your writing skills. It doesn't matter what kind of. You can read romance novels, or you can read self-help books. Fiction or non-fiction. Reading is reading. So, the next time you pick up a favorite book to read, don't feel guilty that the book you are reading is not your biology textbook. If anyone asks what you're doing, say, "I'm improving my writing skills!"

Making the Connection

Reading and writing are connected in numerous ways:

- They are both active processes.
- When you read, you read for the main idea and note the details which support the main idea.
- When you write, you write a topic sentence (main idea) and supply evidence to support the topic sentence.
- Determining the pattern of organization of a reading passage helps you, the reader, understand the flow of ideas.
- Doing the same for a paragraph helps you, the writer, form a paragraph with ideas that are related and with sentences that flow smoothly from one to the next.

Get Ready to Write

Steps in the Writing Process

Draft: the unfinished or "rough" version of a paragraph or essay

There are three stages in the writing process: pre-writing, writing, and post-writing. Although writers may approach the writing process differently, good writers plan before they begin to write. As they write, they stop to read what they have written and make changes, continually improving the presentation of their ideas. Once writers have completed their first draft, they revise and edit their writing, reviewing it for mistakes and checking for the flow of ideas. The final draft is a corrected and properly formatted version.

List the Steps

A. How do you plan your writing? Fill in the boxes with the steps you take in the writing process. Some steps have been listed to get you started.

Pre-writing steps (determine the topic, the main idea, and the supporting details)
Writing steps (organize ideas)
Post-writing steps (rewrite and revise)

B. Share your steps in the process with a classmate. With your class, discuss the writing process. Consider the following questions: Is all writing the same? Do all writers follow the same steps? How do you get ideas for your writing? How many times do you rewrite your paragraphs or essays? How do you know when you have finished? Do you ask someone to read your writing and give you feedback?

Structure of a Paragraph

Although writers may take different approaches to the writing process, most writers follow a common format when writing a paragraph. They begin their paragraph by introducing the main idea or topic sentence. The body of the paragraph contains the details which support the main idea. The paragraph then ends with a concluding sentence. The following chart demonstrates the structure of a paragraph.

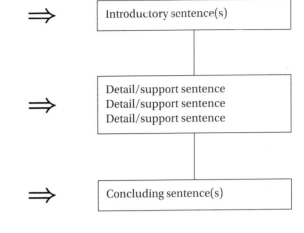

Introduction Topic sentence: includes main idea (topic and what you want the reader to know about the topic)	⟹	Introductory sentence(s)
Body Body of support: includes all the sentences in the paragraph which support the main idea	⟹	Detail/support sentence Detail/support sentence Detail/support sentence
Conclusion Concluding sentence: includes a restatement of the main idea and the conclusion the writer draws	⟹	Concluding sentence(s)

How Did They Do That?

Use the paragraph below for Activities 24-26 to follow the writer's steps in the writing process.

The Definition of Thinking

Thinking is a complex mental activity that is done with purpose. Most thinking is done consciously or with awareness. However, unconscious thinking, while sleeping, for example, can also occur. There are two parts or processes in thinking that complement one another. The first process is creative thinking, which means you widen your focus and try to look for many possible ideas. The second process is critical thinking. In the critical thinking process, you narrow your focus, evaluating all of the possible ideas and choosing the most reasonable ones. Both processes happen naturally, but most people can improve their thinking skills through instruction and diligent practice. Thinking is not daydreaming, nor is it random, uncontrolled fantasizing. Good thinking skills help students succeed in college by enabling them to analyze and synthesize information, make informed conclusions, and solve problems. Thinking is much more than a simple and automatic brain reflex.

Brainstorming

Brainstorming: generating ideas as quickly as possible

Brainstorming is a method writers use to generate ideas for writing. When writers brainstorm a topic, they write down every idea they can think of that is related to the topic. No idea is excluded when brainstorming, so it makes no difference if the idea is good or bad, general or specific, broad or narrow. The goal is to list as many ideas as possible within a short period of time.

Before brainstorming, writers usually have an idea of who the audience or reader will be. They also have in mind the purpose of their writing: a letter for college admission, a research paper for a professor, a classroom project, or even the answer on an essay exam.

After brainstorming, writers go through the list and evaluate each idea based on the appropriateness for the audience and purpose. They reject some ideas right away. They continue to evaluate each idea on the list until they have narrowed the list down to one topic. See Appendix 2 on page 193 for more information about brainstorming.

ACTIVITY 24

Identify the Writer's Idea

Look at the writer's brainstorming ideas for "The Definition of Thinking." In the list below, circle the idea the writer chose. Circle it in the paragraph as well.

Skills needed for college

listening and note-taking	taking essay and multiple-choice exams
reading articles and textbooks	doing math
thinking and analyzing	time management
writing essays and papers	finding a parking place on campus
how to study	finding the money to buy textbooks

Narrowing the Topic

After brainstorming possible topics and choosing one, writers must often narrow the topic if it is too general or too broad. Narrowing the topic means limiting the focus to a specific topic that can be covered completely in one paragraph.

ACTIVITY 25

Identify the Topic

After choosing the very general topic *thinking and analyzing,* the writer brainstormed again to narrow the topic. Look at the writer's ideas for the topic on thinking. In the list below, circle the narrowed topic the writer chose. Underline it in the paragraph as well.

Thinking and analyzing

physiological aspect	analyzing research
purposeful and complex activity	how to improve thinking
Is memory thinking?	courses that require thinking/analyzing

Brainstorming and Narrowing Details

> **Supporting details:** facts, statistics, examples, or personal experience that support the main idea

Once the topic has been narrowed, writers often brainstorm a list of possible details to support the topic. They may also refer to their original brainstorming list of topics to see if there are any supporting details among the list. Details may include facts, statistics, personal experiences, opinions, examples, or reasons.

After brainstorming the details, the writer then narrows them, choosing the ones which will best support the main idea of the paragraph.

Identify the Details

In the list below, circle the details the writer chose to include in the paragraph "The Definition of Thinking" on page 25. Draw two lines under these details in the paragraph as well.

Thinking skills, creative, critical

what it is	harmonious, complementary	for success in college
creative—wide focus, many possibilities	"gifted"	employment
critical—narrow focus, evaluate	conscious, unconscious	for life—wise consumer decisions
generate/produce ideas	choose reasonable ideas	problem solver
natural	what it isn't	avoid neuroses
related to health	daydreaming, fantasizing	analyze knowledge/synthesize data
learned, "learnable"	illogical (critical)	apply previous experience to new experience
vital to success	random	
	purpose	

Choosing Text Structure

Once the writer decides which details to include to support the main idea, a logical text structure or pattern of organization often becomes clear. Common text structures include analysis, classification, compare/contrast, definition, process, and problem/solution. Although writers may combine text structures, they usually use one main pattern of organization.

At times you will decide the structure or pattern of organization to use. Other times an assignment will determine or dictate the text structure for you. For example, an essay exam question might ask you to "compare and contrast the two kinds of thinking" or to "define the concept of thinking." It is important to understand the assignment and use the correct pattern to address it in your writing.

Find the Sentences

Look at the categories the writer used for brainstorming/narrowing the details in Activity 26. Explaining what something is and what it is not suggests a *definition* text structure. Reread the writer's paragraph below and number the seven sentences that explain what *thinking* is and what it isn't.

The Definition of Thinking

Thinking is a complex mental activity that is done with purpose. Most thinking is done consciously or with awareness. However, unconscious thinking, while sleeping, for example, can also occur. There are two parts or processes in thinking that complement one another. The first process is creative thinking, which means you widen your focus and try to look for many possibilities. The second process is critical thinking. In the critical thinking process, you narrow your focus, evaluating all of the possible ideas and choosing the most reasonable ones. Both processes happen naturally, but most people can improve their thinking skills through instruction and diligent practice. Thinking is not daydreaming, nor is it random, uncontrolled fantasizing. Good thinking skills help students succeed in college by enabling them to analyze and synthesize information, make informed conclusions, and solve problems. Thinking is much more than a simple and automatic brain reflex.

The Topic Sentence

The topic sentence is often the first sentence in the paragraph. It contains the topic and what the writer wants the reader to know about the topic. The topic sentence may also give the reader an idea of the text structure or pattern of organization the writer will use.

Although the topic sentence is only now being addressed for the first time in the overall writing process, the writer often has the topic sentence in mind during the pre-writing part of the process. In order to effectively generate details to support the main idea, the writer needs to know the topic and focus of the paragraph.

The topic sentence is the most important sentence in a paragraph. It guides both the writer and the reader. It limits what the writer can include in the paragraph, and it informs the reader of what information the paragraph will contain.

There are several important points to remember about topic sentences:

- A topic sentence is a complete sentence. It must have a subject, a verb, and, in most instances, a complement.

- A topic sentence should be specific. It must let the readers know what they can expect in the paragraph. *Music is entertaining* is not a good topic sentence because it is too general. *The blues developed from the spirituals and work songs sung by African slaves in North America* is a good topic sentence because it is specific.

- A topic sentence should not be too specific, or the writer will have nothing more to add. *The local aquarium is open every day* is too limiting to be a good topic sentence.

- A topic sentence should not be a universally known fact. *The equator divides the Earth into northern and southern hemispheres* is not a good topic sentence.

- A topic sentence should have a controlling or focus idea—words or phrases that limit the content in a paragraph. Look at the following examples:

  1. Florida is home to some of the world's best beaches.

  2. Florida is a leading exporter of strawberries and citrus fruit.

  3. Florida has made many improvements in construction techniques as a result of hurricane damage.

> **Controlling/focus idea:** words or phrases that limit the content of a paragraph

All of these topic sentences share the topic of Florida but have different controlling ideas that let the reader know what will be in the paragraph. Each of these paragraphs would be unique because of the controlling idea.

Choose the Best Topic Sentence

Read the following sentences. Decide which sentence in each group would make the best topic sentence and mark it with an X.

Example: _____ Conserving water is good for the planet.

____X____ There are many ways to practice water conservation.

_____ Using reclaimed water is a way to conserve water.

1. _____ Miami is the most populous city in Florida.

_____ Miami is the home of the Miami Dolphins football team.

_____ People of many countries have influenced the culture of Miami.

2. _____ English is a Germanic language.

_____ It is challenging to learn English.

_____ There are 40,000 words in my English dictionary.

3. _____ Each region of the world experiences its own catastrophic weather.

_____ Meteorologists report the weather forecasts during news reports.

_____ Meteorology is interesting.

4. _____ The first recorded vaccination against disease was in 1796.

_____ Vaccinations have eradicated disease in many parts of the world.

_____ Vaccinations trigger our immune systems to recognize and fight diseases.

5. _____ The Olympics take place every four years.

_____ It takes talent, hard work, and much training to become an Olympic athlete.

_____ People enjoy watching the Olympic Games on television.

6. _____ People use computers at home, at work, and at school.

_____ Computers are helpful to people.

_____ Computers are used to send e-mails to people.

ACTIVITY **29**

Write Topic Sentences

A. Look at the writer's first sentence below. Does it contain the topic? Does it state what the writer wants the reader to know about the topic? Does it suggest a text structure of definition? Label the three parts: topic, focus of topic (what the writer wants the reader to know), and the clue to the text structure.

Thinking is a complex mental activity that is done with a purpose.

B. In a small group, construct possible topic sentences using the components below. Share your sentences with your classmates.

Example: *Thinking can be seen as a multifaceted skill.*

Topic	Clue	Focus	
thinking	refers to	process	mental
	means	exercise	intentional
	can be seen as	multifaceted	deliberate
	is defined as	involved (adj.)	planned

Topic sentences:

_____

_____

_____

C. Write three topic sentences for each of the following topics. Each topic sentence should have a different controlling idea.

1. New York City

a. _____

b. _____

c. _____

2. Fashion

a. _____

b. _____

c. _____

3. Sports

    a. _____

    b. _____

    c. _____

4. Organic food

    a. _____

    b. _____

    c. _____

The Concluding Sentence

The concluding sentence in a paragraph warns the reader that the paragraph is ending. In addition, it summarizes the key points in the paragraph. It is the writer's last opportunity to summarize what is important about the topic. In a paragraph, the concluding sentence is often a restatement of the topic sentence.

Compare and Write

Compare the topic sentence below to the concluding sentence from the paragraph "The Definition of Thinking." Notice how the concluding sentence uses different words to express the idea of the topic sentence. Write your own concluding sentence for one of the topic sentences you created in Activity 29, Part B.

Topic sentence: _Thinking is a complex mental activity that is done with purpose._

Concluding sentence: _Thinking is much more than a simple and automatic brain reflex._

Topic sentence: _____

Concluding sentence (restatement): _____

_____

Outlining

Before writing their first draft, most writers organize their details/support in an outline. Outlines can be formal or informal. They can include Roman numerals (I, II, III, etc.) and letters, or they can simply list the topic and details. Whether you develop a formal or informal outline before you write, be sure your outline contains specific details and is arranged in a logical order, an order that your reader can easily follow and understand.

Compare and Write

A. Look at the outline below for the paragraph "The Definition of Thinking" on page 27. Compare the organization of the outline with the organization of the paragraph. Notice how the author used the outline to arrange the details in a logical order using the text structure of definition.

Topic sentence: Thinking is a complex mental activity that is done with purpose.

    A. Thinking is . . .

       1. conscious and unconscious

       2. creative

a. widen focus

b. think of as many ideas as possible

3. critical

a. narrow focus

b. evaluate ideas

c. choose the best ones

4. natural

a. can be improved with practice and instruction

B. Thinking is not...

1. fantasizing

2. daydreaming

3. uncontrolled or random

C. Purpose: Thinking skills in college

1. analyze data, information

2. synthesize information

3. make conclusions

4. solve problems

B. Using your own words, write sentences using the outline details in Part A. Do not change the order of the details and do not copy the original paragraph. Write the sentences in a paragraph format; do not list or number the sentences. The first sentence, which is the topic sentence, has been provided for you.

The Definition of Thinking

Thinking is a complex mental activity that is done with purpose.

C. When you have finished writing your paragraph, share it with a partner. Look for similarities and differences in your paragraphs. Discuss how two writers with the same information (details) can produce two different paragraphs. Discuss what makes writing a personal and individual activity. Share your answers with the class.

● **On Your Own**

Paragraph of Definition

ACTIVITY 32

Write Your Paragraph

Choose a term or concept from your field of study or from a topic or subject you are interested in. Examples of terms or concepts are *physical therapy, macroeconomics, strength training, hip-hop music,* or *natural disasters.* Follow the steps below to write a paragraph of definition. Your audience is your instructor and your classmates. Your title will be *The Definition of _____.* After you finish writing your paragraph, read the sections on *Revising* and *Editing and Proofreading* and complete the activities.

Steps:

1. Brainstorm the topic. (See Appendix 2 on page 193 for brainstorming techniques.)
2. Narrow the topic.
3. Brainstorm and narrow the details.
4. Choose the text structure (definition: tells what something is and what it isn't).
5. Organize the details.
6. Write the topic sentence.
7. Create an outline with sections for what it is, what it isn't, and purpose.
8. Change outline phrases into sentences.
9. Write concluding sentence (restate topic sentence).
10. Put in paragraph format.

Revising

Revising means rewriting. The purpose of revising is to make your writing better. Each time you re-read your draft, look for ways to improve it. Writers usually focus on the organization and content of their writing first. Questions writers might ask themselves include:

- Does the topic sentence state the main idea clearly?
- Do the details support the main idea?
- Are the details organized logically?
- Do any details need to be added or deleted?
- Is the text structure/pattern of organization clear?
- Does the concluding sentence restate the main idea?

Follow the Steps

A. Use the checklist below to revise the paragraph of definition you wrote.

Revising Checklist

1. Assignment

   ☐ Follows the assignment to write a paragraph of definition for a term or concept from your field of study or area of interest

   ☐ Addresses the instructor and classmates as the audience

   ☐ Follows the ten steps listed in the assignment

2. Topic sentence

   ☐ Is limited to a specific topic

   ☐ Includes the topic

   ☐ Includes what the reader needs to know about the topic

   ☐ Gives a clue to the text structure

3. Details

   ☐ Relate to the topic

   ☐ Are organized in a logical order

   ☐ Follow the outline (what the term is, what it isn't, and the purpose)

   ☐ Enough in number (not too many, not too few)

4. Concluding sentence

   ☐ Restates the topic sentence

   ☐ Alerts the reader to the end of the paragraph

   ☐ Summarizes the key points in the paragraph

B. Share your paragraph with a classmate. Ask your classmate to use the Revising Checklist to check your paragraph and give you some feedback. Make any changes to your paragraph that you feel are necessary. The changes you make should improve your paragraph.

Editing and Proofreading

Editing and proofreading are usually the final steps in the writing process. Editing means looking for errors in grammar, spelling, and punctuation. Editing means making sure that each sentence is complete—that there are no fragments.

Proofreading is taking "one last look" at your draft before you turn it in. You may have included a comma in your original sentence, but cutting and pasting during your final revision may have eliminated it. Proofreading will catch this mistake. It is always good to have someone else proofread your writing before you turn it in—a different set of eyes can be very helpful!

The Final Steps

A. Follow the steps outlined below to edit and proofread the paragraph of definition you wrote.

Editing and Proofreading: looking for and correcting errors in grammar, spelling, punctuation, and formatting

Editing and Proofreading Checklist

1. Grammar
   - ☐ Verb tenses are correct.
   - ☐ Each subject agrees with its verb (singular/plural).
   - ☐ Prepositions are correct.
   - ☐ Pronouns are correct (agree in number/gender).
   - ☐ No articles are missing (a, an, the).

2. Spelling
   - ☐ All words are spelled correctly.
   - ☐ Abbreviations, if any, are used correctly.
   - ☐ First word of each sentence begins with a capital letter.

3. Punctuation
   - ☐ All sentences end with a punctuation mark.
   - ☐ Periods are after statements and question marks are after questions.
   - ☐ Commas, colons, and dashes are used correctly to define terms.

4. Sentences
   - ☐ All sentences are complete.
   - ☐ Each sentence has a subject and a verb.
   - ☐ There are no fragments.

5. Format
   - ☐ Paragraph has a title.
   - ☐ All sentences are in paragraph format (not listed or numbered).
   - ☐ Writer's name is on the paper.
   - ☐ Paper is neat, clean, and legible (easily read).

B. Share your paragraph with a classmate. Ask your classmate to use the Editing and Proofreading Checklist to check your paragraph and mark any errors in grammar, spelling, punctuation, sentences, or paragraph format.

C. Fix any mistakes your paragraph contained. Proofread your paragraph one more time. Turn in your final draft to your instructor.

2 | From the Social Sciences: Psychology

Classes in psychology appeal to students who are interested in learning more about their own behavior or the behavior of others. Studying psychology provides students with insight into gender, cultural, and/or ethical issues. An increased understanding of human behavior will help you in your role as a student, an employee, or even as a parent.

Look at the pictures of the different groups of people. Discuss the following questions with a partner or in a small group.

- How do people influence others in social settings?
- What are some examples of direct and indirect influence people have on others?
- How much does social pressure affect your thoughts and behavior?

This chapter will help you understand some **key concepts** in social psychology, such as:

- social influence
- conformity and compliance
- the trait approach to personality

Get Ready to Read

Social Influence and You

Read the following statements and circle the answer that best reflects your behavior. Discuss your answers and your reasons for them with a partner.

1. If my opinion about something is different from the rest of the group's opinion, I
    a. change my opinion.
    b. don't express my opinion with the others.
    c. express my opinion even if it's different.

2. If someone in the group has a different opinion from mine, I
    a. try to convince the person to change his/her opinion.
    b. let the person have his/her own opinion.
    c. don't express my opinion.

3. If someone in a group asks me to do something I don't want to do, I
    a. usually go along with the group and do what I'm asked.
    b. sometimes go along with the group and do what I'm asked.
    c. usually don't do it.

Surveying and Predicting

Survey and Predict

A. Follow the steps below to survey Reading 1 on page 37.

1. Read the title. Write it here. _____

2. Read the first two paragraphs. Write one or two words which tell the topic or what the paragraph is about. _____

3. Write the main idea here. _____

    _____

4. Read the headings, the titles of the sections in the reading. Write them here.

    _____

5. Look for key (important) terms related to the topic. They are usually in bold. List them here. _____

6. Read the last paragraph. It is a summary of the entire reading.

B. Share your survey answers with a partner and discuss what you think the reading will be about. Then circle the number of the statement below which matches your prediction.

1. The passage will explain the difference between conformity and compliance.

2. The passage will explain three methods of social influence.

3. The passage will explain three methods for obtaining compliance.

Reading 1

The Psychology of Compliance

Individuals and groups can directly and indirectly influence another person's thoughts, feelings, and behavior. The process through which this happens is called **social influence.** There are two types of social influence: conformity and compliance. **Conformity** occurs when people change their behavior and beliefs to match those of the other members of a group. Conformity occurs as a result of *unspoken* group pressure. Unspoken group pressure can be real or imagined.

In contrast, **compliance** occurs when people change what they say or do because of a direct request. Compliance occurs as a result of overt social pressure. There are different methods people use to obtain compliance. Three of those methods are the foot-in-the-door technique, the door-in-the-face procedure, and the low-ball approach.

Foot-in-the-door

The **foot-in-the-door technique** consists of getting a person first to agree to small requests. Later, the requests become larger ones. Why would agreeing to do small favors lead to also doing larger ones? First, people will usually comply with a request that costs little in time, money, effort, or inconvenience. Second, complying with a small request makes people think of themselves as being committed to the cause or issue involved. For some businesses, the foot in the door begins with a request for potential customers to answer a few questions. The larger request, the request to buy something, comes later.

Door-in-the-face

The second approach is known as the **door-in-the-face procedure.** This strategy begins with asking for a favor that will probably be denied. The person who makes the request then concedes that the initial favor was excessive. The person then asks for a smaller favor—which is the favor he or she really wanted in the first place! This approach works for two reasons. The first reason is the person appears willing to compromise. The second reason is the new request seems small compared to the first request. This strategy is often used by groups who bargain or negotiate. Examples of such groups include political groups or labor and management groups.

Low-ball

The third technique is called the **low-ball approach.** It is commonly used by car dealers and other businesses. The first step in this strategy is to get a person to agree to do something, such as to purchase a car. Once this commitment is made, the cost is increased. The person is often told the reason for the increase is because of an "error" in computing the car's price. Why do buyers end up paying much more than originally planned for items like a car? Apparently, once people commit themselves to do something, they feel obligated to follow through.

Compliance is usually generated by a group's spoken norms. Norms are the learned, socially based rules that prescribe what people should or should not do in various situations. Many people believe that the direct approach is always best. They believe that if you want something, you should ask for it. However, salespeople, political strategists, social psychologists, and other experts have learned that often the best way to get something is to ask for something else.

Key Concept Words

compliance – (n.) a change in behavior or beliefs because of a direct request

conformity – (n.) a change in behavior or beliefs because of unspoken (indirect) group pressure

door-in-the-face procedure – (n.) making a large request first and following with a smaller one so as to appear to be willing to compromise

foot-in-the-door technique – (n.) getting people to agree first to small requests and later to larger ones

low-ball approach – (n.) getting someone to make a commitment first and then changing the request

social influence – (n.) a process in which individuals and groups directly and indirectly influence a person's thoughts, feelings, and behavior

Glossed Words

compromise – (v.) to reach agreement with each side giving up some of what it wants; **concedes** – (v.) admits or acknowledges something is true or real; **follow through** – (v.) carry something to completion; **match** – (v.) to be like (something); **overt** – (adj.) open; not hidden or secret; **prescribe** – (v.) rule or guide; order

Summarizing

Share What You Read

A. Use two or three sentences to tell your partner what you thought the reading was about. Then listen to your partner's sentences. Next, read the following statements and circle the number of the statement that best summarizes the reading.

1. Compliance can be obtained directly or indirectly by using one of three specific methods.

2. Individuals and groups both directly and indirectly influence people to either conform to or comply with a group's norms.

3. Obtaining compliance from an individual requires overt social pressure.

B. Did you choose statement 1? If you chose a different answer, go back and review your survey answers. Try to determine why they lead to summary statement 1.

Check Your Comprehension

Read each statement below and circle the word or phrase that best completes it. The first one has been done for you.

1. The door-in-the-face procedure is an example of an approach to *conformity* / *compliance.*

2. Social *norms / influence* can be direct or indirect.

3. Getting a person to agree to do something before changing the request is the first step in the *low-ball / foot-in-the-door* strategy.

4. The spoken or unspoken rules that dictate what people should or should not do in particular situations are called *norms / methods*.

5. When people change their behavior as a result of a direct request, they are *conforming / complying*.

6. Asking first for a small favor and later for a larger one is an example of the *low-ball / foot-in-the-door* approach.

7. Conformity is the changing of behavior or beliefs as a result of *unspoken / spoken* group pressure.

8. Salespeople and political strategists often use techniques to obtain *conformity / compliance*.

Academic Word List

Scan and Define

A. Look at the ten words listed below. Scan the reading and underline the words from the list. Write the definitions for the words you know. Do not use a dictionary. The first one has been done for you.

1. commit *to promise to participate or take action* _____
2. consist _____
3. in contrast _____
4. deny _____
5. initial (adj.) _____
6. items _____
7. occur _____
8. potential (adj.) _____
9. strategist _____
10. technique _____

B. Share your definitions with a partner and then with the rest of your classmates. As a group, try to complete the definitions for all ten words. Use a dictionary to check the definitions if you are unsure about them. Then complete the vocabulary activity.

Vocabulary Challenge

A. Read the words in Columns A and B. Identify the words in Column B as either synonyms (S), words which mean the same as, or antonyms (A), words which mean the opposite of, the words in Column A. Put *S* or *A* in the blank. The first one has been done for you.

Column A	Column B	Synonym or Antonym
1. **potential**	possible; prospective	*S*
2. **items**	units	_____
3. **deny**	agree	_____
4. **consist**	composed of	_____

5. **in contrast**	similarly	_____
6. **strategist**	planner	_____
7. **technique**	method	_____
8. **commit**	obligate	_____
9. **occur**	happen	_____
10. **initial**	final	_____

B. Write sentences using any five phrases below. Be sure to use the correct form of the word. The first one has been done for you.

1. norms consist of <u>Norms consist of rules for appropriate behavior.</u>

2. pay more for items _____

3. potential customers _____

4. an effective technique _____

5. my final thought _____

6. political strategists _____

7. agree to your request _____

8. uninterested in buying _____

9. in contrast _____

10. conformity occurs _____

C. Using your dictionary, work with a partner to find the missing word forms and complete the chart. If no form exists, draw a line in the space. The first one has been done for you.

Noun	Verb	Adjective	Adverb
1. *potential*	---------	potential	*potentially*
2. item			
3.	deny		
4.	consist		
5. contrast			
6. strategist			
7. technique			
8.	commit		
9.	occur		
10.		initial	

Types of Supporting Details

As a reader, your comprehension of a passage will increase if you are able to identify the main idea of a passage and recognize the details which support it. Just as the main idea of a paragraph tells you what the author wants you to know about the topic, the details provide the evidence and support for the main idea. Good readers are able to recognize different types of supporting details.

There are numerous ways to support main ideas. One common way is to use **facts** or **statistics.** A fact is something that is known to be true, to have actually happened. A fact is something that can be proven. *Psychologists study mental processes and behavior* is an example of a fact. A statistic is a piece of numerical data. In the statement "More than 45 percent of the people polled offered a response," *more than 45 percent* is a statistic. Read the paragraph below and study the chart for more examples of facts and statistics.

1. In recent years, an increasing number of minorities have entered the field of psychology, making the professional ranks of psychologists more diverse. <u>Women, who were initially denied doctoral degrees,</u> now account for almost two-thirds of all doctoral degrees awarded in the field. <u>In 1998, ethnic minorities comprised almost eight percent of people holding doctorate degrees in psychology.</u> Despite the increase, however, people of ethnic minorities are still underrepresented in the profession. For example, there is only one Native American psychologist for every 30,000 Native Americans.

fact →

statistic →

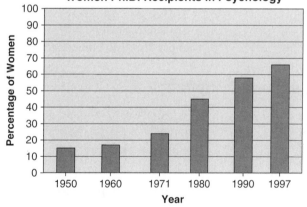

Women Ph.D. Recipients in Psychology

Another way to support a topic sentence is to use **examples**. Read the paragraph below and study the chart to see how examples support the ideas stated in the topic sentence.

2. The field of psychology has identified three major types of phobias: social phobia, specific phobia, and agoraphobia. People with social phobia have intense fears of social interaction. <u>Individuals suffering from social phobia would be greatly distressed when meeting others, dating, or giving a presentation in class</u>. They would have a very difficult time maintaining normal social lives. People with specific phobias have fears of specific objects or situations. Claustrophobia, the fear of small spaces, is a specific phobia. A person with claustrophobia may avoid elevators even if they have to climb many flights of stairs every day. Finally, agoraphobia is the fear of being in open spaces or out in public. Agoraphobics may

example →

literally become housebound, unable even to go to the grocery store or doctor's office. Phobias have a profound impact on the lives of those who suffer from them.

Type of Phobia	Descriptions	Common Symptoms
Social phobia	Fear of social situations or performance situations.	Difficulty in social or public functions such as dating or giving presentations.
Specific phobia	Fear of specific objects or situations. Claustrophobia, for example, is the fear of small spaces.	Avoidance of specific objects or situations. Claustrophobics may avoid elevators at all costs.
Agoraphobia	Fear of public places.	Avoidance of leaving household to be in open spaces or in public.

Personal experience can also be used to support a topic sentence. Read the paragraph below to see how personal experience is used to support a topic sentence.

3. I vividly remember the first time I met with Dr. Henry, the psychologist. <u>I was 6 years old and having difficulty dealing with the trauma of an accident.</u> I was very nervous about meeting him; I thought he would be yet another doctor who would stick me with needles. But I soon learned Dr. Henry was different. His office was painted a soothing yellow and had comfortable chairs instead of an examining table. There were many toys that the doctor brought out; he even played along with me. During the visit, Dr. Henry asked me questions and told me stories instead of looking at my wounds. He had a kind face and laughed easily. At the end of the visit, I looked forward to coming back to see him.

ACTIVITY 7

Find Supporting Details

One fact, statistic, example, and experience have been identified in each of the previous paragraphs. Go back and underline the other facts and statistics in paragraph 1, the examples in paragraph 2, and the experiences in paragraph 3.

Identifying Text Structure—*Classification and Division*

In addition to recognizing the details which support the main idea, recognizing the text structure of a passage also helps increase reading comprehension.

In this chapter, you have read about three different techniques for obtaining compliance. In the opening paragraph of Reading 1, the writer introduces the concept of *social influence* and explains two types: conformity and compliance. Next, the writer explains compliance by dividing it into smaller parts and introducing three methods for obtaining compliance. In separate paragraphs, the writer explains each method and gives examples.

The pattern of organization the writer uses, dividing a topic into groups or categories, is characteristic of the text structure of *classification*. In classification, the members of each group or category have common characteristics. The common characteristic of the three methods of compliance is their use of indirect approaches to obtain compliance. Classification is often used together with *division*, which explains how something is divided into parts.

Study the following diagram to see how the writer divided the topic into groups.

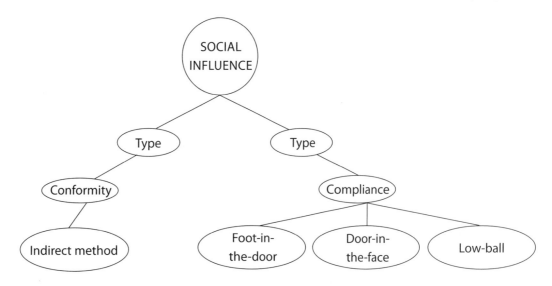

Key Words—*Classification/Division*

Key words and phrases associated with the patterns of classification and division include:

according to	consists of	main types
based on	different types	one, two, three, etc.
be	divided into	parts
category	division	principal types
classified as	first, second, third, etc.	represent
classify	groups	sorted
comprise	kinds of	types of

Examples: Motivation can be *classified as* intrinsic or extrinsic.
There are *three different types* of compliance techniques.
Psychological disorders are *based on* behavior patterns.

 ACTIVITY 8

Recognize Key Words

A. Study the first three examples, which use key words associated with the pattern of classification. Then choose an appropriate key word for sentences 4-7. Make sure you use the appropriate form of the word. Write sentences of your own for the key words and phrases in 8-10.

1. The foot-in-the-door technique ___*consists of*___ two steps.

2. The techniques for obtaining compliance can be ___*divided into*___ three approaches: foot-in-the-door, door-in-the-face, and low-ball approach.

3. ___*Two types of*___ social influence, conformity and compliance, will be outlined in the chapter.

4. Conformity (be/classify) _____ one type of social influence.

5. (Third/Three) _____ techniques are very effective in getting people to change their thoughts, feelings, and behavior.

6. People exert two (kinds/divisions) _____ of pressure on their peers: spoken and unspoken.

7. *Foot-in-the-door* (sort/represent) _____ one kind of sales approach.

8. Two groups of _____.

9. There are three kinds of _____.

10. The principal types of _____.

B. Go back to Reading 1 and find three examples of key words which show the text structure of classification. Write them below.

1. _____

2. _____

3. _____

 **ACTIVITY 9**   *Practice Classifying and Dividing*

Look at the terms below and show how a writer might organize them into groups by putting the terms in the boxes.

1.
Beliefs
Contribute money for a birthday gift
Conformity
Stand up during national anthem
Behavior
Capital punishment is wrong

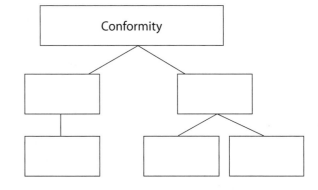

2.
Imagined
Spoken
Group pressure
Real
Unspoken

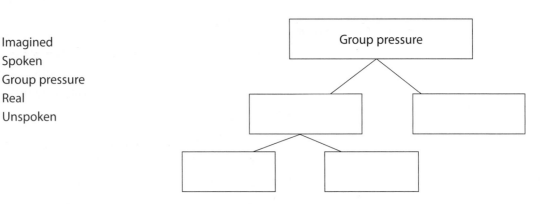

In the first section of this chapter, you practiced surveying, predicting, summarizing, and identifying text structure and supporting details using Reading 1. In this section you will practice the same skills with a new reading.

Get Ready to Read

Agree or Disagree

Read the following statements and decide whether you agree or disagree. Circle your choice. Discuss your answers and your reasons for them with a partner.

1. Each person's personality is unique. AGREE DISAGREE

2. Personality differences can be attributed to inherited differences in the brain. AGREE DISAGREE

3. People from different cultures can have similar personalities. AGREE DISAGREE

Surveying and Predicting

Survey and Predict

A. Survey Reading 2 and predict what information you will find.

1. Read the title. Write it here. _____

2. Read the first two paragraphs. Write one or two words which tell the topic or what the paragraph is about. _____

3. Write the main idea here. _____

4. Read the headings, the titles of the sections in the reading. Write them here.

   _____

   _____

5. Look for any graphic or visual aids in the reading. Graphic aids are charts, graphs, pictures, maps, diagrams, etc. Describe them here. _____

   _____

6. Look for key (important) terms related to the topic. They are usually in bold. List them here. _____

7. Read the last paragraph. It is a summary of the entire reading.

B. Share your survey answers with a partner and discuss what you think the reading will be about. Then circle the number of the statement below which matches your prediction.

1. The passage will describe the four main approaches to personality.

2. The passage will describe the three theories of the trait approach to personality.

3. The passage will describe Allport's trait theory as it applies to personality.

C. Now read the passage to see if your prediction is correct. Try to read as quickly as you can. Do not stop to look up words in your dictionary.

Reading 2

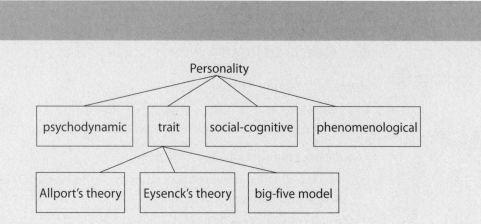

Approaches to Personality

The Trait Approach to Personality

A researcher can choose from among many methods to investigate personality. The method that is used depends on which approach to personality the researcher takes. There are four main approaches: psychodynamic, trait, social-cognitive, and phenomenological. The **trait approach** views personality as the combination of stable internal characteristics. People display these characteristics consistently over time and across situations. In other words, these characteristics do not usually change.

Allport's Trait Theory

Gordon Allport was a trait theorist. He spent 30 years searching for the traits that combine to form normal personality. He believed that the set of labels used to describe a specific person reflects a person's **central traits.** Central traits organize and control behavior in many different situations. They tell what can be expected from a person most of the time. They are also usually apparent to others. Central traits are similar to the descriptive terms used in letters of recommendation. *Reliable* is an example of a central trait.

Allport also believed that people have **secondary traits.** Secondary traits are more specific to certain situations. They control behavior less than central traits do. *Dislikes crowds* is an example of a secondary trait. In his research, Allport focused on the uniqueness of each individual personality. This focus, however, makes it difficult to draw general conclusions about the structure of human personality.

Eysenck's Biological Trait Theory

Another trait theorist was Hans Eysenck, a British psychologist. He used a technique called **factor analysis** to study the structure of both normal and disordered personalities. Factor analysis can reveal, for example, if anxious people are also moody. It can reveal if optimistic people are usually also friendly. Eysenck concluded that personality can be described in terms of three main factors or dimensions. Those factors are **introversion-extraversion, emotionality-stability,** and **psychoticism.**

According to Eysenck, personality can be described in terms of where a person falls along these three dimensions. He believed that differences in personality characteristics can be traced to inherited differences in the brain. He also believed that these biological differences explain why some people are more physiologically aroused or excitable than others. For example, he believed that people who have a low arousal level will be extraverted. He believed that those with more sensitive nervous systems are likely to be introverted.

Big-Five Model of Personality

Other research has led many trait theorists today to conclude that personality is organized around five basic factors, not three. The components of this **big-five model,** or **five-factor model,** of personality are openness, conscientiousness, extraversion, agreeableness, and neuroticism. Some version of the big-five model appears in many countries and cultures. For example, it appears in Canada, China, Germany, Finland, India, Japan, Korea, the Philippines, and Poland. This fact provides more evidence that these factors may represent basic components of human personality.

The emergence of the big-five model is considered a major breakthrough in personality research. Identification of the big-five traits provides a standard way to study the personalities of all people. It no longer matters where people live or what their economic, social, and cultural backgrounds are. The model allows researchers to precisely describe the similarities and differences in people's personalities. It also allows researchers to relate personality characteristics to happiness, or subjective well-being.

The trait approach tends to dominate current research in personality. However, trait theories are better at describing people than at explaining them. Trait theories do not tell much about how traits relate to the thoughts and feelings that precede, accompany, and follow behavior. As a result, some personality psychologists are trying to link their research with that of cognitive psychologists. They hope it will help them to understand better how thoughts and emotions influence, and are influenced by, personality traits.

Key Concept Words

big-five model – (n.) an approach to personality organized around five basic factors; see *five-factor model*

central traits – (n.) features of a person's character which organize and control the person's behavior and which are apparent to others

emotionality-stability – (n.) personality factor with ranges from moody and anxious to calm and relaxed

factor analysis – (n.) a technique used to study personality traits

five-factor model – (n.) an approach to personality organized around five basic factors: openness, conscientiousness, extraversion, agreeableness, and neuroticism; see big-five model

introversion-extraversion – (n.) personality factor with ranges from quiet and thoughtful to sociable and outgoing

psychoticism – (n.) personality factor with ranges from cruel and hostile to warm and accepting

secondary traits – (n.) features of a person's character which are specific to certain situations and which control only some aspects of the person's behavior

trait approach – (n.) a view of personality as a combination of traits or characteristics that people exhibit and which do not change over time

Glossed Words

arouse – (v.) excite or stimulate; **breakthrough** – (n.) a major success or achievement; **conscientiousness** – (n.) a sense of what is right or proper; **falls along . . . three dimensions** – displays characteristics from each of three groups (of personality traits); **link** – (v.) connect or join; **moody** – (adj.) showing low spirits; unhappy; **neuroticism** – (n.) state of being nervous or anxious in an unreasonable way; **precisely** – (adv.) exactly; distinctly; accurately; **stable** – (adj.) not likely to change; steady; **theorist** – (n.) a scholar or scientist who conducts research to explain/prove hypotheses; **uniqueness** – (n.) the quality of being one of a kind; **well-being** – (n.) the state of being healthy, happy, or prosperous

Summarizing

Share What You Read

A. Use two or three sentences to tell your partner what you thought the reading was about. Then listen to your partner's sentences. Next, read the following statements and circle the number of the statement that best summarizes the reading.

1. The trait approach, one of four approaches to personality, includes three prominent theories and dominates contemporary research.

2. Allport's trait theory, Eysenck's biological trait theory, and the big-five model of personality are the three prominent theories in the approach to personality.

3. Allport's trait theory focuses on the uniqueness of each individual personality, Eysenck's on where a person falls along three main factors, and the big-five model on five basic factors.

B. Did you choose statement 1? If you chose a different answer, go back and review your survey answers. Try to determine why they lead to Summary statement 1.

Check Your Comprehension

Read each statement and circle the word or phrase that best completes it. Then share your answers with a partner. The first one has been done for you.

1. People with sensitive, "overaroused" nervous systems are likely to be *extraverted* / *introverted.*

2. *Central* / *Secondary* traits are those that are obvious or noticeable to others.

3. Factor analysis is a technique used both in Eysenck's theory and in *Allport's theory* / *the big-five model theory*.

4. Trait theories are good at *describing* / *explaining* people.

5. "Dislikes crowds" is an example of a *central* / *secondary* trait.

6. According to Eysenck, variations in personality characteristics can be traced to *inherited* / *environmental* differences.

7. Social-cognitive is one of the *three* / *four* approaches to personality.

8. The five-factor model allows researchers to relate personality characteristics to *extraversion* / *happiness.*

9. There is evidence that factor analysis *may / may not* represent basic components of human personality.

10. The trait approach views personality as the combination of stable *internal / external* characteristics that people display over time.

● Academic Word List

Scan and Define

A. Look at the ten words listed below. Scan the reading and underline the words from the list. Write the definitions for the words you know. Do not use a dictionary. The first one has been done for you.

1. apparent *obvious or easily seen* _____

2. approach (n.) _____

3. consistently _____

4. display (v.) _____

5. emergence _____

6. factor (n.) _____

7. individual _____

8. precede _____

9. reliable _____

10. version _____

B. Share your definitions with a partner and then with the rest of your classmates. As a group, try to complete the definitions for all ten words. Use a dictionary to check the definitions if you are unsure about them. Then complete the vocabulary activity.

Vocabulary Challenge

A. Match the words in Column A with their antonyms in Column B. Write the letter of the antonym in the blank. The first one has been done for you.

Column A

___d___ 1. individual

_____ 2. emergence

_____ 3. apparent

_____ 4. version

_____ 5. precede

_____ 6. reliable

Column B

a. hidden

b. undependable

c. original

d. collective

e. departure

f. succeed

g. adaptation

B. Use the words in Column A to complete the sentences. Be sure to use the correct form of the word. The first one has been done for you.

1. It is ___apparent___ from her behavior that she's an introvert.

2. Although they are twins, Michael and Michele have very _____ personalities.

3. Allport's research leading to his trait theory _____ Hans Eysenck's by more than 50 years.

4. The big-five model of personality is an expanded _____ of Eysenck's three-factor model.

5. With the _____ of the big-five model of personality, researchers were able to examine people's personalities in a standard way.

6. Employers want workers who are _____, an example of Allport's definition of a central trait.

C. The following words can be used as nouns and verbs. Read each sentence to determine whether the underlined word is used as a noun or a verb. Then match the word with the correct definition. Put the letter of the definition in the blank. The first one has been done for you.

1. **approach** *verb* **1.** to come near somebody/something in place or time; **2.** to begin to deal with or work on something; **3.** to make a proposal to somebody; *noun* **4.** a way or method of dealing or working with somebody/ something; **5.** a way of reaching a place; an access

___2___ a. Years ago, researchers would <u>approach</u> the study of personality with the goal of discovering the traits that formed normal personality.

_____ b. Looking at personality traits is just one <u>approach</u> which researchers may take when studying human personality.

2. **display** *verb* **1.** to put something to be seen in public; **2.** to show or let something be noticed; *noun* **3.** a show designed to impress or attract attention; **4.** a device, such as a computer screen, that gives information; **5.** the act of displaying

_____ c. People who witnessed the judge's <u>display</u> of anger were shocked.

_____ d. People tend to <u>display</u> the same behavior at work as they do at home.

3. **factor** *verb* **1.** to find one of two or more numbers in a mathematical expression; **2.** to consider something; *noun* **3.** something that helps cause a certain result; **4.** in mathematics, any of two or more numbers which form a product when multiplied together

_____ e. Another <u>factor</u> in the big-five model is agreeableness.

_____ f. Researchers <u>factor</u> in a number of variables as they analyze the data they have collected.

Using Context to Guess Meaning—*Examples*

In Chapter 1, you used key words and punctuation to figure out the meaning of unfamiliar words. Writers often provide examples in their writing to support their main ideas. These examples often help define a term or a concept being presented. Read the example below.

Conformity occurs as a result of **unspoken group pressure**, real or imagined. For example, if everyone in the office contributes money toward a gift for the boss, you may conform by contributing as well, even though no one asked you to do so. You may not even like your boss or you may think buying your boss a gift is an inappropriate gesture, but you feel pressured to follow the group.

From the example, the reader is able to understand that the term *conformity* means "doing the same as others in the group do" and that the concept *unspoken group pressure* means "feeling obligated to do something even though no one asked you to do so." In addition to the key words *for example,* writers may use *for instance, to illustrate,* or *such as* to introduce an example.

Guess Meaning from Context

Use the examples below to define the terms and/or concepts in bold. Underline the key words and then write the definitions of the terms in your own words. The first one has been done for you.

1. **Compliance** occurs as a result of **overt social pressure**. To illustrate, imagine you are on a committee to organize an event. All the committee members except you want to have a live band; you want to hire a DJ to play music. After much debate, the committee chairperson asks you to please go along with the group and vote for the live band. During a short break, all the other committee members take turns asking you to give up the idea of a DJ. Finally, you vote for the live band.

   Compliance = _doing what the group does_

   Overt social pressure = _people ask you to do what they're doing or to agree with them_

2. **The foot-in-the-door approach** is commonly used by charitable organizations. Asking someone first to donate to a charitable cause, for instance, is a small request. Later, asking the same person to help solicit donations from their neighbors is a larger one.

   Foot-in-the-door approach = _____

3. The **low-ball technique** is commonly used by car dealers and other businesses. The first step is to get a person's **oral commitment** to do something, such as to say he/she plans to buy a car. Once the person sits down to sign the papers, the price of the car suddenly increases. The salesperson explains that the increase is the result of an "error" in figuring the price. The customer often agrees to pay the higher price.

   Low-ball technique = _____

   Oral commitment = _____

4. A large, well-known accounting firm wants people with **central traits** of *reliability* or *dependability*, for example. John Temple, who is applying for a position with the company, submits his letter of recommendation in which he is described as "always a dependable and hard-working employee."

   Central traits = _____

5. Career interest tests customarily include questions which identify **secondary traits** such as "dislikes crowds" or "enjoys puzzles" in an effort to target potential career choices. Identifying characteristics that apply to specific situations help narrow the wide range of job possibilities for which a person might be suited.

   Secondary traits = _____

| WRITING 1A | ● **Skills and Strategies** |

In this section, you will learn additional skills and strategies associated with the writing process. This section addresses count and non-count nouns, which are grammatical structures that can be found in the readings. It also addresses writing compound sentences. You will learn about paragraph formatting and supporting details, and you will write a paragraph of classification.

The Grammar of Count and Non-count Nouns

In order to communicate your thoughts clearly when you are writing, make sure the subjects of your sentences agree with their verbs. Although errors in subject and verb agreement rarely prevent the reader from understanding what you have written, they are distracting.

Distinguishing count from non-count nouns in your writing will help you avoid errors in subject-verb agreement. Count nouns are those forms which can be counted: children, shirts, oranges, etc. Count nouns may be singular or plural. Non-count nouns are those forms which cannot be counted: water, flour, intelligence, etc. Non-count nouns are singular.

	Subject	**Verb**	**Object**
Count Nouns			
Singular	*A dream* often	has	meaning.
Plural	People	don't always remember	their *dreams*.
Non-count Nouns			
Singular	*Daydreaming*	is	fun.
	I	have studied	*psychology*.

Sort the Nouns

A. Sort the following list of nouns into count and non-count nouns. Some words may be both count and non-count. The first two have been done for you.

~~behavior~~	factor	request
~~characteristic~~	favor	research
compliance	happiness	similarity
conformity	inconvenience	technique
difference	influence	theory
effort	member	time
emergence	method	trait
error	money	
evidence	openness	

Count Nouns	Non-count Nouns
characteristic	behavior

B. Draw one line under the subject and two lines under the verb in each sentence. Next, check each sentence to make sure the underlined verb agrees with its subject. Make any necessary changes. All of the sentences are in the simple present tense. The first one is done for you.

1. The <u>traits</u> that researchers categorize <u>falls</u> into two groups, central and secondary. *(fall)*

2. People's personality characteristics reflect inherited differences in the brain.

3. Conformity occur as a result of unspoken group pressure.

4. An "error" in computing car prices often follow a person's commitment to purchase a car.

5. Time play a role in the foot-in-the-door technique.

6. Happiness correlate with some personality characteristics.

7. Evidence show there may be five basic components of human personality, not three.

8. Three effective methods for obtaining compliance exist.

9. Openness be one of the five-factor model components.

10. People's behavior reveal much about their personality.

C. Circle the errors in subject-verb agreement in the passage below, and then correct them. The first one has been done for you.

Opposites

My sister seems to have an ever-changing personality. Most of the time she is a very

generous person, but sometimes she ~~refuses~~(*refuse*) to give anyone either her time or her

money. A simple request for a donation from charitable organizations go unanswered.

The welfare of others are often the furthest thing from her mind. My efforts to appeal

to the generous side of her personality fails regularly. The method that she uses to

make decisions about giving gifts are totally beyond me. The similarities between us

are few, and the differences are great. Who would imagine we are twins?

Sentence Essentials

Compound Sentences: Sentence Combining

In Chapter 1 you learned how to write simple sentences containing one
independent clause. It is possible to have more than one independent clause in
a sentence. Combining two or more independent clauses creates a *compound
sentence*. The clauses are joined by a comma and a coordinating conjunction.

Examples: Critical thinkers are valued employees. Critical thinkers are good
problem solvers.
Critical thinkers are valued employees, **for** they are good problem
solvers.

Coordinating Conjunction	Meaning and Use
for	because / introduces reason (formal)
and	additionally / introduces another idea
nor	and not / connects two negative clauses
but	however / introduces contrast
or	alternatively / introduces possibilities
yet	but, despite this / introduces contrast (formal)
so	therefore / introduces result

*Note: An easy way to remember the coordinating conjunctions is to remember the
term **fanboys**. Each letter represents one of the conjunctions: f = for, a = and, etc.*

In compound sentences:

- If the clauses are very short, no comma is needed.
- If the subjects of both clauses are the same, a pronoun is often substituted for
the second subject.
- After the conjunction *nor,* subject and verb order are reversed.

Examples: Unspoken pressure elicits conformity. Direct requests elicit compliance.
Unspoken pressure elicits conformity but direct requests elicit
compliance. (clauses are short)

Group pressure can be real. Group pressure can be imagined.

Group pressure can be real, **or** it can be imagined. (subjects are the same)

Compliance is not a response to unspoken pressure. Compliance is not the same for each culture.

Compliance is not a response to unspoken pressure, **nor** is it the same for each culture. (subject/verb reversed)

 ACTIVITY 18

Use Coordinating Conjunctions

A. Join the two independent clauses with a coordinating conjunction to create a complete sentence. For some sentences, more than one conjunction is possible. Where possible, substitute a pronoun for the second subject. The first one has been done for you.

1. Allport's theory of personality follows the trait approach. Allport's theory of personality uses a set of labels to describe people. _Allport's theory of personality follows the trait approach, and it uses a set of labels to describe people._

2. Eysenck's theory described personality using three factors. Eysenck's theory was rejected in favor of the big-five model. _____

3. Does conformity occur only as a result of real pressure? Can conformity result from imagined pressure? _____

4. Wise consumers recognize the foot-in-the-door approach. Wise consumers don't fall for the door-in-the-face approach. _____

5. Trait theories are good at describing people. Trait theories are not so good at explaining people. _____

6. When using the big-five model, it doesn't matter what people's economic backgrounds are. It doesn't matter what their cultural backgrounds are. _____

7. Salespeople are often adept at using methods of compliance. Salespeople use them eight hours a day, five days a week. _____

8. Most people agree to do small favors. Salespeople make small favors their first request. _____

9. Consumers can follow through on a commitment to purchase something. Consumers can change their minds. _____

10. Trait theories do not provide much information about how thoughts are related to behavior. Personality psychologists are working with cognitive psychologists to understand how thoughts are influenced by personality traits. _____

B. Create compound sentences of your own using each of the seven coordinating conjunctions. Your sentences can be about any topic.

1. _____
_____
2. _____
_____
3. _____
_____
4. _____
_____
5. _____
_____
6. _____
_____
7. _____
_____

Making the Connection

Reading and writing both require paying attention to details. Good readers must be able to distinguish between main ideas and details in order to understand the writer's purpose. Readers use the details to decide whether the writer has supported the main ideas sufficiently and convincingly. Similarly, good writers must be able to supply the reader with enough specific details to support the main idea of a text or passage. If there is no logical relationship between the main idea and the details, the reader will be confused and lose interest in what the writer has to say.

WRITING 1B	● **The Process**

Get Ready to Write

Paragraph Format

Whether you are writing a term paper, business proposal, or letter, your reader will expect you to use the correct format for a paragraph. Follow these steps to ensure your writing is formatted correctly.

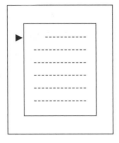

- Make sure there is a margin, or empty space, on each side of the paragraph. A margin is usually 1 inch.
- Indent the first sentence in your paragraph. This means you should start the first sentence 5 spaces or .5 inches to the right.
- Begin all sentences with a capital letter and end each sentence with a punctuation mark.
- Each sentence should immediately follow the previous one. Do not start each sentence on a separate line.
- Double space your paragraph. You can set your word-processing program to do this. If you are writing a paragraph by hand, write on every other line.
- Observe any specific requirements the professor gives you or the project requires.

ACTIVITY 19

Identify Formatting Errors

The following paragraph contains 13 formatting errors. Rewrite the paragraph, correcting any errors.

In this chapter we consider the ideas of several personality theorists. each brings a different perspective to the study of the human personality

Some, including Sigmund Freud, emphasize unconscious influences on personality. other theorists, called trait theorists, view personality as a composition of underlying traits that account for consistencies in behavior
Social-cognitive theorists view personality in terms of an individual's learning history and ways of thinking
finally, humanistic psychologists believe personalities are expressed through our efforts to reach our highest potential as human beings
In the following pages we will explore these different perspectives of the human personality

_____

_____

_____

_____

_____

_____

_____

_____

Identifying Supporting Details

As you know from Chapter 1, the main idea includes the topic and what the author wants the reader to know about the topic. The author supports the main idea by providing specific details: facts, statistics, personal experiences, examples, or reasons. The details convince the reader to accept the viewpoint or information that has been presented.

ACTIVITY 20

Identify Main Idea vs. Supporting Details

A. Read the sentences below. If the sentence contains a topic, it is a main idea. If the sentence provides specific information, it is a detail about the topic. Write *MI* for Main Idea or *SD* for Supporting Detail in the blank. The first one has been done for you.

1. ___MI___ a. The big-five model of personality is organized around five basic factors.

   ___SD___ b. The components of this model are openness, conscientiousness, extraversion, agreeableness, and neuroticism.

2. _____ a. Central traits are those which organize and control behavior in many different situations which are usually apparent to others.

   _____ b. "Reliable" is an example of a central trait.

3. _____ a. "Dislikes crowds" is an example of a secondary trait.

   _____ b. Secondary traits are those which are more specific to certain situations and control far less behavior.

4. _____ a. Gordon Allport, a trait theorist, spent 30 years searching for the traits that combine to form normal personality.

_____ b. He compiled a list of words, many of them adjectives, that could describe people.

The Paragraph Body: Major and Minor Support Sentences

There are two kinds of support sentences in paragraphs: major supporting sentences and minor supporting sentences.

Major supporting sentences contain the main details that support the topic sentence. Minor supporting sentences provide more information, such as facts, statistics, or examples about the statements made in the major support sentences. Both major and minor supporting sentences must be related to the topic sentence.

Read the paragraph below about phobias. Then study the outline showing the paragraph's major and minor supporting sentences.

Phobias

Three major types of phobias are social phobia, specific phobia, and agoraphobia. People with social phobia have intense fears of social interaction. Individuals suffering from social phobia would be greatly distressed when meeting others, dating, or giving a presentation in class. They would have a very difficult time maintaining normal social lives. People with specific phobias have fears of specific objects or situations. Claustrophobia, the fear of small spaces, is a specific phobia. A person with claustrophobia may avoid elevators even if they have to climb many flights of stairs every day. Finally, agoraphobia is the fear of being in open spaces or out in public. Agoraphobics may literally become housebound, unable even to go to the grocery store or doctor's office. Phobias have a profound impact on the lives of those who suffer from them.

Outline for Paragraph on Phobias

Major supporting sentence #1	**Topic Sentence:** Three major types of phobias are social phobia, specific phobia, and agoraphobia.
Minor supporting sentences	A. People with social phobia have intense fears of social interaction. a. Individuals suffering from social phobia would be greatly distressed when meeting others, dating, or giving a presentation in class. b. They would have a very difficult time maintaining normal social lives.
Major supporting sentence #2	B. People with specific phobias have fears of specific objects or situations.
Minor supporting sentences	a. Claustrophobia, the fear of small spaces, is a specific phobia. b. A person with claustrophobia may avoid elevators even if they have to climb many flights of stairs every day.
Major supporting sentence #3	C. Finally, agoraphobia is the fear of being in open spaces or out in public.
Minor supporting sentence	a. Agoraphobics may literally become housebound, unable even to go to the grocery store or doctor's office.

Conclusion: Phobias have a profound impact on the lives of those who suffer from them.

Identify Major and Minor Support Sentences

The sentences below belong to one paragraph. Read the sentences and identify the two major supporting sentences. Then match the minor supporting sentences with the appropriate major supporting sentences. Fill in the outline with your answers. The topic and concluding sentences have been done for you.

- A clinical psychologist evaluates and treats patients with psychological disorders such as depression.
- School psychologists offer children a number of services, including special education programs.
- Many clinical psychologists conduct research as well.
- A school psychologist, on the other hand, specializes in helping children with academic, emotional, and behavioral problems.
- They use a variety of psychological and educational tests along with parent and teacher interviews to evaluate a child's strengths and weaknesses.
- Clinical psychologists can practice in hospitals, clinics, or in private practices.

Topic sentence: A person contemplating a career in psychology has many choices for specialization; clinical psychology and school psychology are two examples of specialty areas.

(major)   1. _____

(minor)   a. _____

(minor)   b. _____

(major)   2. _____

(minor)   a. _____

(minor)   b. _____

Concluding sentence: These specialties are only two of the many opportunities for a person interested in pursuing a career in psychology.

Writing Details from Graphics

Facts and statistics are often shown in the form of graphs or charts. It is important to know how to write details using these kinds of sources.

Earlier in this chapter, you read paragraphs about details and examined a bar graph and chart used for information by the author. Look again at the bar graph titled "Women Ph.D. Recipients in Psychology" from page 41.

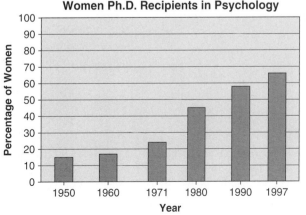

Women Ph.D. Recipients in Psychology

This chart can provide many details to support a topic sentence. Some details can be broad for major supporting sentences, while others can be specific enough for minor support sentences. For example:

Broad: Women earned the majority of Ph.D.s awarded in psychology in 1997.

Two-thirds of the recipients of Ph.D.s awarded in psychology each year are women.

The percentage of women receiving Ph.D.s in psychology has risen dramatically.

Specific: Women earned 66 percent of Ph.D.s awarded in psychology in 1997.

The greatest increase in numbers of women awarded Ph.D.s in psychology occurred between 1971 and 1980.

In 1950, only 15% of Ph.D.s awarded in psychology were earned by women.

What are some other details that can be written from this graph? With a partner, write one broad and one specific detail. Share your details with the class.

_____

_____

_____

ACTIVITY **22**

Use Graphics for Details

Examine each graphic with a partner. Use the information to create supporting sentences with details. Create two broad and two specific details for each graphic.

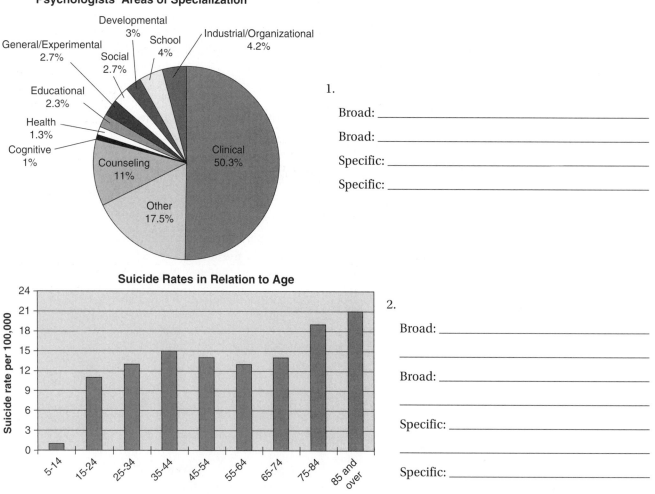

Psychologists' Areas of Specialization

- Developmental 3%
- General/Experimental 2.7%
- Social 2.7%
- School 4%
- Industrial/Organizational 4.2%
- Educational 2.3%
- Health 1.3%
- Cognitive 1%
- Counseling 11%
- Clinical 50.3%
- Other 17.5%

1.

Broad: _____

Broad: _____

Specific: _____

Specific: _____

Suicide Rates in Relation to Age

Suicide rate per 100,000

Age Groups: 5-14, 15-24, 25-34, 35-44, 45-54, 55-64, 65-74, 75-84, 85 and over

2.

Broad: _____

_____

Broad: _____

_____

Specific: _____

_____

Specific: _____

_____

Key Concepts 1: Reading and Writing Across the Disciplines

How Did They Do That?

Review the Steps

First, review *Writing 1B: The Process* on pages 24-32 in Chapter 1, which outlines the steps a writer takes to develop a paragraph. Then read the following classification paragraph about compliance and complete the activity.

Methods of Compliance

The field of psychology has identified three effective methods for evoking compliance in people. When using the first method, the foot-in-the door technique, a person is asked to agree to small requests and then eventually larger ones. The logic behind this method is that people usually agree to requests that do not demand a great deal of time, effort, or money. Agreeing makes people feel committed to the issue, and they are likely to agree to another request. Businesses often employ this approach, asking potential customers to answer simple questions and then asking the person to purchase something. The second approach for eliciting compliance is called the door-in-the-face procedure, whereby a person asks for a favor that is unlikely to be granted. The person then concedes that the request was extreme and suggests a lesser favor as a compromise. This lesser favor is really what the person wanted originally. Because the person seeking the favor appears willing to compromise, the second favor is likely to be granted. The door-in-the-face method is frequently used by politicians. The final technique for eliciting compliance is called the low-ball approach. In this method, a customer is asked to make an oral commitment to purchase something for a price. Once the commitment is made, the initial price is raised due to some computing "error." Customers often pay this higher amount because they feel obligated to uphold their promise. This happens especially if the person making the higher price request was the same person to whom the customer made the original promise. Car salespeople and other businesses often practice this method. Compliance to requests can effectively be evoked by using one of these three proven techniques.

1. Circle the idea the writer brainstormed and used in the paragraph.

2. Underline the narrowed topic in the paragraph.

3. Draw two lines under the details, major and/or minor, in the paragraph.

4. List some key words which identify the text structure. _____
    _____

5. Write the topic sentence here. _____
    _____

6. Write the concluding sentence here. _____
    _____

Paragraph of Classification or Division

Write Your Paragraph

Choose a topic or concept from your field of study or from a topic or subject you are interested in and which can be divided into groups or categories. Examples of concepts are *career options available to graduates in your field, kinds of engineering, types of automobiles,* or *categories of clouds.* Follow the steps below to write a paragraph of classification. Your audience is your instructor and your classmates. After you finish writing your paragraph, complete the two final activities, *Revising* and *Editing and Proofreading.*

Steps:

1. Brainstorm the topic.
2. Narrow the topic.
3. Brainstorm and narrow the details.
4. Choose the text structure (classification).
5. Organize the details.
6. Write the topic sentence.
7. Create an outline with sections for each group/category.

Topic Sentence: _____

_____

A. _____

   1. _____

   2. _____

   3. _____

B. _____

   1. _____

   2. _____

   3. _____

C. _____

   1. _____

   2. _____

   3. _____

Concluding Sentence: _____

_____

8. Change outline phrases into sentences.

9. Write concluding sentence (restate topic sentence).

10. Put in paragraph format.

Revising

ACTIVITY 25

Follow the Steps

A. Follow the steps outlined below to revise the paragraph of classification you wrote.

Revising Checklist

1. Assignment
   - ☐ Follows the assignment to write a paragraph of classification for a topic or concept from your field of study or area of interest
   - ☐ Addresses the instructor and classmates as the audience
   - ☐ Follows the ten steps listed in the assignment

2. Topic sentence
   - ☐ Is limited to a specific topic
   - ☐ Includes the topic
   - ☐ Includes what the reader needs to know about the topic
   - ☐ Gives a clue to the text structure

3. Details
   - ☐ Relate to the topic
   - ☐ Are organized in a logical order
   - ☐ Follow the outline (describe or give examples of each group or category)
   - ☐ Enough in number (not too many, not too few)

4. Concluding sentence
   - ☐ Restates the topic sentence
   - ☐ Alerts the reader to the end of the paragraph
   - ☐ Summarizes the key points in the paragraph

B. Share your paragraph with a classmate. Ask your classmate to use the Revising Checklist to check your paragraph and give you some feedback. Make any changes to your paragraph that you feel are necessary. The changes you make should improve your paragraph.

Editing and Proofreading

ACTIVITY 26

The Final Steps

A. Follow the steps outlined below to edit and proofread the paragraph of classification you wrote.

> ### Editing and Proofreading Checklist
>
> 1. Grammar
>   - ☐ Verb tenses are correct.
>   - ☐ Each subject agrees with its verb (singular/plural).
>   - ☐ Prepositions are correct.
>   - ☐ Pronouns are correct (agree in number/gender).
>   - ☐ Articles are correct (a, an, the).
> 2. Spelling
>   - ☐ All the words are spelled correctly.
>   - ☐ Abbreviations, if any, are used correctly.
>   - ☐ First word of each sentence begins with a capital letter.
> 3. Punctuation
>   - ☐ All sentences end with a punctuation mark.
>   - ☐ Periods are after statements and question marks are after questions.
>   - ☐ Commas are used with independent clauses joined by coordinating conjunctions.
> 4. Sentences
>   - ☐ All sentences are complete.
>   - ☐ Each sentence has a subject and a verb.
>   - ☐ There are no fragments.
> 5. Format
>   - ☐ Paragraph has a title.
>   - ☐ First line is indented.
>   - ☐ All sentences are in paragraph format (not listed or numbered).
>   - ☐ Writer's name is on the paper.
>   - ☐ Paper is neat, clean, and legible (easily read).

B. Share your paragraph with a classmate. Ask your classmate to use the Editing and Proofreading Checklist to check your paragraph and mark any errors in grammar, spelling, punctuation, sentences, or paragraph format.

C. Fix any mistakes your paragraph contained. Proofread your paragraph one more time. Turn in your final draft to your instructor.

3 From Business: International Trade and Marketing

Classes in business and marketing have always been popular choices for college and university students. With today's global economy, the focus of many companies has widened to include the international consumer.

Using your general knowledge about business, discuss the following questions with a partner or in a small group.

- How do companies compete for business?
- Is there anything to prevent one company from becoming a monopoly?
- Should all businesses follow the same set of rules? Why or why not?
- How do international companies affect domestic ones?

This chapter will help you understand some of the **key concepts** in international trade and marketing such as:

- protectionism
- trade restrictions
- ethics
- social responsibility

Get Ready to Read

Business Decisions

Read the paragraph below and follow the instructions.

You have a small business that makes and sells picture frames. Another store, located next to yours, imports picture frames from outside the country and is able to sell them for a lower price. Now people are buying picture frames from your competitor. You cannot lower your prices or you will go out of business. With a partner, discuss the advantages and disadvantages of the solutions listed below and rank them from best (1) to worst (5). Share your answers with the class.

1. _____ Encourage the government to charge taxes on all imported picture frames.

2. _____ Form a partnership with your competitor and sell frames together.

3. _____ Ask the government to limit how many picture frames your competition can import.

4. _____ Sell all of your frames and then close your store.

5. _____ Move to another location where no one sells picture frames.

Surveying and Predicting

Survey and Predict

A. Follow the steps below to survey Reading 1 on page 67.

1. Read the title. Write it here. _____

2. Read the first paragraph. Write one or two words which tell the topic or what the paragraph is about. _____

3. Write the main idea here. _____

4. Read the headings, the titles of the sections in the reading. Write them here.
   _____

5. Look for any graphic or visual aids in the reading. Graphic aids are charts, graphs, pictures, maps, diagrams, etc. Describe them here. _____
   _____

6. Look for key (important) terms related to the topic. They are usually in bold. List them here. _____

7. Read the last paragraph. It is a summary of the entire reading.

B. Share your survey answers with a partner and discuss what you think the reading will be about. Then circle the number of the statement below which matches your prediction.

1. The passage will describe various types of protectionist legislation.

2. The passage will discuss the benefits and losses associated with free trade.

3. The passage will discuss the problems of and the efforts to control protectionism.

C. Now, read the passage to see if your prediction is correct. Try to read as quickly as you can. Do not stop to look up words In your dictionary.

Reading 1

Protectionism and Trade Restrictions

Free trade is like all competitive or technological changes. It creates and destroys. It gives and it takes away. Free trade lowers the price of the imported goods (products) by increasing competition. It also raises the demand for efficiently produced domestic goods. In the export industries, sales will increase, profits will rise, and stock prices will climb. It is clear that two groups will benefit from these new conditions. The consumers of the imported goods will benefit, as will the producers of the exported goods.

However, it is clear that there are groups that are harmed as well. One of the most visible groups is the domestic producers. They must compete with the producers of the imported goods. The domestic producers are harmed in various ways. They experience noticeable declines in **market share,** falling profits, and deteriorating stock prices.

Benefits vs. Losses

It is a fact of life that there are both beneficiaries and victims of free trade. There are beneficiaries and victims when almost any change is made. The true test, however, is not to determine if victims exist. The true test is whether the benefits of change outweigh the inevitable losses. The same is true for the issue of **protectionism**. Do the benefits of protectionism outweigh the losses?

Herein lies the major reason for protectionist legislation. The victims of free trade are highly visible. Their losses are quantifiable. The governments use protectionism to lessen or reduce the harm done to this easily identified group. Protectionist legislation tends to take one of three forms. It may be in the form of **tariffs, quotas,** or **qualitative trade restrictions.**

> **World Trade Organization Facts**
> - founded January 1, 1995
> - headquarters in Geneva, Switzerland
> - 148 members (in 2005)
> - administers WTO trade agreements
> - monitors national trade policies
> - provides technical assistance and training for developing countries
> - handles trade disputes

Tariffs

Tariffs are taxes on goods which move across an economic or political boundary. They can be imposed on imports and exports. They can also be imposed on goods in transit. In other words, goods are taxed as they move through a country on their way to some other destination. The most common type of tariff is the import tariff.

Import tariffs usually raise the price of imported goods. This protects domestic industries from foreign

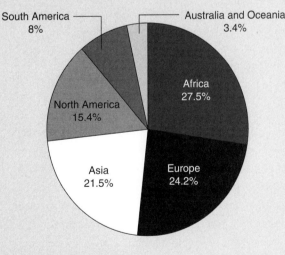

WTO Members by Continent in 2005

- South America 8%
- Australia and Oceania 3.4%
- Africa 27.5%
- North America 15.4%
- Asia 21.5%
- Europe 24.2%

competition. Import tariffs also generate tax revenues for the governments who impose them.

Quotas

Quotas are physical limits on the *amount* of goods that can be imported into a country. Tariffs restrict trade by directly increasing prices. Unlike tariffs, quotas increase prices by directly restricting trade. For domestic producers, quotas are a much surer means of protection. For consumers, quotas mean limited choices and higher prices.

Qualitative Trade Restrictions

Qualitative trade restrictions are non-tariff barriers. They are not taxes on goods. Instead, they include a wide range of charges, requirements, and restrictions. Examples are surcharges at border crossings, licensing regulations, or packaging and labeling regulations. Other restrictions might be size and weight requirements. Not all of these barriers are discriminatory and protectionist. Those that deal with public health and safety are legitimate. However, the line between social well-being and protection is a fine one.

World Trade Organization

The harmful effects of protectionism were felt most during the Great Depression in the 1930s. As a result, 23 nations formed the General Agreement of Tariffs and Trade **(GATT)** in 1948. GATT worked to liberalize and promote nondiscriminatory international trade between its members. In 1995, the World Trade Organization **(WTO)** replaced GATT. The WTO continues to pursue reductions in tariffs on manufactured goods today. It also continues to seek liberalization of trade in agriculture and services. In 2000, the WTO had 135 member countries. Thirty more countries wanted to join. The WTO is considered the global watchdog for free trade.

Key Concept Words

free trade – (n.) unrestricted exchange of products/services

GATT – (n.) General Agreement of Tariffs and Trade

market share – (n.) a company's share as a percent of the sales for the total industry

protectionism – (n.) restricting imports in order to help domestic producers

qualitative trade restriction – (n.) charge, requirement, or restriction on imports

quotas – (n.) limits on the amount of goods or products that can be imported

tariffs – (n.) taxes on goods or products which are imported, exported, or cross through a country

WTO – (n.) World Trade Organization

Glossed Words

barrier – (n.) obstacle to prevent success; **beneficiaries** – (n.) those who benefit from something; **deteriorating** – (adj.) becoming worse; **harm** – (v.) to hurt or damage; **legitimate** – (adj.) based on common sense; lawful; **noticeable** – (adj.) easy to see or observe; **pursue** – (v.) to try to accomplish; **surcharge** – (n.) an extra charge; **the line ... is a fine one** – (idiom) the difference between two things is difficult to see; **watchdog** – (n.) a person or group that guards against bad or illegal practices

Summarizing

Share What You Read

A. Use two or three sentences to tell your partner what you thought the reading was about. Then listen to your partner's sentences. Next, read the following statements and circle the number of the statement that best summarizes the reading.

1. The WTO was formed to address the problem of protectionism, which can harm free trade between countries.

2. The WTO has served to promote legislation consisting of tariffs, quotas, and qualitative trade restrictions.

3. The WTO supports protectionism when dealing with public health and safety issues.

B. Did you choose statement 1? If you chose a different answer, go back and review your survey answers. Try to determine why they lead to summary statement 1.

Check Your Comprehension

Read each statement below and decide if the statement is true or false. If it is true, put *T* in the blank; if it is false, put *F*. Correct any false statement to make it true. The first one has been done for you.

                         raise

_**F**_ 1. Import tariffs ~~lower~~ the price of imported goods.

_____ 2. Examples of qualitative trade restrictions include packaging and labeling regulations, and size and weight requirements.

_____ 3. Free trade hurts consumers who buy imported goods and the producers who exported them.

_____ 4. Today, WTO promotes non-discriminatory international trade among and between the members.

_____ 5. Domestic producers must compete with the producers of exported goods.

_____ 6. Quotas restrict trade and mean higher prices.

_____ 7. Tariffs, quotas, and qualitative trade restrictions are examples of protectionism.

Academic Word List

Scan and Define

A. Look at the ten words listed below. Scan the reading and underline the words from the list. Write the definitions for the words you know. Do not use a dictionary. The first one has been done for you.

1. domestic _in or from this country_

2. declines (n.) _____

3. export (adj./n.) _____

4. generate _____

5. global _____

6. impose _____

7. qualitative _____

8. range (n.) _____

9. restrictions _____

10. transit _____

B. Share your definition with a partner and then with the rest of your classmates. As a group, try to complete the definitions for all ten words. Use a dictionary to check the definitions if you are unsure about them. Then complete the vocabulary activity.

 Vocabulary Challenge

A. Circle the word that best completes the sentence. The first one has been done for you.

1. The *transit / (range)* of restrictions includes size and weight requirements.

2. Governments may use protectionism to support *domestic / export* producers.

3. Tariffs *generate / impose* money for the government.

4. The WTO is a *qualitative / global* organization formed in 1995.

5. Taxes which are *imposed / generated* on imports, exports, or goods in transit/range are called tariffs.

6. As a result of free trade, *qualitative / export* industries often see increased sales, rising profits, and climbing stock prices.

7. Quotas increase prices by directly imposing trade *ranges / restrictions*.

8. Tariffs are taxes on imported goods; quotas are physical limits on the amount of goods imported; and *export / qualitative* restrictions include packaging and labeling regulations as well as size and weight requirements.

9. An increase in sales for one group may mean a *range / decline* in market share for another.

B. Write your own sentences using the phrases below. Be sure to use the correct form of the word(s). The first one has been done for you.

1. global issue <u>An international meeting in Switzerland identified pollution as a</u>
   <u>global issue.</u>

2. range of products _____
   _____

3. sharp decline in prices _____
   _____

4. domestic producers _____
   _____

5. export industries _____
   _____

6. goods in transit _____
   _____

7. qualitative difference _____
   _____

8. generate revenue _____

_____

9. impose tariffs _____

_____

10. restrictions on imports _____

_____

Making Inferences and Drawing Conclusions

Inference: to use facts to determine the writer's message

In Chapter 1, you learned that sometimes writers do not state the main idea in one topic sentence. They imply the main idea through the details in the sentences. As the reader, you have to infer the main idea from the stated details.

Making inferences is often defined as "reading between the lines" to discover the writer's message. Making inferences applies to more than just the main idea, however. It is an analytical skill that you can use to guess the meaning of an unfamiliar word or even to predict questions when you study for a test.

To make an inference, you

- begin with the facts and the information the writer supplies
- add your own background knowledge and personal experiences to the writer's information
- consider all the possible meanings of the writer's message
- choose the best, most logical meaning

Writers present facts and information to convey their messages in different ways. They may use examples, facts, or statistics, for instance. Becoming familiar with these different methods will help you choose the best, most logical meaning the writer is trying to convey. Study the following examples and the accompanying analyses to become familiar with four different methods writers use.

Inferring from Examples

Example: Protectionist legislation can take many forms. For instance, imagine that the government of Kidds imposes a 10 percent tax on all children's shoes imported from the country of Footwear. The same government also allows only 200,000 pairs of children's shoes from the country of Boots to come into the country each year. Finally, the government of Kidds requires all imported shoes from the country of Soles to be packaged in boxes instead of in cheaper plastic bags. Shoes made in Kidds, however, are not subject to any tax or package requirements, and companies can manufacture as many shoes as they wish.

Analysis: Using the government of Kidds as an example, the writer implies that protectionist legislation is used to protect a country's domestic industries from foreign competition. The writer states that one country has to pay a 10 percent tax, another can only export 200,000 pairs of shoes, and the third country has to use special packaging. As the reader, you infer from the examples that protectionist legislation benefits Kidds's companies and hurts foreign companies.

Inferring from Facts or Statistics

Example: The World Trade Organization (WTO) is the global watchdog for free trade. The WTO had 135 members in 2000, and 30 additional countries were waiting to join. In 2005, the membership numbered 148 countries.

Analysis: The writer uses statistics (numbers) to show that the membership increased less than expected: the membership increased by only 13 countries over five years instead of the expected 30. As the reader, you try to infer the reason. In this case, the increase in numbers may mean more countries value free trade. However, the smaller-than-expected increase between 2000 and 2005 might mean that some countries changed their minds about joining; the small increase may also mean that the entry requirements changed and it takes longer to become a WTO member.

In this case, you, the reader, do not have enough information to draw a conclusion about the meaning of the numbers. You will need more information in order to choose the best, most logical meaning.

Inferring from Cause and Effect

Example: Free trade increases competition. Increased competition lowers the prices of imported goods and products because producers must compete for the same customers, and customers typically consider quality and price when they purchase a product. Increased competition also raises the demand for efficiently produced domestic goods and products. Domestic producers have to manufacture products that can compete with the lower-priced products imported into the country.

Analysis: The writer uses cause and effect to show the relationship between free trade and competition. As the reader, you can infer that consumers benefit from free trade by paying less for imported products. You may also draw the conclusion that free trade affects producers of domestic products, perhaps in a negative way.

When making inferences based on cause and effect, you, as the reader, will need to have enough information to be certain that one event causes another.

Inferring from Specific Details or Statements

Example: The government of a country has to decide whether to charge a tax on all cars imported into the country or to limit the number of cars allowed to be imported. Taxes restrict trade by directly increasing prices. Quotas increase prices by directly restricting trade.

Analysis: The writer makes direct statements to present the facts. Based on the statements, you, the reader, can infer that automakers in the home country prefer the government to issue quotas because fewer import cars will be available to consumers.

ACTIVITY **7**

Identify the Method

Read the situations and choose the method the reader must use to make an inference or draw a conclusion. Sometimes more than one method is possible. The first one has been done for you.

1. Kat Krunchies, Inc. was founded in 1987 and sold its cat snacks in small pet stores in the Midwest. Today, the company sells its snacks in all 50 states and publishes a catalogue of cat food, snacks, toys, and clothing.

   _____ examples

   _____ cause and effect

   ___X___ facts or statistics

2. Quotas are one type of protectionist legislation. If, for instance, the domestic manufacturers of calculators cannot compete with the lower prices of imported calculators, the government can limit the number of calculators imported into the country. Domestic manufacturers, however, can produce as many calculators as they wish.

_____ examples

_____ specific details or statements

_____ cause and effect

3. A small company in Italy produces leather goods and exports its products to the United States. The average price for its purses is about $95. Similar purses, manufactured by Bags & Co. in the U.S., cost $115. Over a six-month period, as demand for the Italian purses grew in the U.S., Bags & Co. lowered the price of its purses to $90.

_____ examples

_____ specific details or statements

_____ cause and effect

4. The government is trying to decide whether to limit the number of flat-screen televisions imported into the country. Consumers will be unhappy if they have fewer televisions to choose from and have to pay higher prices. The government decides not to impose a limit on the number of televisions allowed into the country, but it does charge a tariff on imported televisions.

_____ facts or statistics

_____ specific details or statements

_____ examples

 Make Inferences

Read the situations and the possible inferences that follow. With a partner, discuss each choice and circle the letter of the inference you feel is the best, based on the information given. If there is not enough information to choose one best option, suggest what kind of information is still needed to be able to draw a conclusion. The first one has been done for you.

1. Your neighbor owns a small factory that produces sports clothing. He has a bumper sticker on his car that reads "Victim of free trade."
   a. Your neighbor supports protectionist legislation.
   b. Your neighbor's business is hurt by foreign competition.
   c. Your neighbor supports free trade.

2. Records show that import car sales were strong and increased during the first six months of the year. However, even though prices remained the same, car sales decreased dramatically during the last six months of the year. In June, the government imposed a 23-percent surcharge on all cars brought into the country.
   a. The surcharge caused car sales to drop.
   b. Qualitative trade restrictions hurt import car sales.
   c. Higher prices are the result of qualitative trade restrictions.

3. Food for Today, Inc. wants to export meat and poultry to Canada. Canada has specific requirements that need to be met before meat and poultry can be imported into the country.
   a. Canada is using qualitative trade restrictions to protect its companies.
   b. Canada is imposing qualitative trade restrictions to protect the health of its citizens.
   c. Food for Today, Inc. has inferior products.

4. The United States imposes a tariff on all fruit brought into the country. The price of imported fruit, however, is not always higher than the price of domestic fruit.
   a. The tariff generates tax revenue for the government without raising fruit prices.
   b. Importers are losing money on the fruit they sell in the U.S.
   c. Consumers as well as domestic producers of fruit are being harmed by the tariff.

5. Japan exports computer software to the United States. The exported software is the same price as the software manufactured in the United States. Profits in domestic software manufacturing are falling.
   a. Free trade is responsible for falling profits.
   b. Domestic software producers are victims of free trade.
   c. The government is not practicing protectionism in this case.

Identifying Text Structure—*Problem/Solution*

Writers may use more than one pattern of organization in their writing, but there is usually one overall pattern. In Reading 1, the author introduces the topic of *protectionism* by explaining the effects of free trade on the cost of imported goods.

In the first two paragraphs of the reading, the author acknowledges who benefits from and who is harmed by free trade, and supports the information with details. In the third paragraph, the writer introduces responses to the problems of free trade. The remainder of the passage explains/outlines specific kinds of protectionist solutions: tariffs, quotas, and qualitative trade restrictions. The writer concludes the passage by introducing the formation of GATT/WTO as a solution to protectionism.

These characteristics are common to the text structure of problem/solution. The writer often begins with a definition or description of the problem and explains why it is a problem. The writer then offers possible solutions and their expected results, and ends the passage with the preferred solution.

Key Words—*Problem/Solution*

Recognizing the key words improves the reader's speed and increases comprehension of the material. Key words which may be associated with the pattern of problem/solution are listed in the chart below.

Neutral Key Words	Positive Key Words	Negative Key Words	Idea Connectors
effect of/on	alternative to	adverse	as a result
impact on	answer	harmful	because of
influence	benefits of	negative	but
issue	positive	problem	in conclusion
option	right	serious	for these reasons
recommend	solution	victim	however
situation	solve	wrong	nevertheless
warranted			

ACTIVITY **9** **Use Key Words**

A. Fill in the blanks with an appropriate key word associated with problem/solution. Choose from the words listed in the chart on the previous page. More than one answer may be possible for some of the sentences. The first one has been done for you.

1. Those who end up going out of business feel they may be the _victims_ of free trade.

2. Free trade benefits consumers; _____, it can hurt domestic manufacturers.

3. The Board of Directors met to discuss the _____ of raising prices.

4. Governments need to limit the _____ that is done to domestic producers of goods.

5. _____, the WTO is one possible solution to the problems associated with protectionism.

6. One possible _____ is to make agreements with neighboring countries to limit imports and exports.

B. Go back to Reading 1 and find examples of key words which show the pattern of problem/solution. Write the examples below.

1. _____

2. _____

3. _____

READING 2 ● **On Your Own**

In the first section of this chapter, you were introduced to the skills of and strategies for making inferences and drawing conclusions and to identifying the text structure of problem/solution. In this section, you will practice inferring the meaning of words in context with a new reading.

Get Ready to Read

ACTIVITY **10** **Agree or Disagree**

Read the following statements and decide whether you agree or disagree. Circle your choice. Discuss your answers and your reasons for them with a partner.

1. Business ethics are the same across countries.	AGREE	DISAGREE
2. Culture determines what is ethical or unethical.	AGREE	DISAGREE
3. "When in Rome, do as the Romans do" is good advice for international business managers.	AGREE	DISAGREE
4. International businesses should not do business with governments that violate human rights.	AGREE	DISAGREE

Surveying and Predicting

Survey and Predict

A. Survey Reading 2 and predict what information you will find.

1. Write the title here. _____

2. Read the first paragraph. Write one or two words which tell the topic or what the paragraph is about. _____

_____

3. Write the main idea here. _____

4. List the subheadings here. _____

5. List any key (important) terms related to the topic here. _____

_____

6. Read the last paragraph.

B. Share your survey answers with a partner and discuss what you think the reading will be about. Then circle the number of the statement below which matches your prediction.

1. The passage will describe the need for universal ethics in international management.

2. The passage will describe possible ways/methods to approach ethics in international management.

3. The passage will present different views on ethics in international management.

C. Now, read the passage to see if your prediction is correct. Try to read as quickly as you can. Do not stop to look up words in your dictionary.

Reading 2

Ethics and Social Responsibility in International Management

It is common for U.S. companies to have standards of conduct for their employees. Some business activities are considered wrong even if they do not violate any legal codes or political norms. Multinational companies face similar ethical issues around the globe. As **trade barriers** fall, international business increases. This means that more firms will face ethical issues in the future.

Universalism

How we act and how we feel others should act have been debated for years. Two perspectives are **universalism** and relativism. Universalism holds there are widespread and objective "rules." These rules are a part of all countries and cultures. Advocates of this position agree that there are moral rules that everyone should follow. They point to behaviors that almost every culture considers wrong. An example of one behavior is harming others or their property.

A common strategy is to develop a set of behaviors that constitute universal guidelines. In fact, global codes of ethics have been developed for managers in multinational companies. These codes include minimal rights for international workers. Included are the rights to physical security, free speech, subsistence, and nondiscriminatory treatment.

Problems

However, at least two problems emerge with implementing universal principles. First, it is not clear how they should be interpreted. This is because the codes try to be broad and universal. A second issue is that many countries and companies have not officially adopted all of these ethical obligations. Many countries and companies have not adopted even some of them.

Cultural Relativism

For these reasons, **cultural relativism** has become a popular alternative to universalism. Proponents of relativism believe that ethical behavior differs among countries. They believe ethical behavior is determined by a country's own unique culture, laws, and business practices. They believe "when in Rome, do as the Romans do." Their belief is often justified on several counts. The most important one is respect. Not to follow the practices of the country is to disrespect the culture in which you are a guest. This implies that international managers should follow the practices of the country where they are doing business.

An example of this situation occurred in Moscow. American actress Michelle Pfeiffer was filming the movie *The Russia House.* She left the movie set after a few weeks of filming. She protested the fact that Russian extras were not allowed to eat the catered food given to foreign actors. Local officials were called in to beg Ms. Pfeiffer to return to the set. They explained that this was the way things were done in Russia. Pfeiffer was eventually convinced. She stated,

"Whether I was right or wrong wasn't the issue. The issue was, do I have the right as an outsider to come in and force my sensibilities on this culture?"

Problems for Managers

Nevertheless, being a relativist could cause big problems for international managers. Just because a country has different customs doesn't make it immune to analysis or judgment. It can still be studied or judged. For example, most people would not agree that suppressing political freedom is morally acceptable anywhere. Using slave or prison labor, and other violations of human rights, are not morally acceptable because it is "Rome" rather than Paris or New York.

Possible Approaches

There are different ways to approach ethical issues across countries. Some multinationals believe they can have more influence by remaining in a country. If they remain, they are engaged in the economy. Others believe that pulling out is the answer. Multinationals also need to realize that their actions may have negative effects on the local populations of those countries making an ongoing transition to a market-based economy. What are some solutions? Investments in the community may help lessen the social impact of economic change. Helping the governments of emerging nations to develop and implement policies similar to those that exist in many Western industrialized countries is another. All in all, a greater emphasis on ethical behavior and social responsibility by multinationals is warranted.

Key Concept Words

cultural relativism – (n.) the belief that ethical behavior is determined by the unique culture, laws, and business practices of each individual country

trade barriers – (n.) obstacles to prevent trade between nations

universalism – (n.) the belief that there are moral rules that everyone should follow that cut across countries and cultures

Glossed Words

cater – (v.) to provide and serve food and drinks; **harming** – (n.) hurting or injuring; **on several counts** – (idiom) for many reasons; **proponents** – (n.) supporters or advocates; **pulling out** – (v.) leaving; **subsistence** - (n.) the ability to live from; **warranted** – (v.) justified or called for

Summarizing

Share What You Read

A. Use two or three sentences to tell your partner what you thought the reading was about. Then listen to your partner's sentences. Next, read the following statements and circle the number of the statement that best summarizes the reading.

1. Developing universal rules is the solution to avoiding unethical business behaviors.

2. Respecting the culture of the country in which you are doing business solves the issue of potentially unethical business behaviors.

3. Universalism and cultural relativism are possible solutions to the ethics and social responsibility issues that international business managers face.

B. Did you choose statement 3? If you chose a different answer, go back and review your survey answers. Try to determine why they lead to summary statement 3.

Check Your Comprehension

Read each statement and fill in the blank with a word or phrase below that best completes it. The first one has been done for you.

approach	moral
cultural relativism	pull out of
customs	universalists
ethical issues	"When in Rome, do as the Romans do"
interpret	wrong

1. Investing in the community is one ___approach___ to solving ethical issues for multinational companies.

2. Following the customs and culture of the country you are in is referred to as _____.

3. As international business increases, more multinational companies will face _____ abroad.

4. The incident with Michelle Pfeiffer on the movie set of *The Russia House* is an example of _____.

5. One method of influencing a country and its ethical issues is to _____ or leave the country.

6. Cultural relativism implies that international managers should follow the practices or _____ of the country where they live.

7. There are some behaviors that every culture considers _____, for example, hurting others.

8. _____ believe there is a common group of behaviors that can be developed for international managers.

9. One of the problems with universalism is how to _____ the very broad guidelines.

10. Universalists also believe that there are _____ rules that everyone should follow.

● Academic Word List

Scan and Define

A. Look at the ten words listed below. Scan the reading and underline the words from the list. Write the definitions for the words you know. Do not use a dictionary. The first one has been done for you.

1. advocates (n.) *people who support a cause* _____

2. codes (n.) _____

3. constitute _____

4. debate (v.) _____

5. ethics _____

6. interpreted _____

7. norms (n.) _____

8. ongoing _____

9. perspectives _____

10. widespread _____

B. Share your definition with a partner and then with the rest of your classmates. As a group, try to complete the definitions for all ten words. Use a dictionary to check the definitions if you are unsure about them. Then complete the vocabulary activity.

Vocabulary Challenge

A. Circle the word that does not belong. The first one has been done for you.

1. proponents	supporters	advocates	(protesters)
2. nationality	morals	ethics	rules
3. widespread	confined	scattered	dispersed
4. views	judgments	perspectives	outlooks
5. argue	discuss	debate	exist
6. understood	accepted	interpreted	translated

B. Read the definitions of the words below. Then decide which meaning is the one used in the sentence. Put the definition number next to the sentence. The first one has been done for you.

1. **interpret** *verb* **1.** to understand in one's own way; **2.** to translate from one language to another

   ___1___ First, it is not clear how universal principles should be interpreted.

2. **code** *noun* **1.** a system of words, symbols, or letters to keep messages secret; **2.** a system or collection of laws or rules and regulations

   _____ Although certain business activities may not violate any legal codes, they are often seen as simply the wrong thing to do.

3. **constitute** *verb* **1.** to set something up; establish; **2.** to be the elements or part of something; compose

   _____ A common strategy has been to develop a set of behaviors that constitute universal guidelines.

---

4. **norms** *noun* **1.** a standard or pattern that is considered to be typical of a group; **2.** an average or a statistical mode

_____ Certain business activities may violate political norms in one country or culture but not in another.

5. **ongoing** *adjective* **1.** open-ended; without specific limits; **2.** continuing or progressing

_____ There are social costs associated with many nations' ongoing transitions to more competitive, market-based economies.

Using Context to Guess Meaning—*Inference*

Sometimes it is possible to guess the meaning of an unfamiliar word simply by using other words in the sentence. Other times, however, you will need to use your background knowledge and experiences in order to guess the meaning.

Read the following sentence and how you might use your background knowledge to infer the meaning of the word *immune.*

*Just because a country has different customs than a manager is used to doesn't make it **immune** to analysis or judgment.*

Your past experience might include being *immunized* or vaccinated against a disease such as measles. You know that being immunized gives you protection. From this knowledge, you can infer that *immune* in the sentence above means "protected" or "safe."

Your past experience may have included reading about a court case in which one of the defendants was given *immunity* in exchange for testimony about a crime. You know that this person will be protected from being charged with the crime. From this knowledge, you can infer that *immune* means "protected from."

Without this knowledge, you would depend on a dictionary to give you the meaning of the word. Together with the information in the sentence, your knowledge of *immune* can also help you infer the larger meaning of the sentence: *A country is not protected or safe from analysis or judgment just because it has different customs.*

Guess Meaning from Context

Read the sentences below. Use the information in each sentence and your background knowledge to determine the meaning of the word in bold. On the line, write the definition of the word. Share your definitions with a partner and explain how you inferred the meanings.

1. International workers need guaranteed **minimal** rights, including safe working conditions, enough money to pay living expenses, and nondiscriminatory treatment.

   minimal = _____

2. In an effort to establish standards of ethical behavior, an international committee will meet to outline basic **principles** that are common to all cultures.

   principles = _____

3. Because cultures are so different around the world, it is difficult to develop a **transnational** set of behaviors that all international managers should follow.

    transnational = _____

4. People's behavior is determined by the culture, laws, and business practices that are **unique** to their country.

    unique = _____

5. Most people would agree that **suppression** of political freedom and discrimination are not good, morally acceptable behaviors.

    suppression = _____

6. **Proponents** of relativism believe ethical behavior differs among countries.

    proponents = _____

7. Universalism holds there are widespread and **objective** "rules."

    objective = _____

8. If they remain, they are **engaged** in the economy.

    engaged = _____

WRITING 1A • Skills and Strategies

In this section, you will learn additional skills and strategies associated with the writing process. This section addresses articles, a grammatical structure used in the readings, and writing compound sentences with conjunctive adverbs. You will practice different steps in the writing process and will write a paragraph of problem/solution.

The Grammar of Articles

Articles can be either indefinite (*a, an*) or definite (*the*). Nouns in English are preceded by indefinite or definite articles, or no article. Study the overview of article usage in the information below.

Indefinite Articles: A, An
Used with singular count nouns that:

- identify or classify
    A *tariff* is **a** *tax* on goods which move across an economic or political boundary.
- are not specified or not previously mentioned
    Goods are taxed as they move through **a** *country*.
- refer to one of a group
    Does the U.S. charge **an** *import tax* on clothing items from Canada?
- make generalizations
    A *quota* increases prices by directly restricting trade.

Indefinite articles generally are not used with non-count nouns.

Definite Article: The

Used with singular and plural count nouns that:

- are identified in the sentence by a modifier, such as an adjective clause
  The *barriers* that deal with public health are legitimate.

- have been previously mentioned
  A code of ethics has been developed for managers. **The** *code* includes minimal rights for international workers.

- refer to a member of a group or class in general
  The *surcharge* is a common trade restriction.

- are unique
  The *World Trade Organization* had 135 members in 2000.

- are familiar to the reader/listener
  Consider **the** *culture* of our country.

- refer to the entire group or class
  The *domestic producers* of goods are harmed by free trade.
  The *Americans* tend to support free trade.

- plural proper nouns and some place names
  The *United States* imports goods from South America.

Used with non-count nouns that:

- are identified in the sentence by a modifier, such as an adjective clause
  The *conduct* that managers display is often tied to the culture of the country.

No article

Used with plural count nouns that:

- refer to a member of a group or class in general
  Surcharges are examples of non-tariff barriers.

- refer to the entire group or class
  Domestic producers are harmed by free trade.
  American business owners value competition.

- make generalizations
  Governments impose trade restrictions to limit harm done to domestic producers.

Used with non-count nouns that:

- are not specified
  Universalism holds that there are widespread and objective "rules."

- follow gerunds
  Using *slave or prison labor* is not morally acceptable.

Use Articles

A. Read the paragraph below. Fill in the blanks with *a, an,* or *the.* Share your answers with a partner. Use the information on articles to explain the reasons for your choices.

The World Bank

(1) _____ World Bank gives long-term loans mainly to developing nations. In this sense, it functions like (2) _____ merchant banker (that is, (3) _____ supplier of capital) for (4) _____ developing nations. (5) _____ World Bank acts as (6) _____ intermediary between (7) _____ private capital markets and (8) _____ developing nations. It makes long-term loans, carrying rates that reflect prevailing market conditions. (9) _____ World Bank is able to borrow private funds at relatively low market rates and pass (10) _____ savings to (11) _____ developing nations.

B. Read the paragraph below. Fill in the blanks with *the* or a line (---) to show that no article is needed. Share your answers with a partner. Use the information on articles to explain the reasons for your choices.

Cross-National Differences

There are widely different ways to approach (1) _____ ethical issues across (2) _____ countries. For instance, one study found that (3) _____ American managers were more likely to view certain personnel issues (such as employee theft and misuse of company information) in ethical terms than their counterparts from Austria and Germany. On the other hand, (4) _____ Austrian and German managers were more likely to view (5) _____ involvement in local politics in ethical terms. These differences may reflect (6) _____ cultural values. (7) _____ Americans tend to be highly individualistic and, as a result, may feel that (8) _____ individual is (9) _____ main source of ethical values. (10) _____ Germans and Austrians, however, tend to be more community-oriented. In fact, (11) _____ business ethics in these countries has been described in terms of (12) _____ relationship between businesses and their local environments.

C. Read the paragraphs below. Decide whether article usage in the underlined item is correct or incorrect. If the item is incorrect, fix it. Share your answers with a partner. Use the information on articles to explain the reasons for your choices.

A Study of International Ethics

Another interesting study compared the reactions of managers in (1) <u>the United States</u>, France, and Germany to several important ethical concerns, including illegal payments. Here is (2) <u>the example</u> of one of the stories that the managers read:

Rollfast Bicycle Company has been barred from entering the market in (3) the large Asian country by collusive efforts of the local bicycle manufacturers. Rollfast could expect to net five million dollars per year from sales if it could penetrate the market. Last week, (4) a businessman from the country contacted the management of Rollfast. (5) A businessman stated that he could smooth the way for the company to sell in his country for (6) price of $500,000.

(7) The managers were then asked whether they would pay the bribe. In most cases, U.S. managers were less likely to pay the bribe than either of (8) the European managers, who in turn did not really differ all that much from one another. The managers were also asked about the reasons for their behavioral reactions. Not surprisingly, (9) the reasons varied across countries. For example, nearly 50 percent of the U.S. managers said they would not pay (10) bribe because they thought it was unethical, illegal, or against company policy. Only 15 percent of the French and 9 percent of the Germans mentioned these reasons. Instead, the Europeans were much more likely to say that it was (11) a competition that forced them to act that way. Overall, the U.S. managers were more concerned about (12) an ethical issues, while the Europeans were more concerned about maintaining a competitive business presence.

Sentence Essentials

Compound Sentences with Conjunctive Adverbs

In Chapter 2 you learned how to create compound sentences with coordinating conjunctions. Now you will learn how to form compound sentences using conjunctive adverbs.

It is important to note the punctuation of sentences connected by conjunctive adverbs: a semicolon (;) follows the first independent clause, and a comma follows the conjunctive adverb.

Example:

Some governments believe protectionism is the solution to the problems caused by free trade; ***however,*** *protectionism has its own problems.*

Just like the coordinating conjunctions, conjunctive adverbs show the relationship between clauses. The following chart shows the coordinating conjunctions and conjunctive adverbs that share similar meanings. See Appendix 3 on page 198 for sample sentences with conjunctive adverbs.

Coordinating Conjunction	Use and Meaning	Conjunctive Adverb
and	introduces another idea or more information	also besides furthermore moreover
or	introduces an alternative	otherwise
so	introduces a result	accordingly consequently hence therefore thus
but yet	introduces contrast	however instead nevertheless nonetheless on the other hand

When joining clauses with a conjunctive adverb, it is important to understand the relationship between the clauses. Is additional information given? Is a contrast, result, or alternative offered? Understanding the relationship between the clauses helps you choose an appropriate conjunctive adverb.

Examine the relationship between the two clauses in the compound sentence below. Decide which conjunctive adverb(s) can correctly join the clauses.

Consumers and importers benefit from the conditions brought by free trade; _____ domestic producers are harmed by those same conditions.

The first clause says some individuals and companies benefit (are helped by) free trade. The second clause mentions a group that is harmed by free trade. The two clauses have a *contrasting* relationship. Therefore, *however, nevertheless,* and *on the other hand* are the most appropriate conjunctive adverbs.

Use Conjunctive Adverbs in Sentences

A. Match the independent clauses (listed a-g) to the appropriate corresponding sentences (1-7). After matching, choose any three and write them underneath the activity. Use correct punctuation to join the two clauses with the conjunctive adverb given. Make any necessary changes.

Example: Small business owners are sometimes hurt by free trade. (furthermore)
They expect the government to restrict trade in order to help them.

Small business owners are sometimes hurt by free trade; furthermore, they expect the

government to restrict trade in order to help them.

_____ 1. The World Trade Organization works to promote nondiscriminatory international trade. (however)

_____ 2. A small dress factory must keep its costs low. (otherwise)

_____ 3. Cultures around the world vary. (consequently)

_____ 4. Some people believe that international managers should follow the practices of the country in which they are doing business. (moreover)

_____ 5. Tariffs and surcharges are forms of trade restrictions and hurt free trade. (nevertheless)

_____ 6. Importing food requires attention to public health and safety. (therefore)

_____ 7. There are some behaviors that almost every culture considers wrong. (thus)

a. Not following the customs is disrespecting the culture.

b. Some countries impose qualitative trade restrictions such as licensing and labeling regulations.

c. Many governments impose these restrictions to generate revenue.

d. It won't be able to compete with larger domestic or import clothing manufacturers.

e. It may be possible to develop a universal set of behavioral guidelines for international managers.

f. International managers need to be trained in the customs of the new culture.

g. Not all countries are interested in joining the organization.

1. _____

_____

2. _____

_____

3. _____

_____

B. Add a conjunctive adverb and an independent clause to the sentences below to make compound sentences.

Example: Computer literacy is required in today's business world.

Computer literacy is required in today's business world; consequently, computers are being installed in classrooms for even the youngest students.

1. Someday I want to open my own business.

_____

_____

2. International business requires a person to understand other cultures.

_____

_____

3. Exporting coffee to other countries is a major business in Colombia.

_____

_____

4. It is important for governments to protect their own businesses.

_____

_____

5. People who are bilingual and bicultural are needed in multinational companies.

_____

_____

Compound Sentences with Semicolons

It is not always necessary to use a conjunctive adverb if the two clauses are closely related. A semicolon (;) can be used between the clauses. See the example below.

> *Advocates of universalism agree that there are moral rules that everyone should follow; efforts have been made to develop a transnational code of ethics.*

If the second clause provides further definition, explanation, or description of the first clause, a colon (:) can be used.

> *Advocates of universalism agree that there are moral rules that everyone should follow: there are many behaviors that almost every culture considers wrong.*

ACTIVITY 19

Use Semicolons in Compound Sentences

A. Read each of the following statements. If the clauses are closely related, form a compound sentence using a semicolon. If the second clause explains or describes the first, use a colon.

1. Differing customs in countries are not immune to judgment. Most people would not agree that violations of human rights are acceptable because the occurrence is in "Rome."

   _____

   _____

2. Relativists believe ethical behavior in any country is determined by that country's culture and laws. An outsider behaving differently would be disrespectful of the host country.

   _____

   _____

3. It is a fact that there are beneficiaries and victims from free trade. The true test is whether the benefits outweigh the losses.

   _____

   _____

4. Quotas are limits on the amount of goods that can be imported into a country. They increase prices by directly restricting trade.

   _____

   _____

5. There are social costs with many nations' transitions to market-based economies. Investments in the community may reduce the social impact of economic change.

   _____

   _____

B. Use semicolons in three compound sentences of your own.

1. _____

2. _____

3. _____

C. Use colons in three compound sentences of your own.

1. _____

2. _____

3. _____

Punctuation: Run-on Sentences and Comma Splices

Two common errors in sentences are run-ons and comma splices. In a **run-on** sentence, two independent clauses have been joined without any punctuation.

Tariffs raise the price of goods the most common tariff is the import tariff.

Joining two independent clauses with only a comma results in a **comma splice.**

Tariffs raise the price of goods, the most common tariff is the import tariff.

To correct run-ons and commas splices, you can:

1. Separate the clauses into two simple sentences by adding a period.

   Tariffs raise the price of goods. The most common tariff is the import tariff.

2. Create a compound sentence by adding a coordinating conjunction or a semicolon.

   *Tariffs raise the price of goods, **and** the most common tariff is the import tariff.*
   Tariffs raise the price of goods; the most common tariff is the import tariff.

Correct Sentence Errors

Read each sentence carefully and identify whether the error is a run-on sentence or comma splice. Correct the errors by adding a period, coordinating conjunction, or semicolon.

1. Universalists are trying to develop a standard set of behaviors they want a code of ethics for multinationals to follow.

   _____

   _____

2. Many companies have not adopted universalist codes, this is a problem.

   _____

   _____

3. The "When in Rome" perspective is justified on many accounts, to do otherwise is disrespectful of the culture in which you are a guest.

   _____

   _____

4. International commerce is on the rise companies will have to confront ethical issues on a global level.

   _____

   _____

5. The reading "Ethics and Social Responsibility in International Management" explains different views on ethics, it cites problems for each view.

_____

_____

Making the Connection

Readers and writers focus on the conclusion of a passage for the "final word" on the subject. For readers, the conclusion often serves as a short summary of the entire passage: it may contain a restatement of the main idea and topic sentences and the writer's final opinion on the subject. For writers, the conclusion is the last opportunity to tie all of the details together to lead readers to the "right" conclusion.

| **WRITING 1B** | ● **The Process** |

Get Ready to Write

Conclusions

In Chapter 1 you learned how to conclude a paragraph by restating your topic sentence. As you continue to write, however, you will want to vary your conclusions to make your writing more interesting and to better suit the purpose of your paragraph.

Other ways to conclude a paragraph include:

- Summarizing the paragraph
- Calling for action
- Making a prediction
- Posing a question

Summarize your paragraph

A writer can conclude a paragraph by summarizing it, or reducing it to its main points.

Example: Many businesses are creating education projects in an effort to be good corporate citizens. S.C. Johnson, Phillips Petroleum, Lockheed Martin, and other firms have created the Young Eagles program, which teaches basic flying principles to students to encourage interest in flying careers. The pharmaceutical company Bayer promotes science education with its Bayer Science Forum. The Forum allows students to work alongside scientists conducting experiments. Mathematics and science education is also promoted by Toyota, which sponsors teacher grants. _Whether they're teaching flying or science, these education projects are giving corporations the opportunity to show their commitment to social responsibility._

Call for action

Writers use this method to conclude a paragraph if they want the readers to *do something* in response to the information they just read.

Example: The aftereffects of Hurricane Katrina are widespread. Some businesses have tried to take advantage of the situation by raising their prices unreasonably on items such as food and fuel. Profiting through price gouging is illegal and offenders should be punished. *If you are aware of any price gouging in your area, contact the Attorney General's office.* Your information will help the Attorney General prosecute these unethical businesses.

Make a prediction

You can end your paragraph by stating what will or may happen in the future.

Example: All around the globe, e-business is changing the way businesses process purchase orders, ship merchandise, and handle customer requests. Companies that use e-business to increase productivity and sales see their profits increase. Doing business electronically used to be reserved for only high-tech companies. *Now it is apparent that those companies that refuse to join the e-business revolution will be left behind.*

Pose a question

If you want your reader to think about a final problem or issue, you can end your paragraph with a question.

Example: Reducing our dependency on fossil fuels will be an expensive venture. Companies are spending millions of dollars around the world developing alternative energy sources such as fuel cells and hydrogen fuels. Converting our current energy infrastructure to use these new sources will also be costly. The expense will be a significant burden on governments and corporations. *Knowing, however, that fossil fuels are a finite source of energy, do we really have a choice?*

 ACTIVITY 21

Write Conclusions

Write new concluding sentences for each of the paragraphs on pages 89-90. Use one of the four techniques you have read about. The first one has been done for you.

1. Whether they're teaching flying or science, these education projects are giving corporations the opportunity to show their commitment to social responsibility.

   New concluding sentence: <u>What better way is there for corporations to show their commitment to social responsibility?</u>

   New concluding sentence: <u>We will see the benefits of these projects as those students choose future careers in mathematics and science.</u>

2. If you are aware of any price gouging in your area, contact the Attorney General's office.

   New concluding sentence: _____

   _____

   New concluding sentence: _____

   _____

3. Now it is apparent that those companies that refuse to join the e-business revolution will be left behind.

New concluding sentence: _____

_____

New concluding sentence: _____

_____

4. Knowing, however, that fossil fuels are a finite source of energy, do we really have a choice?

New concluding sentence: _____

_____

New concluding sentence: _____

_____

How Did They Do That?

Follow the Steps

First, review *Writing 1B: The Process* on pages 24-32 in Chapter 1, which outlines the steps the writer took to develop a paragraph. Then read the following problem/solution paragraph about free trade and protectionism to complete the activity.

Protectionism as a Response to Free Trade

The most apparent victims of free trade are the domestic producers of import-competing goods. The losses they suffer due to deteriorating stock prices, declines in market share, and falling profits are considerable. Tariffs, quotas, and trade restrictions are some of the ways governments can protect this very visible group. Placing tariffs on imported goods will raise prices and protect domestic producers from foreign competition. These tariffs will also generate revenue for the government. Imposing quotas will limit the amount of goods that foreign producers can import. This method will directly increase prices. Finally, qualitative trade restrictions can be used to ensure the domestic producers share in the market. Restrictions might be in the form of surcharges, or size and weight requirements. The above examples of protectionist legislation can reduce the harmful effects of free trade on domestic producers.

1. Circle the idea the writer brainstormed and used in the paragraph.

2. Underline the narrowed topic in the paragraph.

3. Draw two lines under the details, major and/or minor, in the paragraph.

4. List some key words which identify the text structure. _____

_____

5. Write the topic sentence here. _____

_____

6. Write the concluding sentence here. _____

_____

Paragraph of Problem/Solution

Write Your Paragraph

Choose a problem from your field of study or from a topic or subject you are interested in and offer potential solutions. Examples of problems are *counterfeiting of luxury items, testing new medications,* or *world dependence on fossil fuels.* Follow the steps below to write a paragraph of problem/solution. Your audience is your instructor and your classmates. After you finish writing your paragraph, complete the two final activities, *Revising* and *Editing and Proofreading.*

Steps:

1. Brainstorm the topic.
2. Narrow the topic.
3. Brainstorm and narrow the details.
4. Choose the text structure (problem/solution).
5. Organize the details.
6. Write the topic sentence.
7. Write an outline with sections for the problem and the solution.

Topic Sentence:

_____

_____

A. Problem _____
1. _____
    _____
2. _____
    _____
3. _____
    _____

B. Solution _____
1. _____
    _____
2. _____
    _____
3. _____
    _____

Concluding Sentence:

_____

_____

8. Change outline phrases into sentences.

9. Write concluding sentence (restate topic sentence, summarize, call for action, make a prediction, pose a question).

10. Put in paragraph format.

Revising

Follow the Steps

A. Follow the steps outlined below to revise the paragraph of problem/solution you wrote.

Revising Checklist

1. Assignment
   - ☐ Follows the assignment to write a paragraph of problem/solution for a topic or concept from your field of study or area of interest
   - ☐ Addresses the instructor and classmates as the audience
   - ☐ Follows the ten steps listed in the assignment

2. Topic sentence
   - ☐ Is limited to a specific topic
   - ☐ Includes the topic
   - ☐ Includes what the reader needs to know about the topic
   - ☐ Gives a clue to the text structure

3. Details
   - ☐ Relate to the topic
   - ☐ Are organized in a logical order
   - ☐ Follow the outline (describe the problem and possible solutions)
   - ☐ Enough in number (not too many, not too few)

4. Concluding sentence
   - ☐ Restates the topic sentence
   - ☐ Alerts the reader to the end of the paragraph
   - ☐ Summarizes the key points in the paragraph, calls for action, makes a prediction, or poses a question

---

B. Share your paragraph with a classmate. Ask your classmate to use the Revising Checklist to check your paragraph and give you some feedback. Make any changes to your paragraph that you feel are necessary. The changes you make should improve your paragraph.

Editing and Proofreading

The Final Steps

A. Follow the steps outlined below to edit and proofread the paragraph of problem/solution you wrote.

> **Editing and Proofreading Checklist**
>
> 1. Grammar
>   - ☐ Verb tenses are correct.
>   - ☐ Each subject agrees with its verb (singular/plural).
>   - ☐ Prepositions are correct.
>   - ☐ Pronouns are correct (agree in number/gender).
>   - ☐ Articles are correct (a, an, the).
> 2. Spelling
>   - ☐ All words are spelled correctly.
>   - ☐ Abbreviations, if any, are used correctly.
>   - ☐ First word of each sentence begins with a capital letter.
> 3. Punctuation
>   - ☐ All sentences end with a punctuation mark.
>   - ☐ Periods are after statements, and question marks are after questions.
>   - ☐ Commas are used with independent clauses joined by coordinating conjunctions.
>   - ☐ Semicolons and commas are used with independent clauses joined by conjunctive adverbs.
> 4. Sentences
>   - ☐ All sentences are complete.
>   - ☐ Each sentence has a subject and a verb.
>   - ☐ There are no fragments.
> 5. Format
>   - ☐ Paragraph has a title.
>   - ☐ First line is indented.
>   - ☐ All sentences are in paragraph format (not listed or numbered).
>   - ☐ Writer's name is on the paper.
>   - ☐ Paper is neat, clean, and legible (easily read).

B. Share your paragraph with a classmate. Ask your classmate to use the Editing and Proofreading Checklist to check your paragraph and mark any errors in grammar, spelling, punctuation, sentences, or paragraph format.

C. Fix any mistakes your paragraph contained. Proofread your paragraph one more time. Turn in your final draft to your instructor.

From the Social Sciences: American Government

Classes in American government typically focus on institutions and policies. Examples of institutions include local government, public schools, and the U.S. Supreme Court. Policies may be economic, foreign, military, or environmental.

Look at the photograph of the two political candidates above. Using your general knowledge about U.S. government, discuss the following questions with a partner or in a small group.

- What are the major U.S. political parties?
- How do people who hold a political office get their positions?
- What purpose do laws serve?
- What are some examples of laws that exist?

This chapter will help you understand some of the **key concepts** of American government such as:

- liberalism
- conservatism
- criminal law
- civil law

Skills and Strategies

Get Ready to Read

Liberal or Conservative

Read the following statements and decide whether they represent liberal or conservative views in the U.S. Circle your choice. Discuss your answers and your reasons for them with a partner.

1. The U.S. government should play an active role in foreign affairs.   LIBERAL   CONSERVATIVE

2. People who are unemployed should receive government support as long as necessary.   LIBERAL   CONSERVATIVE

3. The military force of a country needs to be strong.   LIBERAL   CONSERVATIVE

4. Prayer in public schools is acceptable.   LIBERAL   CONSERVATIVE

5. We need laws which guarantee equality of opportunity among races.   LIBERAL   CONSERVATIVE

Surveying and Predicting

Survey and Predict

A. Follow the steps below to survey Reading 1 on page 97.

1. Read the title. Write it here. _____

2. Read the first paragraph. Write one or two words which tell the topic or what the paragraph is about. _____

3. Write the main idea here. _____

4. Read the headings, the titles of the sections in the reading. Write them here.

    _____

5. Look for any graphic or visual aids in the reading. Graphic aids are charts, graphs, pictures, maps, diagrams, etc. Describe them here. _____

    _____

6. Look for key (important) terms related to the topic. They are usually in bold. List them here. _____

7. Read the last paragraph. It is a summary of the entire reading.

B. Share your survey answers with a partner and discuss what you think the reading will be about. Then circle the number of the statement below which matches your prediction.

1. The passage will discuss the meanings of the terms *liberalism* and *conservatism* and how they have changed over time.

2. The passage will describe the terms *liberalism* and *conservatism* as they are used in government today.

3. The passage will compare liberals and conservatives and what makes them support their political views.

C. Now, read the passage to see if your prediction is correct. Try to read as quickly as you can. Do not stop to look up words in your dictionary.

Reading 1

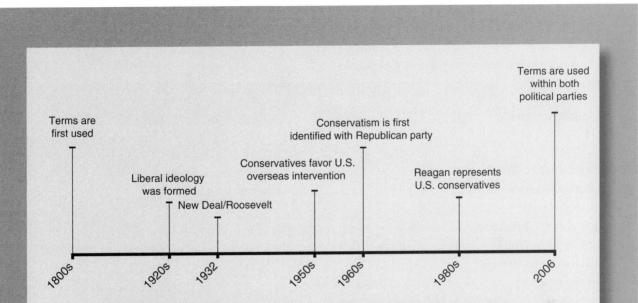

Terms are used within both political parties

Terms are first used

Conservatism is first identified with Republican party

Liberal ideology was formed

Conservatives favor U.S. overseas intervention

New Deal/Roosevelt

Reagan represents U.S. conservatives

1800s · 1920s · 1932 · 1950s · 1960s · 1980s · 2006

What Do Liberalism and Conservatism Mean?

The definition of these words has changed since they first came into use in the early nineteenth century. At that time, a **liberal** was a person who favored personal and economic liberty. That is, a liberal favored freedom from the controls and powers of the state. An economical liberal, for example, supported the **free market** and opposed government regulation of trade. In contrast, a conservative was originally a person who opposed the excesses of the French Revolution and its emphasis on personal freedom. A conservative favored instead restoring the power of the state, the church, and the **aristocracy**.

Meanings begin to change

Beginning around the time of Franklin Roosevelt and the **New Deal** in 1932, the meaning of these terms began to change. Roosevelt used the term *liberal* to refer to his political program. His program called for an active national government that would intervene in the economy and create social welfare programs. It would also help certain groups (such as **organized labor**)

acquire greater bargaining power. In time, the opponents of an active national government began using the term *conservative* to describe themselves. In general, a conservative favored a free market rather than a regulated one. A conservative also favored states' rights over **national supremacy** and greater reliance on individual choice in economic affairs.

Current meanings

Two persons may describe themselves as liberals even though one favors the **welfare state** and a strong national defense, and the other favors the welfare state but wants a sharp reduction in military spending. Similarly, one conservative may favor enforcement of laws against drug abuse. Another may believe that the government should let people decide for themselves what drugs to take. Once, liberals favored laws guaranteeing equal opportunity among the races. Now some liberals favor "**affirmative action**" plans involving racial quotas or goals. Once, conservatives opposed American intervention abroad. Today many conservatives believe the United States should play an active role in foreign affairs.

Identifying differences

In view of this confusion one is tempted to throw up one's hands in disgust and consign words like *liberal* and *conservative* to the garbage can. While understandable, such a reaction would be a mistake. In spite of their ambiguities, these words remain in general use and convey some significant meaning. They point to real differences between, for example, the liberal and conservative wings of the **Democratic** and **Republican** parties. One way to clarify the differences is to consider how self-described liberals and conservatives differ in their opinions on prominent issues. Prominent issues include 1) government policy with regard to the economy, 2) civil rights and race relations, and 3) public and political conduct.

Key Concept Words

affirmative action – (n.) a requirement to increase the number of minorities (racial quotas) in jobs/schools

aristocracy – (n.) a social class, usually one of wealth and nobility

conservative – (adj.) the tendency, usually political, to oppose change in customs, traditions, and existing institutions

Democratic party – (n.) one of two major U.S. political parties

free market – (n.) unrestricted exchange of products and services

national supremacy – (n.) the belief that the powers of the national government should be broadly defined

New Deal – (n.) Franklin Roosevelt's policy of government intervention in the economy to help American people

organized labor – (n.) labor unions

Republican party – (n.) one of two major U.S. political parties

welfare state – (n.) a system or government that provides economic assistance to those in need due to illness, unemployment, or age

Glossed Words

consign – (v.) to deliver or give up; **favor** – (v.) to support or approve of; **oppose** – (v.) to be against or not approve of; **prominent** – (adj.) widely known; **regulated** – (adj.) controlled by law; **reliance** – (n.) dependence on; **restore** – (v.) to return to previous state; **support** – (v.) to favor or approve of

Summarizing

Share What You Read

A. Use two or three sentences to tell your partner what you thought the reading was about. Then listen to your partner's sentences. Next, read the following statements and circle the number of the statement that best summarizes the reading.

1. The meanings of *liberalism* and *conservatism* have changed over the years but continue to be used today and signify real differences.

2. *Liberalism* and *conservatism* used to define a person's political beliefs about specific issues but are not used anymore today.

3. Liberals and conservatives differ in three ways: economically, ethnically, and behaviorally.

B. Did you choose statement 1? If you chose a different answer, go back and review your survey answers. Try to determine why they lead to summary statement 1.

Check Your Comprehension

Read the following statements. Circle the letter of the answer that best completes the statement.

1. In the 1930s, people who believed that states' rights were less important than national supremacy were classified as

   a. liberals.
   b. conservatives.
   c. organized labor.

2. Although today the terms *liberal* and *conservative* contain ambiguities, they

   a. are no longer generally used.
   b. communicate some important meaning.
   c. describe very different political programs.

3. In the early nineteenth century, a *liberal* favored freedom

   a. for the country, state, and church.
   b. from the controls and powers of the state.
   c. for the individual person.

4. One way that people can be identified as *liberal* or *conservative* is through their

   a. membership in a political party.
   b. opinions of government economic policy.
   c. opposition to military spending.

5. Which of the following does not fit Roosevelt's definition of a liberal political program? "An active national government that would..."

   a. create social welfare programs.
   b. help certain groups acquire bargaining power.
   c. avoid intervening in the economy.

6. Today, some liberals favor affirmative-action plans, including racial quotas. In the past, liberals favored laws guaranteeing

   a. equal opportunity among races.
   b. a free market over a regulated one.
   c. an active role in foreign affairs.

7. Which of the following is not a prominent political issue?

   a. national parks and roadways
   b. public and political conduct
   c. civil rights and race relations

8. A person considered to be conservative in the 1800s typically

   a. favored American intervention abroad and a strong national defense.
   b. opposed a regulated market and national supremacy.
   c. favored restoring the power of the state, the church, and the aristocracy.

Academic Word List

Scan and Define

A. Look at the ten words listed below. Scan the reading and underline the words from the list. Write the definitions for the words you know. Do not use a dictionary. The first one has been done for you.

   1. acquire *to get or obtain* _____
   2. ambiguities _____
   3. clarify _____
   4. conduct (n.) _____
   5. enforcement _____
   6. intervene _____
   7. liberal (n.) _____
   8. policy _____
   9. significant _____
   10. welfare (adj.) _____

B. Share your definition with a partner and then with the rest of your classmates. As a group, try to complete the definitions for all ten words. Use a dictionary to check the definitions if you are unsure about them. Then complete the vocabulary activity.

Vocabulary Challenge

A. Using your dictionary, work with a partner to find the missing word forms and complete the chart. If no form exists, draw a line in the space. The first one has been done for you.

Noun	Verb	Adjective	Adverb
1. acquisition	acquire	acquired/acquiring	---------
2. ambiguity			
3.	clarify		
4. conduct			
5. enforcement			
6.	intervene		
7. liberal			
8. policy			
9.		significant	
10.		welfare	

B. Read the sentences and determine whether the underlined word form is used correctly. If it is used correctly, put a *C* in the blank; if it is used incorrectly, put an *I* in the blank and correct the word form. The first one has been done for you.

_____I_____ 1. When asked about her stand on welfare reform, the candidate

ambiguously

answered <u>ambiguous</u>.

_____ 2. The neighborhood group <u>acquired</u> 10,000 signatures on a petition.

_____ 3. <u>Welfare</u> agencies across the country are understaffed and underfunded.

_____ 4. The senator's <u>liberally</u> message was greeted with boos and hisses.

_____ 5. During an election year, each candidate's <u>conducted</u> is under scrutiny from the press.

_____ 6. The U.S. presidential election, which takes place every four years, is a <u>significantly</u> event for the nation.

C. Decide whether the following statements are true or false based on the meaning of the underlined word. If a statement is true, put a *T* in the blank; if it is false, put an *F* in the blank. Share your answers with a partner and explain the reasons for your *False* answers. The first one has been done for you.

_____T_____ 1. A politician who wins with 85 percent of the vote has won by a <u>significant</u> majority.

_____ 2. If the U.S. government sends the U.S. National Guard to an American city to restore order, the government has <u>intervened</u> in city governance.

_____ 3. If a reporter asks a political candidate to explain her views on the environment, and the candidate's response focuses on health care issues, the candidate has <u>clarified</u> her position.

_____ 4. Letting people decide for themselves what drugs to take is an example of <u>enforcement</u> of laws against drug use.

_____ 5. The government's plan for social security for retired workers in the U.S. constitutes a <u>policy</u>.

_____ 6. A conservative who favors an individual's choice in economic affairs is expressing an opinion on public and political <u>conduct.</u>

Making Inferences and Drawing Conclusions

In Chapter 3, you learned that making inferences is "reading between the lines" in order to discover the writer's message. You practiced making inferences/drawing conclusions based on the writer's use of examples, facts or statistics, cause and effect, and specific details or statements.

In addition to those methods, writers may also use assumptions, opinions, and tone and bias to convey their message. These techniques are more subtle or abstract and not as easy to identify as examples or facts are. Because much of the academic reading you will do will be in textbooks, whose purpose is to provide information, you will seldom find assumptions, opinions, or tone and bias in the readings.

However, other readings related to the course subject may be assigned; recognizing the writer's assumptions or opinions will help you choose the best, most logical meaning of the passage. To become familiar with these additional methods, study the following examples and accompanying analyses.

Inferring Assumptions

Example: Once again, those few social welfare programs that are actually doing some good are in danger of being cut by the federal government next year. In an effort to reduce federal spending, the President has targeted a number of programs to eliminate: the preschool learning program, the hot lunch program, and the after-school arts and recreation program are just three. Democrats are outraged and have vowed to fight the proposed cuts, while Republicans are heralding the move.

Analysis: The writer makes the assumption that the three social welfare programs mentioned are all working successfully and that there is no reason to discontinue them. The writer provides no proof, however. The writer also assumes that the role of the government is to offer and fund such programs.

The writer also makes a generalization: "Democrats are outraged…Republicans are heralding the move." Are _all_ Democrats outraged? Are _all_ Republicans heralding the move? The writer gives no evidence to support this statement.

Assumptions, then, are ideas the writer accepts as true, ideas for which the writer provides no proof. They may be based on generalizations, but these generalizations may or may not be correct. Any generalization the writer makes needs to be supported by evidence. Because the assumptions are unstated, they are sometimes difficult to detect. Your job as the reader is to "uncover" the writer's assumptions and to infer meaning using your background knowledge and/or personal experiences.

Inferring Opinions

Example: Social order takes a back seat to equality in the ideal government of today's liberals. As long as the emphasis continues to be on equality, the federal budget will suffer. Government spending in support of education, welfare, and environmental protection programs is the mainstay of the liberals' platform. In time, it will also be the downfall of this great nation. No one is saying that equality is unimportant. It's just not government's job to enforce it. The more that government is involved, the weaker the nation becomes. Government should stay out of the business of enforcing equality.

Analysis: The writer shares an opinion about the role of government. The writer believes that social order is more important than equality; this statement can be disputed but not proven true or false, making it a statement of opinion. The writer also makes claims about consequences: "the budget will suffer," and "it will be the downfall of this great nation." The writer also uses the phrase "should stay out of." The author does not offer any facts to support the statements.

An opinion is a belief based on a person's judgments, attitudes, feelings, or thoughts. Because they are beliefs, opinions can be disputed. Do not infer anything that is not supported or that cannot be supported with facts. You as the reader must separate fact from opinion. Because a topic may have a range of opinions, determine what the range of opinions on an issue is before drawing a conclusion. Be careful not to accept the writer's view simply because you have the same view or because you are familiar with the writer's view.

Facts	Opinions
• can be confirmed or verified	• cannot be confirmed or verified
• cannot be disputed or disagreed with	• can be disputed or disagreed with
• can be proven true or false	• cannot be proven true or false
• are not based on the writer's beliefs	• are what the writer believes is true

Note: Opinions are different from personal preferences: "Classical music is more popular than jazz" is an opinion; "I like listening to classical music" is a preference.

Inferring Tone and Bias

Examples:

1. The prospective candidate for governor spent the weekend crisscrossing the state, meeting constituents, discussing the issues, and encouraging people to vote for her instead of the incumbent.

2. The wannabe governor gallivanted all over the state last weekend, glad-handing voters, lambasting her opponent, and painting a picture of gloom and doom if the incumbent is re-elected.

Analysis: In the first example, the writer is very matter-of-fact; that is, the writer states what the candidate did. The writer expresses the subject in a factual, objective way; the tone the writer has toward the subject is neutral. The author's word choices do not generate any specific emotion and so the statement does not reflect any bias either toward (positive) or against (negative) the candidate.

In the second example, the writer's approach is very subjective. The author's use of "wannabe" and "glad-handing," informal words of criticism, conveys a negative tone. "Gallivant," (to travel in search of pleasure) and "lambaste," (to criticize negatively) connote a candidate who is unfit for the office of governor. The author's word choices reflect an overall negative bias toward the candidate.

Tone, then, is the specific attitude or feelings the author expresses toward a subject. Tone is discerned through the writer's choice of words. It can be positive, negative, or neutral, as in the chart shown below.

Positive	Negative	Neutral
eager	angry	impartial
excited	arrogant	factual
happy	critical	objective
humorous	cynical	respectful
optimistic	pessimistic	serious
sympathetic	sarcastic	statistical

You as the reader need to consider the writer's purpose, main idea, and words used in order to determine tone. Read the example sentence below to see how word choice can change the tone of a sentence.

Example:

As expected, conservatives $\left\{\begin{array}{l}\text{dutifully}\\\text{wisely}\\\text{gleefully}\\\text{selfishly}\end{array}\right\}$ voted against the bill in the Senate.

Bias is closely connected to tone in that it is conveyed through the author's choice of words. These words tend to be emotional ones, and they make the reader feel either positive or negative toward the subject. Textbooks and reports are usually written in formal language; they present the subject as important. Writing that is more informal, that is "conversational" in nature, reflects an author's less-serious approach to the subject.

The sentences below all address the issue of welfare programs. Read each sentence and notice how word choice, specifically the italicized words, reflects the author's bias.

Elected officials are *entrusted with* public money to deliver needed services.

Baby-kissing, arm-waving officials *dole out* public money as they see fit.

Social welfare programs benefit those who are ill, unemployed, or elderly.

Handouts for the poor *are a free ride* paid for by the hard-working taxpayer.

When making inferences, consider 1) assumptions the writer makes, along with any supporting evidence; 2) opinions, along with facts to support them; and 3) tone and bias, conveyed through word choice.

 ACTIVITY **7**

Making Inferences

Read the passages and the statements which follow. Based on the information in the passage, decide whether the statement is an assumption (A), an opinion (O), or a fact (F). Put *A, O,* or *F* in the blank. Identify the tone and bias of each passage as well.

A. The Bureaucracy

One of the most remarkable revelations in the wake of the September 11 attack on the United Sates was that six months after the tragedy, the U.S. government's Immigration and Naturalization Service (INS) mailed a notice to a Venice, Florida, flight school, informing it that Mohamed Atta and Marwan Al-Shehhi had been approved for student visas. Atta and Al-Shehhi were two of the hijackers who flew planes into the World Trade Center. The approval of visas for terrorists who had died six months earlier was a symbol of the bureaucratic mistakes that allowed the terrorists to succeed in their mission on September 11.

Criticism is also warranted for the Federal Aviation Administration (FAA). It had received numerous warnings of possible terrorist attacks and had issued four information circulars to commercial airlines asking them to "use caution." But these bulletins sent to the airlines do not require any response, and the airlines did nothing. The FAA could have mandated changes in airline safety. The Central Intelligence Agency (CIA), which gathers intelligence outside the United States, made its share of mistakes, too. After identifying two foreigners as being involved with Al Qaeda, it waited twenty months, until right before September 11, before it placed these two hijackers on a federal watch list. By the time the men went on the watch list, they were already in the United States and could not be located by law enforcement officials.

The FBI made blunders as well. When Zacarias Moussaoui was arrested on an immigration charge in Minneapolis in August 2001, the local FBI office asked headquarters in Washington for permission to search his laptop computer because agents there believed he might be a part of a terrorist plot involving airplanes. FBI officials in Washington refused the request.

As investigations unearthed more and more failures of various federal agencies, it quickly became apparent that major changes in our national security apparatus were needed. The solution to all these bureaucratic failings was a new bureaucracy, the Department of Homeland Security. It is easy to criticize bureaucracies for their failings while at the same time overlooking underlying causes for their shortcomings. Like the INS, they may be understaffed and underfunded. They may have conflicting goals. Our expectations may be unrealistic. If any agency lacks sufficient resources or is given conflicting tasks, isn't that the responsibility of Congress and the president? Agencies don't set their own budgets and are not free to set their own goals.

Assumption, Opinion, or Fact?

_____ 1. The FBI is a government organization.

_____ 2. Bureaucratic mistakes resulted in terrorists entering the United States.

_____ 3. The World Trade Center was an economic center in New York.

_____ 4. Congress and the U.S. president should provide resources to government agencies.

_____ 5. Immigration officials mailed notices to a Florida flight school six months after the attack.

_____ 6. Government agencies do not set their own budgets.

_____ 7. The INS, FAA, CIA, and FBI are all to blame for the terrorist attacks.

_____ 8. The attack on the World Trade Center occurred in 2001.

_____ 9. Major changes in national security are needed.

_____ 10. Twenty months passed before the CIA placed the hijackers on a watch list.

Tone and Bias

11. Is the tone positive, negative, or neutral? _____

12. What words convey the tone? _____

13. List three words that convey the author's bias. _____

B. Uncle Sam Needs You

The government's talent shortage should worry us all. Government employees research asthma at the CDC; they keep planes from crashing at the FAA; and they're the ones who decide when it's safe to set off the Forest Service–controlled burns near your house.

Moreover, without top young talent, government is no match for the private sector it is supposed to regulate. Corporations that don't want to pay taxes hire lawyers who compete with the IRS. Mining companies that don't want to pay royalties hire smart lawyers who work wonders with federal law. Does anyone really want first-rate people on the corporate side and second-rate people on the public's side?

In addition, a great deal of government work is now contracted out. But contracting work out doesn't preclude the need for smart people in government. You still need smart people to make sure that the public isn't sold a bill of goods. Many of the security problems at the Los Alamos nuclear laboratory in New Mexico, for example, weren't just caused by the Department of Energy, but rather by lax oversight from the University of California at Berkeley, the main contractor running the lab.

This isn't to say that there's something bad about working for corporate America and the private sector. We're lucky that Henry Ford didn't work for the Department of Commerce, just as we're lucky that executives like IBM's Lou Gerstner and private inventors like Linus Torvalds are improving the ways that America runs. The growth of our private businesses is a primary reason for the current economic boom and its bounties.

The problem is one of balance. A society in which every ambitious environmentalist goes to work for the EPA or a nonprofit would fall apart because there would be no one to help develop non-polluting effluent systems. A society in which every ambitious environmentalist goes to work for [consulting firm] McKinsey and GE would fall apart because there would be no one to write regulations and to test pollution levels. Unfortunately, we seem to be shifting to the latter.

Assumption, Opinion, or Fact?

_____ 1. Private business is good for the nation's economy.

_____ 2. Government employees research health issues.

_____ 3. Some government work is performed through contracts with private businesses.

_____ 4. Private businesses are regulated by the U.S. government.

_____ 5. Henry Ford was responsible for creating a mass market for cars.

_____ 6. The EPA is a government agency.

_____ 7. Lou Gerstner worked for IBM.

_____ 8. It's too bad that young people don't want to work for the government.

_____ 9. The FAA keeps planes from colliding in the air.

_____ 10. The University of California at Berkeley should be blamed for some of the problems that occurred at Los Alamos in New Mexico.

Tone and Bias

11. Is the tone positive, negative, or neutral? _____

12. What words convey the tone? _____

13. List three words that convey the author's bias. _____

Identifying Text Structure—*Comparison/Contrast*

Writers sometimes introduce important terms or concepts by explaining the similarities and differences between them. In Reading 1, the author introduces the term *liberal* by explaining its meaning in the early nineteenth century. This is immediately followed by a definition of the term *conservative*. The remainder of the passage continues the format: each paragraph contains details about liberals and conservatives. This format follows the text structure of *comparison/contrast*. A paragraph may focus on only the similarities or only the differences between things, or it may contain both, as Reading 1 does.

When writing paragraphs of comparison/contrast, the writer may address the points or details of the first subject, followed by the points or details of the second subject. For example, Reading 1 could have contained all the information about liberals and liberalism in the first paragraph and all the information about conservatives and conservatism in the second paragraph. However, the writer chose to present the two concepts by alternating between the two, comparing and contrasting the same points for each concept. Short readings often present the information subject-by-subject, while longer readings are often organized point-by-point. Identifying how a passage is organized helps you anticipate what the writer will say, making you a more efficient reader.

Key Words—*Comparison/Contrast*

Good readers recognize the key words that are used with different patterns of text structure. Recognizing the key words improves the reader's speed and increases comprehension of the material. Key words associated with the pattern of comparison/contrast include:

Comparison		Contrast	
alike	same	but	instead
also	similar	contrast with	on the other hand
and	similarly	differ from	unlike
compared to	too	difference	versus
likewise		different / different from	whereas
		however	while
		in contrast to	

ACTIVITY 8

Use Key Words

A. Read the sentences below and decide whether the underlined comparison/contrast key word is used correctly. If it is, put *C* in the blank; if it is incorrect, put *I* in the blank and write the correct word above it. Make any necessary changes. The first one has been done for you.

unlike

_____I_____ 1. Pre-casino life in Greenbucks was quiet and uneventful, <u>like</u> now with non-stop traffic racing through the small downtown streets 24/7.

_____ 2. At first, the townspeople were very interested in the idea of offering 24-hour access to slot machines. The tourists, <u>in contrast</u>, found the idea attractive and exciting.

_____ 3. The casino's presence increased the number of jobs available in the town <u>but</u> increased the amount of tax revenue paid to the city.

_____ 4. Unemployment in Greenbucks decreased, <u>whereas</u> the crime rate, unfortunately, went up.

_____ 5. A national health care policy would benefit employers by reducing the cost of manufactured goods. <u>Likewise</u>, a national health care policy would be good for employees, many of whom currently have no coverage.

_____ 6. Most Democrats are in favor of a nationalized health care insurance plan; <u>similarly</u>, upper-middle-class workers do not support such a plan.

_____ 7. Instituting a national health care plan means the federal government would pay for the medical care of all its citizens. <u>Similar to</u> plans in some European countries, a U.S. plan would also regulate doctors and hospitals providing the care.

_____ 8. Young people entering the job market are eager to learn and make a difference in the way things are done. This attitude is <u>the same</u> for older workers, who reject innovation and focus only on making it to retirement age.

_____ 9. Public and private sector employment are <u>alike</u>. Promotions in government agencies are limited; promotions in private corporations can be unlimited for those who make a company's goals their own.

B. Go back to Reading 1 and find examples of key words which show the pattern of comparison/contrast. Write the examples below.

1. _____

2. _____

3. _____

READING 2 ● **On Your Own**

In the first section of this chapter, you were introduced to the skills of and strategies for making inferences and drawing conclusions and to identifying the text structure of comparison/contrast. You practiced those skills and strategies with Reading 1. In this section you will practice using synonyms and antonyms to guess the meaning of words in context with a new reading.

Get Ready to Read

Criminal or Civil

Read the following statements and decide whether they are examples of criminal or civil offenses. Circle your choice. Discuss your answers and your reasons for them with a partner.

1. The suspect was charged with murder.   CRIMINAL CIVIL

2. He signed a lease and then didn't pay the rent.   CRIMINAL CIVIL

3. She was driving 80 mph in a 60 mph zone.   CRIMINAL CIVIL

4. The man was driving while under the influence of alcohol.   CRIMINAL CIVIL

5. The woman was living and working in the country illegally.   CRIMINAL CIVIL

Surveying and Predicting

Survey and Predict

A. Survey Reading 2 and predict what information you will find.

1. Read the title. Write it here. _____

2. Read the first paragraph. Write one or two words which tell the topic or what the paragraph is about. _____

3. Write the main idea here. _____

   _____

4. Read the headings, the titles of the sections in the reading. Write them here.

   _____

5. Look for any graphic or visual aids in the reading. Graphic aids are charts, graphs, pictures, maps, diagrams, etc. Describe them here. _____

   _____

6. Look for key (important) terms. They are usually in bold. List them here.

_____

7. Read the last paragraph. It is a summary of the entire reading.

B. Share your survey answers with a partner and discuss what you think the reading will be about. Then circle the number of the statement below which matches your prediction.

1. The passage will compare and contrast the consequences of breaking the law, both criminal and civil.

2. The passage will outline the similarities and differences between criminal and civil law.

3. The passage will outline the similarities and differences between felonies and misdemeanors.

C. Now, read the passage to see if your prediction is correct. Try to read as quickly as you can. Do not stop to look up words in your dictionary.

Reading 2

Criminal vs. Civil Law

The distinction between criminal and civil law is a very important concept in our legal system. A criminal action is brought by the government against an individual who has allegedly committed a crime. Crimes are classified as **treason, felonies, and misdemeanors.** Their classification depends on the punishment attached to the crime. A civil suit involves a dispute between private individuals. The dispute involves a breach (breaking) of either a legal agreement or a legal obligation.

Government role

Criminal and civil cases differ in who brings the action. In criminal cases, unlike in most civil cases, the government brings the action. This means that, regardless of the victim's financial condition, the government will pay the costs of the action. It will pay for the investigation of the crime and for the prosecutors. If evidence requires scientific analysis, the government pays for the services of forensic scientists. If expert witnesses are needed, they are also paid for by the government. This involvement of the government is generally not found in civil cases.

Private parties

Governmental bodies can both sue and be sued in civil actions. However, most civil suits are between private parties. The private parties may be businesses, associations, or individuals. In civil cases, the parties determine whether to pursue a lawsuit or to seek some other non-judicial resolution. Each party is responsible for any costs and expert witnesses fees. In the civil justice system, a person's financial condition can make an enormous difference. Many people feel shut out of the civil justice system because of the cost involved in litigation.

Procedural rules

All states and the federal government have extensive rules that govern criminal and civil litigation. In both types, procedural rules help ensure that decisions are made in a fair and reasonable manner.

In criminal cases, procedural rules play a major role. They place limits on police investigative techniques, for example. In addition, they outline how criminal trials should be conducted. In order to find a person guilty of a crime, guilt must be proved beyond a reasonable doubt. This is a stricter standard than is usually required in a civil case. Since a crime is an act against society, the criminal court punishes a guilty defendant by imposing a fine or imprisonment or both.

Civil suits

Civil remedies, burden of proof, and court procedures all differ greatly from those in criminal cases. In a civil suit, the court attempts to remedy the dispute between individuals. This is accomplished by first determining their legal rights. Awarding money damages to the injured party may be part of the remedy. Directing one party to perform or refrain from performing a specific act is another possible remedy.

The burden of proof in civil cases requires that the **preponderance of evidence** show guilt. Guilt beyond a reasonable doubt does not have to be proved. Procedural rules ensure that the court has **jurisdiction** over the parties and that proper notice has been given to defendants. The rules also ensure that the parties have an equal opportunity to present evidence and arguments to the decision maker. Criminal actions are also recognized as violations of the civil law. As a result, victims in criminal cases often maintain or file separate civil suits against their attackers.

While both criminal and civil cases offer remedies, require burden of proof, and follow specific procedural rules, there are differences between them, including who brings the action and who pays the costs.

Key Concept Words

burden of proof – (n.) responsibility for proving the facts

civil remedy – (n.) resolution of a civil suit

felonies – (n.) very serious crimes, e.g. murder

jurisdiction – (n.) authority or power to decide

misdemeanors – (n.) less serious crimes, e.g. shoplifting

preponderance of evidence – (n.) superior proof

treason – (n.) help given to an enemy of one's country

Glossed Words

allegedly – (adv.) said to be true, but not proved; **dispute** – (n.) disagreement; **distinction** – (n.) difference; **forensic scientists** – (n.) scientists whose work is used in court; **guilt** – (n.) responsibility for committing an offense; **imprisonment** – (n.) confinement in jail or prison; **litigation** – (n.) suing; taking legal action against; **non-judicial** – (adj.) not in a court of law; outside of court; **sue** – (v.) to take legal action against

Summarizing

Share What You Read

A. Use two or three sentences to tell your partner what you thought the reading was about. Then listen to your partner's sentences. Next, read the following statements and circle the number of the statement that best summarizes the reading.

1. There are a number of similarities between criminal and civil law, two of which are who can sue and be sued, and what role procedural rules play.

2. There are more differences than similarities between criminal and civil law, including who brings the action, with whom the burden of proof lies, and what the court procedures are.

3. The only difference between criminal and civil law is who brings the action: the government in criminal law and private individuals in civil cases.

B. Did you choose statement 2? If you chose a different answer, go back and review your survey answers. Try to determine why they lead to summary statement 2.

Check Your Comprehension

Read each description and determine whether it is associated with criminal or civil law. Write *criminal* or *civil* before each item. The first one has been done for you.

_____criminal_____	1. rules for how trials should be conducted
_____	2. may include money awarded to the injured party
_____	3. costs and witness fees paid for by each party
_____	4. action brought by the government against an individual
_____	5. punished with a fine and/or imprisonment
_____	6. guilt proved by preponderance of evidence
_____	7. treason, felonies, misdemeanors
_____	8. government pays for cost of action
_____	9. dispute between private individuals
_____	10. brought by individuals, businesses, or associations
_____	11. guilt proved beyond a reasonable doubt
_____	12. breaking a legal document or legal obligation

Academic Word List

Scan and Define

A. Look at the ten words listed below. Scan the reading and underline the words from the list. Write the definitions for the words you know. Do not use a dictionary. The first one has been done for you.

1. analysis _a study or report on the parts of a problem, situation, or matter_

2. civil _____

3. concept _____

4. enormous _____

5. ensure _____

6. injured (adj.) _____

7. pursue _____

8. resolution _____

9. seek_____

10. violations _____

B. Share your definitions with a partner and then with the rest of your classmates. As a group, try to complete the definitions for all ten words. Use a dictionary to check the definitions if you are unsure about them. Then complete the vocabulary activity.

ACTIVITY ⑭ *Vocabulary Challenge*

A. Substitute one of the words from the Academic Word List for the underlined word. You may have to change the form of the word.

                               resolution

1. When the parties were unable to agree on a <u>solution</u>, the attorney advised her
              pursue
client to <u>carry on</u> the matter by filing a lawsuit.

2. The evidence in their case was overwhelming, <u>guaranteeing</u> a victory in court.

3. The judge had such a <u>large</u> number of cases to try that he <u>looked for</u> additional help from the district.

4. The <u>idea</u> of suing his own brother Thomas in an action related to <u>a citizen's</u> rights was unthinkable to Gerard.

5. The jury spent three days conducting its own <u>detailed examination</u> of the evidence before it rendered its guilty verdict.

6. Citing the defendant's <u>breaking</u> of multiple agreements, the prosecutor

asked the judge to award the <u>harmed</u> party a large settlement in the matter.

B. For the words below, put an *X* on the line in front of the definition as used in the reading.

1. **analysis**   ___X___ a. the separation of something into its parts to determine its nature

                         _____ b. a written report of information

2. **civil**   _____ a. relating to a citizen or citizens

                         _____ b. polite; courteous

3. **pursue**   _____ a. to follow someone or something in order to catch up with or capture

                         _____ b. to try to gain or accomplish something

                         _____ c. to carry something further

4. **resolution**   _____ a. firm determination

                         _____ b. a decision to do something

                         _____ c. a formal statement of a decision or opinion by a legislature or organization

                         _____ d. a solution or explanation; an answer

5. **seek** _____ a. to try to locate something; search for

_____ b. to try to obtain or get something

_____ c. to make an attempt to do something; to try

C. Using your dictionary, work with a partner to find the missing word forms and complete the chart. If no form exists, draw a line in the space. The first one has been done for you.

Noun	Verb	Adjective	Adverb
1. concept	conceive	conceptual	conceptually
2.		enormous	
3.	ensure		
4.		injured	
5. violations			

Using Context to Guess Meaning—*Synonyms and Antonyms*

In Chapter 1, you learned how key words and punctuation can help identify the meaning of unknown words. As writers seek ways to add variety to their writing, they often turn to synonyms and antonyms. You, as the reader, can take advantage of this by using the synonyms and antonyms as context clues to help you define other words in the passage. Read the following sentences to see how context clues help define the words *allege* and *breach*.

Without offering any proof, the police **alleged** *Ralph had participated in the bank robbery and arrested him. An hour later, the police had no choice but to release him.*

In this example, the police believed that Ralph had participated in a bank robbery. In fact, they were so certain that he had participated that they arrested him. However, the police did not provide any evidence (proof) of his participation. Thus, *allege* is a synonym for "saying or stating something without proof."

The businessman insisted that he had met all of his contractual obligations and that he had not **breached** *any part of the agreement as the lawsuit alleged. He produced copies of cancelled checks and signed receipts.*

In this example, the businessman stated that he did everything he was obligated to. If he met all of his obligations, he did not break or fail to meet any. Thus, *breach* is an antonym for "meet an obligation," and means, in fact, "to break or not meet an obligation or promise."

Guess Meaning from Context

Read the sentences below. Underline the synonym or antonym of the word in bold. Then write the word or phrase below the sentence, and tell whether it is a synonym or an antonym. Share your answers with a partner and explain how you guessed the meanings.

1. They charged him with <u>a very serious crime</u>. In the legal system, anyone who is convicted of a **felony** faces spending a number of years in jail. He's looking at 20 to 30 years in prison.

    felony = *a very serious crime (synonym)*

2. A **preponderance** of the evidence showed the landlord had not followed the terms of the lease. The tenant presented photos, videotapes, recorded messages, and written notes related to the case. The landlord's evidence was inferior; he presented just one witness.

    preponderance = _____

3. Although many people threaten to **sue** their employers for discrimination or their doctors for malpractice, most of them end up neither filing a lawsuit nor going to court.

    sue = _____

4. Jason **disputed** the fraud charges filed against him in a lawsuit by the investors of his company. He argued that he had paid the shareholders every penny they were owed.

    dispute = _____

5. Evidence discovered three years after his **imprisonment** showed that the young man could not have committed the crime for which he was found guilty. The judge ordered the man's immediate release from jail.

    imprisonment = _____

6. A local judge has no authority over matters pertaining to federal crimes. Only federal judges have such **jurisdiction.**

    jurisdiction = _____

7. She was charged with shoplifting, a less-serious offense than robbery. However, the **misdemeanor** will remain on her record until she successfully completes her community service.

    misdemeanor = _____

8. The woman stood before the judge and admitted she had made threatening phone calls to her ex-boyfriend. The judge ordered her to **refrain** from contacting her ex-boyfriend in the future or risk going to jail.

    refrain = _____

9. The courts rely on **forensic** scientists to present findings which are used as evidence during criminal trials. These scientists who testify in a court of law are employed by police labs, customs offices, and other government agencies.

    forensic = _____

10. The **prosecutor**'s opening statement outlined the government's case against the defendant. The defendant's attorney followed with a statement that her client was innocent and that the evidence would support that statement.

    prosecutor = _____

In this section, you will learn some skills and strategies associated with the writing process. This section addresses adjective clauses, a grammatical structure used in the readings, and writing complex sentences. You will practice different steps in the writing process and will write a paragraph of comparison/contrast.

The Grammar of Adjective Clauses

Like adjectives, adjective clauses modify a noun in a sentence. Adjective clauses are dependent clauses and are connected to independent clauses by relative pronouns or relative adverbs. Study the use of the relative pronouns and relative adverbs in the example sentences below.

Relative Pronoun	Use	Adjective Clause
who / that	subject (people)	Earlier, a liberal was a ***person* who favored personal and economic liberty.**
which	subject (things)	*Liberal* and *conservative*, ***terms* which were first used in the early nineteenth century,** began to change in meaning in 1932.
whom / that	object (people)	The ***conservative* whom I voted for** ran on a platform of American intervention abroad.
which	object (things)	Members of the political ***party* which I belong to** are holding a fundraiser next week.
whose	subject/object (possessive)	***People* whose votes were not counted** demanded a judicial hearing. ***Voters* whose names I didn't know** appeared on the voter registration list.

Relative Adverb	Use	Adjective Clause
when	object (time)	There were ***days* when people weren't allowed to vote.**
where	object (place)	People must vote in the ***district* where they live.**

 16 *Identify Adjective Clauses*

Underline the adjective clause in the sentences below. Circle the noun that the adjective clause modifies. The first one has been done for you.

1. A conservative was originally a (person) who opposed the excesses of the French Revolution.

2. Some people believe that the United States is a country which typifies freedom.

3. A criminal action may result in a person being fined and/or sent to jail.

4. I have never met a voter whose sole reason for voting was to be able to go into work late.

5. A prosecutor is a lawyer who represents the government in a criminal trial.

6. Some cases that are scheduled for court end up being settled before the court date.

7. During the last election, some of the candidates whom liberals supported barely won a majority.

Restrictive and Non-restrictive Adjective Clauses

There are two types of adjective clauses: restrictive and non-restrictive. They differ in how they affect the meaning of the sentence and in how they are punctuated.

Imagine you are in a room filled with newspaper reporters. One of the reporters was awarded a Pulitzer Prize. How do you know which reporter won? You need more information to identify the specific reporter. The following sentences use adjective clauses to identify a specific reporter.

> *The reporter who is standing in the doorway was awarded a Pulitzer Prize.*
>
> *The reporter whose picture is on the wall was awarded a Pulitzer Prize.*
>
> *The reporter who is carrying a black portfolio was awarded a Pulitzer Prize.*

Each of the three sentences contains a restrictive adjective clause. Taking out the adjective clause would make it impossible to identify which reporter won the prize. Restrictive adjective clauses 1) provide information that is essential or important to the meaning of the sentence, 2) limit or restrict the noun that is modified, and 3) are not set off by commas.

Now imagine that you are in a room filled with people in a variety of occupations: teachers, police officers, nurses, electricians, waiters, truck drivers, etc. Only one of the people in the room is a reporter. The reporter was awarded a Pulitzer Prize. Do you need more information in order to identify the reporter? No. The following sentence provides additional information about the reporter:

> *The reporter, who is shaking hands with the mayor, was awarded a Pulitzer Prize.*

Because you already know who the reporter is, the information *who is shaking hands with the mayor* is extra information. The sentence above contains a non-restrictive adjective clause. Non-restrictive adjective clauses 1) provide additional information, information that is not essential or important to the meaning of the sentence, 2) do not change the meaning of the sentence if they are omitted, and 3) are set off by commas to show that the information they provide is extra.

Identify Restrictive and Non-restrictive Adjective Clauses

Read each sentence. Underline the adjective clause. If the adjective clause is restrictive, write *R* in the blank. If it is non-restrictive, write *NR* in the blank and add the necessary commas to the sentence. The first one has been done for you.

__NR__ 1. The candidate, <u>who had been trailing in the polls,</u> was unexpectedly the winner of the election.

_____ 2. Liberal politicians who valued economic freedom did not want the government to regulate trade.

_____ 3. Early conservatives who did not approve of the French Revolution's emphasis on personal freedom wanted to restore the power of the state, church, and aristocracy.

_____ 4. Journalists protect their sources who often don't want their identity known publicly.

_____ 5. People who provide journalists with inside information often have their own motives.

_____ 6. International diplomacy which is my favorite subject is covered extensively on the 10:00 PM news program.

Sentence Essentials

Introduction to Complex Sentences

In previous chapters you learned that simple sentences are made up of independent clauses that can stand alone. Compound sentences are formed with two or more independent clauses joined by a conjunction, semicolon, or colon. *One candidate agreed to the debate, but the other did not* is an example of a compound sentence, i.e., two independent clauses joined by a conjunction.

> An **independent clause** completes a thought and can stand alone as a sentence.
>
> A **dependent clause** does not complete a thought and *cannot* stand alone.

- A dependent clause cannot stand alone because it does not express a complete thought.

  Until the judge takes her seat.

  That the definition of liberalism has changed.

  Whose homes were damaged by the tornado.

- A dependent clause must be connected to an independent clause to complete a thought. This kind of sentence is called a complex sentence.

  The courtroom audience will stand <u>until the judge takes her seat.</u>
  dependent

  Some people argue <u>that the definition of liberalism has changed.</u>
  dependent

  The people <u>whose homes were damaged by the tornado</u> voted to re-elect the mayor.
  dependent

- There are three kinds of dependent clauses: adverb clauses, noun clauses, and adjective clauses.

Identify Dependent and Independent Clauses

Read the sentences and determine whether the underlined clauses are independent or dependent. The first one has been done for you.

___D___ 1. The accused was held in jail <u>until the trial was over.</u>

_____ 2. The jury found the defendant guilty, and <u>they sentenced him to prison.</u>

_____ 3. <u>Before this campaign,</u> I was never interested in politics.

_____ 4. The students <u>who were old enough to vote</u> were allowed to watch the debate.

_____ 5. Defendants <u>who cannot afford an attorney</u> have one appointed for them.

_____ 6. The popular governor entered the convention, <u>where he announced his bid for the presidency</u>.

_____ 7. <u>News cameras were allowed into the courtroom</u> so everyone could watch the verdict.

More Practice with Adjective Clauses

Use Adjective Clauses

Connect the two clauses with the relative pronoun or adverb in parentheses to form an adjective clause. Do not repeat the underlined noun you replace with the pronoun or adverb.

1. The governor announced his candidacy for president. <u>The governor</u> was very popular in his state. (who)

   The governor, who was very popular in his state, announced his candidacy for president.

2. The President flew on a jet. <u>The jet</u> is called Air Force One. (which)

   _____

3. A rival network hired the news anchor. <u>The news anchor's</u> contract was about to expire. (whose)

   _____

4. The senator was running for re-election. I met <u>the senator</u> at the fundraiser. (whom)

   _____

5. Photographers waited at the courthouse. The defense lawyer would speak <u>at the courthouse</u>. (where)

   _____

6. News stories are perceived to be unbiased. <u>News stories</u> are viewed on television. (that)

   _____

7. Witnesses are paid for their time in court. <u>Witnesses</u> testify for the government. (who)

   _____

Create Complex Sentences with Adjective Clauses.

Use the relative pronoun or relative adverb in parentheses to create a sentence with a restrictive or non-restrictive adjective clause.

1. (that) *The book that the reporter wrote made the best-seller list.* _____

2. (who) _____

3. (whom) _____

4. (which) _____

5. (whose) _____

6. (where) _____

7. (when) _____

8. (that) _____

Making the Connection

Readers and writers alike pay close attention to the purpose and tone of a passage. In order to read critically, readers must decide the author's purpose. Is it to inform or share information with the reader? Is it to convince the reader to accept a specific viewpoint? Or is the purpose simply to entertain the reader? Writers who have a clear purpose are better able to use facts, statistics, and examples to support their main idea. Writers who choose words which express their attitude toward the subject help the reader understand the tone of their writing. If either the purpose or the tone is unclear, the reader will not benefit from what the writer is trying to share.

WRITING 1B ● The Process

Get Ready to Write

Identify Purpose and Select a Tone

Effective writing is more than just grammatical sentences and correct format. A good writer also identifies a purpose for writing and then chooses an appropriate tone.

Purpose

A writer's purpose is the reason he or she is writing. Different purposes require different styles of writing. Non-academic writing styles include reporting, reviewing, and creative writing. In academic writing, students often write to inform, instruct, or persuade. The chart below lists some writing styles and their purposes.

Style	Purpose or Reason
reporting	to document actions or events of interest to the audience
reviewing	to evaluate a product, movie, restaurant for the audience
creative	to entertain the audience
informational	to teach an audience about a subject by providing information
instructional	to teach an audience how to do something by giving instructions
persuasive	to convince an audience to do or to believe something

Determine the Writer's Purpose

Read the following descriptions and decide the style the author would use as well as the author's purpose for writing. Some may have more than one purpose.

Example: a blog about the adventures of raising triplets _entertain, possibly inform_

1. an editorial titled "Oil fuels tension between nations" _____

2. a letter to the editor titled "Open park to four-legged residents" _____

3. a comedian's monologue about being a minority _____

4. a manual for a computer software program _____

5. an article on hurricane preparedness _____

6. an editorial titled "Where do our tax dollars go?" _____

7. a satire about the current political climate _____

8. meeting minutes _____

9. an article comparing different types of laptop computers _____

Tone

In conversation, your tone of voice says a great deal to the listener. It conveys your attitude not only about the subject, but also toward the listener. The tone in your writing also conveys your attitude. Thus, it is important to write with a tone that is appropriate for your purpose.

For academic writing, you should:

1. use a professional tone
   - Be polite and respectful.

     Unprofessional: *The prosecutor who lost the case is lazy and stupid.*
     Professional: *The prosecutor who lost the case made critical and avoidable errors.*

2. use formal language
   - Conversational language is not appropriate for academic work.

     Informal: *That network's coverage of the election dispute was awesome. People were totally into it.*
     Formal: *People were captivated by the network's coverage of the election dispute.*

3. be consistent with your tone
   - Do not mix tones or change tone in a single piece of writing.

You should avoid:

1. sarcasm

   Not: *The government's response to the disaster was **so** coordinated.*
   But: *The government's reaction to the disaster showed flaws in organization.*

2. over- or under-exaggeration

   Not: *Only rich people can win in the civil justice system.*
   But: *Costs associated with legal action can make the civil justice system seem like it is only for the wealthy.*

Revising Statements for Tone

Read the following statements. With a partner, discuss why the tone in the original statement is inappropriate. Rewrite the statements with an academically appropriate tone.

Example: This news program is the best in the world.

Rewrite: This news program received the highest rating from viewers.

1. The congressman is very healthy for a man his age.

   Rewrite: _____

2. You should know better than to vote for that candidate.

   Rewrite:_____

3. That reporter couldn't find a story if he tripped on it.

   Rewrite: _____

4. Anyone who could defend that murderer is a jerk.

   Rewrite: _____

5. I didn't vote for her 'cause I don't like her ideas about taxes.

   Rewrite: _____

How Did They Do That?

ACTIVITY **23**

Follow the Steps

Read the following comparison/contrast paragraph that is a summary of Reading 2. Then, review *Writing 1B: The Process* on pages 24-32 in Chapter 1, which outlines the steps the writer took to develop the paragraph, to complete the activity.

Criminal vs. Civil Law I

The U.S. legal system houses two kinds of courts: criminal and civil courts. Knowing their roles and characteristics is crucial to understanding how the legal system works. Criminal cases are tried in courtrooms at the state or federal level. The trials are presided over by a judge, and often held in front of a jury. In criminal cases, action originates with the government charging a defendant with a crime. The government assumes responsibility for all costs of the prosecution, including attorney salaries and costs of evidence testing. When a defendant cannot afford an attorney, the government supplies one at its own cost. Procedural rules for criminal courts require that guilt beyond a reasonable doubt must be proved by the government in order for a conviction. They also guide how a trial is conducted. Like criminal cases, civil suits are also tried in courtrooms in front of a judge if they cannot be resolved privately. There may also be a jury. Action in a civil case originates when a private party sues another over a breach of a legal agreement or obligation. In a civil case, each party, whether an individual, business, or association, is responsible for their own legal costs, making some people feel they are shut out of the civil justice system. Unlike in criminal cases, the procedural rules in civil cases ensure that the court has jurisdiction over the parties and that proper notice has been given to defendants. The rules also ensure that each party has an opportunity to present evidence. Venue, origin of action, financial obligation, and procedural rules are characteristics that define the roles of criminal and civil courts.

1. Circle the idea the writer brainstormed and used in the paragraph.

2. Underline the narrowed topic in the paragraph.

3. Draw two lines under the details, major and/or minor, in the paragraph.

4. List some key words which identify the text structure. _____

   _____

5. Write the topic sentence here. _____

   _____

6. Write the concluding sentence here. _____

   _____

Format Options for Comparison/Contrast

When writing a comparison/contrast paragraph about two or more subjects, you have two options for formatting.

In the **block** format, a writer first discusses one subject entirely before discussing the next one. In a **point-by-point** format, the writer organizes information around the points compared. Both (or all) subjects are discussed with regard to each point.

Block Format

The sample paragraph on the previous page was written using block formatting. Criminal cases were discussed completely before the author wrote about civil cases. The author's outline for the paragraph would look like this:

Topic Sentence: The U.S. legal system houses two kinds of courts: criminal and civil courts. Knowing their roles and characteristics is crucial to understanding how the legal system works.

I. Criminal cases

  A. Venue

    1. tried in courtrooms at the state or federal level

    2. presided over by a judge

    3. most often in front of a jury

  B. Origin of action - government

    1. Defendant is charged with a crime.

  C. Financial obligation

    1. Government is responsible for all costs of the prosecution, including attorney salaries and costs of evidence testing.

    2. Attorney is provided for defendants who cannot pay.

  D. Procedural rules

    1. Guilt beyond a reasonable doubt must be proved by the government in order for a conviction.

    2. guide trial

II. Civil cases

  A. Venue

    1. tried in courtrooms if they cannot be resolved privately

    2. presided over by a judge

    3. sometimes in front of a jury

  B. Origin of action – private party

    1. breach of a legal agreement or obligation

C. Financial obligation
1. Each party is responsible for own costs.
2. Costs cause some to feel shut out.
D. Procedural rules
1. ensure the court has jurisdiction
2. proper notice given to defendants
3. Each party has opportunity to present evidence.

Conclusion: Venue, origin of action, financial obligation, and procedural rules are characteristics that define the roles of criminal and civil courts.

Point-by-Point Format

If the sample paragraph had been written using the point-by-point format, it would look like this:

Criminal vs. Civil Law II

The U.S. legal system houses two kinds of courts: criminal and civil courts. Knowing their roles and characteristics is crucial to understanding how the legal system works. Criminal cases are tried in courtrooms at the state or federal level. The trials are presided over by a judge, and often held in front of a jury. Likewise, civil suits are also tried in courtrooms in front of a judge if they cannot be resolved privately. There may also be a jury in civil cases. In criminal cases, action originates with the government charging a defendant with a crime, while a civil case begins when a private party sues another over a breach of a legal agreement or obligation. In criminal cases, the government assumes responsibility for all costs of the prosecution, including attorney salaries and costs of evidence testing. When a defendant cannot afford an attorney, the government supplies one at its own cost. In contrast, each party in a civil case, whether an individual, business, or association, is responsible for their own legal costs. As a result, some people feel they are shut out of the civil justice system. Procedural rules for criminal courts require that guilt beyond a reasonable doubt must be proved by the government in order for a conviction. They also guide how the trial is conducted. The procedural rules in civil cases, however, ensure that the court has jurisdiction over the parties and that proper notice has been given to defendants. The rules also ensure that each party has an opportunity to present evidence. Venue, origin of action, financial obligation and procedural rules are characteristics that define the roles of criminal and civil courts.

The author's outline for the point-by-point paragraph would look like this:

Topic Sentence: The U.S. legal system houses two kinds of courts: criminal and civil courts. Knowing their roles and characteristics is crucial to understanding how the legal system works.

I. Venue
A. Criminal: state or federal court
1. presided over by a judge
2. most often in front of jury

B. Civil

    1. in court with judge if not settled privately

    2. sometimes in front of jury

II. Origin of action

  A. Criminal – government files charges against defendant

  B. Civil – private party sues another over breach

III. Financial obligation

  A. Criminal – government assumes all prosecutorial costs

    1. will also provide attorney for those who cannot afford one

  B. Civil – each party responsible for own costs

    1. Some feel shut out due to costs.

IV. Procedural rules

  A. Criminal

    1. outline how trial should be conducted

    2. guilt beyond reasonable doubt for conviction

  B. Civil

    1. ensure jurisdiction

    2. proper notification

Concluding Sentence: Venue, origin of action, financial obligation, and procedural rules are characteristics that define the roles of criminal and civil courts.

Highlight the Format

Use two different colored highlighters to compare block and point-by-point formats.

1. Re-read the block format paragraph and outline *Criminal vs. Civil Law I* on page 122.

2. Highlight all of the sentences about criminal law in Color 1.

3. Highlight all of the sentences about civil law in Color 2.

4. Repeat the steps for *Criminal vs. Civil Law II*: Color 1 for criminal law, Color 2 for civil law.

5. Compare the two formats.

Complete the Outlines

The following sentences make up a comparison/contrast paragraph titled *Stories on the News*. Read the sentences and organize them in the block and point-by-point outlines. Use highlighters to help you. The topic and concluding sentences have been identified for you.

The first kind of news story discussed is the routine story. Highlight all of the sentences for this subject in Color 1.

The second kind of story is the inside story. Highlight all the sentences for this subject in Color 2. Then complete the outlines.

Topic Sentence: Network news programs show a variety of stories to their viewers. All of the stories are meant to provide information, but they differ in the manner in which they are produced and how susceptible they are to bias.

A journalist working on an inside story obtains information from a source who has inside access.

A routine story provides viewers with information about a regularly covered, public event that is easy to describe.

A president's trip abroad, for example, would be a routine story.

These stories can differ in length and headlines, but because the media receives the same information from wire sources, routine stories are less likely to be affected by a journalist's opinion or bias on the subject.

One kind of story featured on news programs is the routine story.

Wire sources provide the media with routine stories every day.

Insider stories cover topics a journalist or network believes are interesting or should be interesting to viewers, making inside stories vulnerable to bias.

On the other hand, an insider story covers information not generally public, such as a company's illicit financial practices.

It takes hard work to find sources to provide inside information.

Conclusion: Knowing the difference between the two kinds of stories can help a viewer watch for possible bias.

Stories on the News—*Block Format*

Topic Sentence: Network news programs show a variety of stories to their viewers. All of the stories are meant to provide information, but they differ in the manner they are produced and how susceptible they are to bias.

A. Subject One: _____

   1.

   2.

   3.

   4.

B. Subject Two: _____

   1. _____

   2. _____

   3. _____

Concluding Sentence: Knowing the difference between the two kinds of stories can help a viewer watch for possible bias.

Stories on the News—*Point-by-point Format*

Topic Sentence: Network news programs show a variety of stories to their viewers. All of the stories are meant to provide information, but they differ in the manner they are produced and how susceptible they are to bias.

A. Point One: There are two kinds of news stories. _____

   1. _____

   2. _____

   3. _____

   4. _____

B. Point Two: The kinds of stories also differ in their sources of information.

   1. _____

   2. _____

   3. _____

C. Point Three: The differences in the stories' sources affect the potential for bias.

   1.

   2.

Concluding Sentence: Knowing the difference between the two kinds of stories can help a viewer watch for possible bias.

Signaling Similarities and Differences

Whether you use the block or point-by-point format, you need to alert the reader to which points or subjects are similar and which are different. Transitions serve this purpose. Study the chart below. Then circle all the transitions in the sample block paragraph *Criminal vs. Civil Law I* and the sample point-by-point paragraph *Criminal vs. Civil Law II*. Which format uses more transitions? Why?

Transitions for Comparison/Contrast

Comparison		Contrast	
and, also, in addition	like	although	on the other hand
as well as	neither	but	unlike
both	similarly	conversely	whereas
each (of)	the same	however	while
just as	too	in contrast	yet

WRITING 2   ● On Your Own

Paragraph of Comparison/Contrast

Write Your Paragraph

Choose two topics or subjects from your field of study that you are interested in and compare and contrast them. Examples of subjects to compare are *private and public universities, liberal and conservative approaches to funding education,* and *e-mail and handwritten letters.* Follow the steps below to write a paragraph of comparison/contrast. Your audience is your instructor and your classmates. After you finish writing your paragraph, complete the two final activities, *Revising* and *Editing and Proofreading.*

Steps:

1. Brainstorm the topic.

2. Narrow the topic.

3. Brainstorm and narrow the details.

4. Choose the text structure (comparison/contrast).

5. Choose block or point-by-point format.

6. Organize the details.

7. Write the topic sentence.

8. Write an outline in the format of your choice (see pages 123-125 for sample outlines).

9. Change outline phrases into sentences.

10. Write concluding sentence (restate topic sentence).

11. Put in paragraph format.

Revising

Follow the Steps

A. Follow the steps outlined below to revise the paragraph of comparison/contrast.

Revising Checklist

1. Assignment
   - ☐ Follows the assignment to write a paragraph of comparison/contrast for subjects from your field of study or area of interest
   - ☐ Addresses your instructor and classmates as your audience
   - ☐ Follows the ten steps listed in the assignment

2. Topic sentence
   - ☐ Is limited to a specific topic
   - ☐ Includes the topic
   - ☐ Includes what the reader needs to know about the topic
   - ☐ Gives a clue to the text structure

3. Details
   - ☐ Relate to the topic
   - ☐ Are organized in a logical order
   - ☐ Follow the outline (makes comparison/contrast)
   - ☐ Enough in number (not too many, not too few)

4. Concluding sentence
   - ☐ Restates the topic sentence
   - ☐ Alerts the reader to the end of the paragraph
   - ☐ Summarizes the key points in the paragraph, makes a prediction, or poses a question

---

B. Share your paragraph with a classmate. Ask your classmate to use the Revising Checklist to check your paragraph and give you some feedback. Make any changes to your paragraph that you feel are necessary. The changes you make should improve your paragraph.

Editing and Proofreading

The Final Steps

A. Follow the steps outlined below to edit and proofread the paragraph of comparison/contrast you wrote for the *On Your Own* section.

> ### Editing and Proofreading Checklist
>
> 1. Grammar
>   - ☐ Verb tenses are correct.
>   - ☐ Each subject agrees with its verb (singular/plural).
>   - ☐ Prepositions are correct.
>   - ☐ Pronouns are correct (agree in number/gender).
>   - ☐ Articles are correct (a, an, the).
> 2. Spelling
>   - ☐ All words are spelled correctly.
>   - ☐ Abbreviations, if any, are used correctly.
>   - ☐ First word of each sentence begins with a capital letter.
> 3. Punctuation
>   - ☐ All sentences end with a punctuation mark.
>   - ☐ Periods are after statements, and question marks are after questions.
>   - ☐ Commas are used with independent clauses joined by coordinating conjunctions and with non-restrictive adjective clauses.
>   - ☐ Semicolons and commas are used with independent clauses joined by conjunctive adverbs.
> 4. Sentences
>   - ☐ All sentences are complete.
>   - ☐ Each sentence has a subject and a verb.
>   - ☐ There are no fragments.
>   - ☐ There are transitions and key words.
> 5. Format
>   - ☐ Paragraph has a title.
>   - ☐ First line is indented.
>   - ☐ All sentences are in paragraph format (not listed or numbered).
>   - ☐ Writer's name is on the paper.
>   - ☐ Paper is neat, clean, and legible (easily read).

B. Share your paragraph with a classmate. Ask your classmate to use the Editing and Proofreading Checklist to check your paragraph and mark any errors in grammar, spelling, punctuation, sentences, or paragraph format.

C. Fix any mistakes your paragraph contained. Proofread your paragraph one more time. Turn in your final draft to your instructor.

From the Biological Sciences: Biology

5

Classes in biology focus on the study of living organisms and their life processes and develop a student's understanding and appreciation for the unity and diversity of life. Biology classes include learning about the origin, physical characteristics, growth, and habits of plants and animals.

Using your general knowledge about biology, discuss the following questions with a partner or in a small group.

- How can studying biology help you in everyday life?
- What are some of the biological systems of the human body?
- How are botany and zoology related to biology?
- What environmental factors affect the growth of plants and animals?

This chapter will help you understand some of the **key concepts** of biology such as:

- the respiratory system in humans
- inhalation and exhalation
- ecosystems
- producers, consumers, and decomposers

Get Ready to Read

 Activity 1

True or False

Read the following statements and decide whether they are true or false. Circle your choice. Discuss your answers and your reasons for them with a partner.

1. Respiration (breathing) in the human body happens automatically.	TRUE	FALSE
2. Blood carries oxygen to the body's tissues.	TRUE	FALSE
3. The stomach is one of the organs of the respiratory system.	TRUE	FALSE
4. The air we take in is filtered by tiny hairs in the nose.	TRUE	FALSE
5. The air we breathe contains carbon dioxide.	TRUE	FALSE

Surveying and Predicting

 **Activity 2**

Survey and Predict

A. Follow the steps below to survey Reading 1 on page 133.

1. Read the title. Write it here. _____

2. Read the first paragraph. Write one or two words which tell the topic or what the paragraph is about. _____

3. Write the main idea here. _____

4. Read the headings, the titles of the sections in the reading. Write them here.

   _____

5. Look for any graphic or visual aids in the reading. Graphic aids are charts, graphs, pictures, maps, diagrams, etc. Describe them here. _____

   _____

6. Look for key (important) terms related to the topic. They are usually in bold. List them here. _____

7. Read the last paragraph. It is a summary of the entire reading.

B. Share your survey answers with a partner and discuss what you think the reading will be about. Then circle the number of the statement below which matches your prediction.

1. The passage will discuss the different life processes in humans, including the process of inhalation and exhalation.

2. The passage will define all the parts of the respiratory system in humans and compare the system to other biological systems.

3. The passage will describe how the human body inhales oxygen and exhales carbon dioxide as part of the respiratory process.

C. Now, read the passage to see if your prediction is correct. Try to read as quickly as you can. Do not stop to look up words in your dictionary.

Reading 1

The Respiratory Process

The process of taking in air, which is made up of several gases including oxygen, is called **inhalation** or inspiration. The process of breathing it out is called **exhalation** or expiration. The human body breathes in and out thousands of times each day. Because it is unable to store very much oxygen, the body relies on the respiratory system—the nose, **pharynx** (throat), **trachea** (windpipe), lungs, ribs, and **diaphragm**—to get oxygen from the environment and remove carbon dioxide and other waste products from the body. Without the respiratory system, the human body would die.

Nose, throat, and trachea

The process of inhalation begins when air is taken in through the nose and/or mouth. Inside the nose, tiny hairs called **cilia** filter dirt, pollen, and other particles out of the air. These particles are then either pushed toward the nostrils and expelled, or pushed toward the pharynx, carried to the stomach, and then eliminated by the body. Before the air moves down the throat toward the trachea, the nasal cavity warms the air slightly. A structure called the epiglottis prevents air from entering the stomach.

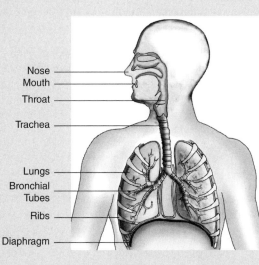

Nose
Mouth
Throat
Trachea
Lungs
Bronchial Tubes
Ribs
Diaphragm

Lungs

Next, the air moves from the trachea and into the **lungs** through structures called **bronchial tubes**. These bronchial tubes branch throughout the lungs into smaller and smaller tubes called bronchioles. At the ends of the bronchioles, the air enters tiny air sacs called **alveoli**. The walls of the alveoli are very thin, only one **cell** thick, and are lined with capillaries—tiny blood vessels. Oxygen passes from inside the alveoli through the thin walls and diffuses into the blood. Once the oxygen gets into the bloodstream, it is picked up by the **hemoglobin**, a molecule in the red blood cells. The blood flows back to the heart and then out to the body's **tissues** through the **arteries**. Once in the tissues, the oxygen moves from the hemoglobin in the capillaries into the body's cells.

At the same time, carbon dioxide waste passes from the blood into the alveoli to be exhaled. First it moves out of the cells into the capillaries. Here, much of it is dissolved in the **plasma** of the blood. Through the **veins**, the blood returns to the heart and is pumped to the lungs. In the lungs, carbon dioxide passes into the alveoli to be exhaled.

Diaphragm and ribs

During the inhalation process, a large muscle called the diaphragm contracts and pulls downward, expanding the thoracic (chest) cavity. This movement causes the lungs to push downward, filling the extra space. At the same time, other muscles draw the ribs outward and expand the lungs. Air then rushes into the lungs.

During exhalation, the process is reversed, and the diaphragm and other muscles relax. The diaphragm moves upward and the thoracic cavity contracts. This causes air to flow from the lungs upward, where it then flows out through the nose or the mouth.

Respiration, the process of inhalation and exhalation, happens automatically, thousands of times each day, and is one of the most important processes the human body performs

Key Concept Words

alveoli – (n.) tiny air sacs in the lungs

arteries – (n.) tubes or vessels that carry blood from the heart to parts of the body

bronchial tubes – (n.) one of two branches from the trachea to the lungs

cell – (n.) the basic unit of living matter in organisms

cilia – (n.) tiny hairs inside the nose

diaphragm – (n.) large muscle between chest and abdominal cavities

exhalation – (n.) breathing out

hemoglobin – (n.) the red matter of blood that carries oxygen to parts of the body

inhalation – (n.) breathing in

lungs – (n.) one of two respiratory organs in the chest cavity

pharynx – (n.) throat (leads from nose/mouth to esophagus)

plasma – (n.) fluid part of blood

tissues – (n.) a system of cells that makes up plants/animals

trachea – (n.) windpipe (carries air to bronchi in lungs)

veins – (n.) tubes or vessels that carry blood to the heart from parts of the body

Glossed Words

branch – (v.) to divide or separate; to go in a new direction; **breathe** – (v.) to take air in and let it out; **diffuse** – (v.) to spread out or go in many directions; **dirt** – (n.) dust or unclean matter/material; **dissolve** – (v.) to merge with a liquid; to break up and disappear; **filter** – (v.) to remove solids or separate solids from liquids; **flow** – (v.) to move in a stream, like water; **particle** – (n.) a tiny piece of matter/material; **pollen** – (n.) yellow powder-like substance from flowers; **store** – (v.) to put away for future use

Summarizing

Share What You Read

A. Use two or three sentences to tell your partner what you thought the reading was about. Then listen to your partner's sentences. Next, read the following statements and circle the number of the statement that best summarizes the reading.

1. The diaphragm contracts during inhalation and the lungs fill with air, while during exhalation, the diaphragm relaxes and air flows from the lungs upward.

2. In the respiratory system, exhalation is the reverse process of inhalation, both of which are automatic processes.

3. During respiration, oxygen is taken into the body, enters the lungs and moves into the cells, while carbon dioxide passes from the blood to the lungs and out through the nose.

B. Did you choose statement 3? If you chose a different answer, go back and review your survey answers. Try to determine why they lead to summary statement 3.

Check Your Comprehension

Read the statements below and put them in the correct order. Part A explains the inhalation process and Part B explains the exhalation process. The first step has been done for you.

Part A

_____ a. From the trachea, air enters the lungs through the bronchial tubes.

___1___ b. Air first enters the nose or mouth.

_____ c. Next, air moves from the smaller tubes into the alveoli and then into the blood.

_____ d. The blood flows to the heart and then out to the tissues and cells through the arteries.

_____ e. Air then moves down the throat to the trachea.

Part B

_____ a. The air flows from the lungs upwards and then out through the nose or mouth.

_____ b. Carbon dioxide first moves out of the cells into the capillaries and is dissolved in the plasma of the blood.

_____ c. Once carbon dioxide is in the lungs, it passes into the alveoli to be exhaled.

_____ d. The blood returns to the heart and is pumped to the lungs through the veins.

● Academic Word List

 ACTIVITY **5**   **Scan and Define**

A. Look at the ten words listed below. Scan the reading and underline the words from the list. Write the definitions for the words you know. Do not use a dictionary. The first one has been done for you.

1. automatically _involuntarily; happening without anyone's control_____

2. contract (v.) _____

3. eliminate _____

4. environment _____

5. expand _____

6. relax _____

7. rely _____

8. remove _____

9. reverse (v.) _____

10. structure (n.) _____

B. Share your definitions with a partner and then with the rest of your classmates. As a group, try to complete the definitions for all ten words. Use a dictionary to check the definitions if you are unsure about them. Then complete the vocabulary activity.

 ACTIVITY **6**   **Vocabulary Challenge**

A. Read the statements and then circle the correct answer or answers. Sometimes more than one answer is possible.

1. The process of respiration happens automatically in the human body. Which of the following can also happen <u>automatically</u>?
   a. eating of food   b. blinking of eyes   c. beating of heart

2. During inhalation, the diaphragm contracts and pulls downward, expanding the chest cavity. Which of the following can also <u>contract</u>?
   a. bones   b. muscles   c. nerves

3. Particles we inhale are either expelled through the nose or carried to the stomach and then eliminated by the body as waste products. Which of the following can also be used by the body to <u>eliminate</u> waste products?
   a. the hair   b. the skin   c. the nerves

4. Humans get oxygen from the environment. Which of the following can represent interaction with the <u>environment</u>?
   a. obtaining food   b. migrating to a new region   c. giving birth

5. As the lungs expand, air rushes in to fill them. Which of the following parts of the body cannot <u>expand</u>?
   a. the stomach   b. the skull   c. the heart

6. As the diaphragm and other muscles relax, air flows upward from the lungs and out through the nose or the mouth. Which of the following parts of the body cannot <u>relax</u>?
   a. the blood   b. the shoulders   c. the bones

B. Study the sentence patterns below. Next, on a separate sheet of paper create sentences from the words provided, using the underlined words to follow the same sentence patterns. You may need to add some words of your own.

1. The body <u>relies on</u> the respiratory system <u>to</u> get oxygen.
   a. body, carbohydrates, energy <u>*The body relies on carbohydrates to get energy.*</u>
   b. companies, employees, jobs
   c. patients, doctors, illnesses

2. The respiratory system <u>removes</u> carbon dioxide <u>from</u> the body.
   a. kidneys, chemical waste, the blood
   b. doctors, cancerous growths, skin
   c. businesses, duplicate names, mailing lists

3. During exhalation, the process <u>is reversed, and</u> air flows out of the lungs.
   a. during exocytosis, endocytosis, waste materials push out of cell
   b. in hypothyroidism, symptoms, body functions slow down
   c. in bottom-up organizations, flow, many decisions made by teams

4. In the throat, <u>a structure called the</u> epiglottis prevents air from entering the stomach.
   a. in the brain, hippocampus, be important for learning and memory
   b. in English, tag question, used to ask for confirmation
   c. in business, corporation, issue shares of stock

5. Foreign particles <u>are eliminated by</u> the body.
   a. body heat, sweat glands
   b. minerals in water, filtering systems
   c. business competition, offering better products

Tools for Interactive Reading

Reading an academic text differs from reading a novel not only in purpose but also in approach. The purpose of reading an academic text is to get information which will add to your knowledge and understanding of a particular subject. Reading a novel, unless it is an assignment for a literature class, is usually for enjoyment and not for information. Academic texts require you to read carefully and to understand what you have read as well as to retain what you have read. You will not be tested on the contents of a novel you have read for pleasure.

Reading an academic text requires interacting with it. Surveying a passage and predicting its content are examples of interacting with a text that you are already familiar with. This section will introduce you to additional ways to actively read a passage, namely, by marking a text.

Marking a Text: Highlighting, Underlining, Commenting

Marking a text helps you in numerous ways:

- It helps you understand the material by making you focus on what you are reading.
- It improves your concentration and, thus, your comprehension of the material.
- It increases your retention of the material, making it easier to study or review for exams.
- It forces you to think about what you have read and decide whether or not it is important enough to mark.
- It makes it easy to recognize key ideas and points when you review the material.

What to Mark

The biggest problem you will encounter is deciding what to mark, and at first you will be tempted to mark everything as important. The best way to avoid this is to read *before* you mark anything.

First, survey the entire chapter: read the title, the introduction, the headings, any words in bold, and the chapter summary. Look at any pictures, charts, or graphs in the chapter, and read the captions. This step gives you a general idea of the chapter and prepares you for a closer reading. Next, focus on one section of the chapter at a time. Read the entire section (not the entire chapter) without marking anything. Then go back and re-read the section. Now you are ready to mark. Here are some suggestions to guide you in marking the text as you re-read:

- Mark the main ideas—use the headings and subheadings to help identify them. Look for numbers or letters that the writer may have used to organize and introduce the major points.
- Mark the topic sentence in each paragraph.
- Mark important parts such as introductions, conclusions, and/or summaries. These sections often include the main points addressed in the passage.
- Mark important facts which support the main ideas. These are the minor support details and could be facts, statistics, or examples.
- Mark phrases that contain numbers and which introduce lists. For example, mark, *The respiratory system is composed of six organs.* Then number and mark each of the items as it is described or explained to make sure you have the entire list.
- Mark definitions and examples. In the margin of the page, note *def* or *e.g.* for later reference.
- Mark any graphic or visual aids. Mark the title of the graphic, and in the margin of the page, make a note that summarizes what the graphic shows.
- Mark any information that you find surprising or contrary to what you expected and in the margin, make a note of it.

How to Mark

There is no single way to correctly mark text. Some people use markers to highlight text. Others use a pen or pencil to underline text. Some use both markers and pencils. Some people highlight main ideas in one color and details in another color. Some people use one underline for the topic sentence and a double underline for the thesis statement or main idea. Some people write comments in the margins, and others do not.

Your goal is to separate the main ideas from the supporting details. Here are some guidelines for you to follow. In time, you will develop your own system—use what works for you. Whatever system you choose, be consistent.

Highlight or underline:

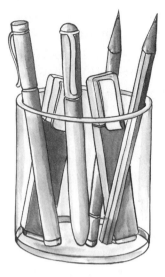

- main ideas
- key words
- topic sentence in each paragraph
- one example, if more than one is given
- words and phrases instead of complete sentences

Use abbreviations and symbols:

- *def.* for definitions
- *e.g.* for examples
- *?* for statements you question or doubt
- *!* for statements you find surprising or contrary to what you expected
- → for ideas that are related

Comments in the margin:

- key words or concepts
- summary of important information in section
- numbers or letters for lists contained in section
- important names and dates
- note patterns of organization: cause/effect, comparison/contrast, process
- questions that you want to ask the instructor

After you have highlighted or underlined a section and made comments in the margins, read what you've marked. Does it make sense? Does it cover the meaning of the passage? If it doesn't, go over it again. Can you explain the section using the information you marked? If you can't, go over it again. While there is no rule on how much of the text you should mark, if you focus on the key points, you will probably mark no more than ten or fifteen percent of the material.

Look at the following examples of marked text from Reading 1.

1) Text is not marked enough

The process of taking in air, which is made up of several gases including oxygen, is called **inhalation** or inspiration. The process of breathing it out is called **exhalation** or expiration. The human body breathes in and out thousands of times each day. Because it is unable to store very much oxygen, the body relies on the respiratory system—the nose, **pharynx** (throat), **trachea** (windpipe), lungs, ribs, and **diaphragm**—to get oxygen from the environment and remove carbon dioxide and other waste products from the body. Without the respiratory system, the human body would die.

The key words *inhalation* and *exhalation* are important, but what do they mean? *Get oxygen from the environment* is a key point, but how does this occur?

2) Text is marked too much

The process of taking in air, which is made up of several gases including oxygen, is called **inhalation** or inspiration. The process of breathing it out is called **exhalation** or expiration. The human body breathes in and out thousands of times each day. Because it is unable to store very much oxygen, the body relies on the respiratory system—the nose, **pharynx** (throat), **trachea** (windpipe), lungs, ribs, and **diaphragm**—to get oxygen from the environment and remove carbon dioxide and other waste products from the body. Without the respiratory system, the human body would die.

It is difficult to know what is important in the passage because almost the entire paragraph has been highlighted.

3) Text is marked sufficiently

def. → The process of taking in air, which is made up of several gases including oxygen, is called **inhalation** or inspiration. The process of breathing it out is called **exhalation** or expiration. The human body breathes in and out thousands of times each day. Because it is unable to store very much oxygen, the body relies on the

parts of respiratory system → respiratory system—the nose, **pharynx** (throat), **trachea** (windpipe), lungs, ribs, and **diaphragm**—to get oxygen from the environment and remove carbon dioxide and other waste products from the body. Without the respiratory system, the human body would die. ← process

Marking Text

Using the guidelines above, go back to Reading 1 and mark the text. Share your marking with a classmate and discuss how you chose what to highlight, underline, or comment on.

Identifying Text Structure—*Process*

As mentioned in the preceding section on how to mark text, it is helpful to note the text structure or pattern of organization of an academic passage while you are reading. Noting the text structure can help you predict what might come next and thus read more efficiently.

In this chapter you read about the workings of the respiratory system. In the opening paragraph of the passage, the writer first defines *inhalation* and *exhalation* and then states that the respiratory system is responsible for taking in oxygen and removing carbon dioxide. Next, the writer explains, step by step, how the respiratory system works. Explaining how to do something (how to give CPR, for example) or how something happens (how the body takes in oxygen, for instance) is characteristic of the text structure of *process*. In this structure (or pattern), the writer divides the topic into stages or steps. Each step is then presented in chronological (time) order.

Key Words—*Process*

Because *process* involves a method with steps and sequences, key words and phrases may include chronological or time words. Some of the key words associated with the pattern of *process* include:

Process	Sequence	
how to	after/before	last
method	beginning with	meanwhile
phase	during	next
procedure	eventually	once X happens
process	for X amount of time	starting with
stage	finally	(at) the same time
step	first, second, third, etc.	then

Examples: *First,* air is taken in through the nose or mouth.

In the *next step,* the air passes from the trachea to the lungs.

At the same time, carbon dioxide passes from the blood into the alveoli.

Recognize Key Words

A. Read the following steps in the respiratory process. Underline the key words. Then, using the key words as a guide, number the steps in the correct order. The first step has been done for you.

_____ a. The blood flows back to the heart and then out to the body's tissues and cells.

_____ b. Next, air moves from the throat through the trachea and into the lungs.

_____ c. At the same time, carbon dioxide passes from the blood into the alveoli to be exhaled.

___1___ d. The process <u>begins</u> with air entering through the nose and/or mouth.

_____ e. Once that happens, the blood returns to the heart and is pumped to the lungs.

_____ f. In the final phase, air flows from the lungs and out through the nose or mouth.

_____ g. In the third step, oxygen passes from the lungs and diffuses into the blood.

B. Go back to Reading 1 and find three examples of key words which show the text structure of process. Write them below.

1. _____

2. _____

3. _____

Use Key Words

Read the paragraph and fill in the blanks with the key words/phrases below. More than one answer may be possible. Some words/phrases may be used twice.

after	next
in the final step	in the next step
during this interactive process	during this part of the process

How the Heart Interacts with the Respiratory System

The heart is the organ that pushes blood throughout the circulatory system. The right side of the heart pumps blood to the lungs to receive oxygen, and the left side pumps blood to the entire body. The lungs receive oxygen when you inhale, and remove carbon dioxide when you exhale. Inside the lungs, the respiratory system interacts with the circulatory system.

(1) _____ blood from the body with less oxygen flows to the right side of your heart, into a filling chamber called the right atrium. (2) _____ with each heartbeat, blood flows from the right atrium into a pumping chamber, the right ventricle. (3) _____ it leaves the right ventricle, it moves into the lungs. There the blood releases carbon dioxide waste and absorbs oxygen.

(4) _____ the blood picks up oxygen. (5) _____ picking up oxygen, blood is pushed back to the heart, filling another chamber, which is called the left atrium. (6) _____ blood moves from the left atrium to the left ventricle, a pumping chamber. (7) _____ the blood again begins its trip out to the rest of the body.

READING 2 ● **On Your Own**

In the first section of this chapter, you were introduced to the skills of and strategies for marking text and identifying the text structure of process. In this section you will practice these same skills on your own with a new reading.

Get Ready to Read

Energy and the Ecosystem

Discuss your answers to the following questions with a partner.

1. What is meant by the term *ecosystem*?

2. How do plants and animals get energy?

3. What happens to dead branches, leaves, and other plants in the forest?

Surveying and Predicting

Survey and Predict

A. Survey Reading 2 and predict what information you will find.

1. Write the title here. _____

2. Read the first paragraph. Write one or two words which tell the topic here.

   _____

3. Write the main idea here. _____

4. List the subheadings here. _____

5. Describe any graphic or visual aids in the reading here. _____

   _____

6. List any key (important) terms related to the topic here. _____

   _____

7. Read the last paragraph.

B. Share your survey answers with a partner and discuss what you think the reading will be about. Then circle the number of the statement below which matches your prediction.

1. The passage will classify plants and animals as producers, consumers, or decomposers in the ecosystem.

2. The passage will describe how producers, consumers, and decomposers capture and move energy in the ecosystem.

3. The passage will compare and contrast the roles of producers, consumers, and decomposers in the ecosystem.

C. Now, read the passage to see if your prediction is correct. Try to read as quickly as you can. Do not stop to look up words in your dictionary.

Reading 2

How Energy Flows through Ecosystems

Energy is vital to all living things. Most of that energy comes either directly or indirectly from the Sun. To use the Sun's energy, living things must first capture that energy and store it in some usable form. Because energy is continuously used by the activities of living things, it must be continuously replaced in the ecosystem. In the process, energy is captured by producers and then moved through the **ecosystem** by consumers and decomposers.

Producers

A **producer** is an **organism** that captures energy and stores it in food as chemical energy. The producers of an ecosystem make energy available to all the other living parts of an ecosystem. Most energy enters ecosystems through **photosynthesis**. Plants and other photosynthetic organisms take water and carbon dioxide from their environment and use energy from the Sun to produce sugars. The chemical energy stored in sugars can be released when sugars are broken down. Producers do just as their name suggests—they produce food for themselves and for the rest of the ecosystem. Organisms that cannot produce their own food must get their food from other sources.

Consumers

Consumers are organisms that cannot produce their own food and that get their energy by eating, or consuming, other organisms. Consumers are classified by their position in a feeding relationship. For instance, in a meadow ecosystem, animals such as antelopes and grasshoppers feed on grasses. They are primary consumers because they are the first link between the producers and the rest of the consumers in an ecosystem. The wolves that eat the antelopes and the meadowlarks that eat the grasshoppers are secondary consumers. There are also tertiary consumers, such as the prairie falcon that eats the meadowlark. Ecosystems also have special consumers called scavengers, such as the vulture, which is a consumer that feeds on dead animals.

Studying feeding relationships helps to more easily understand how energy is transferred from a producer to a consumer as it flows through an ecosystem. A hike through a forest or a walk through a park offers additional examples of the interaction between producers and consumers. Tall trees and leafy shrubs are home to many insects and the birds that feed upon the insects. Energy, via photosynthesis, enters the ecosystem through a tree, which is a producer. A caterpillar that gets Its energy by feeding on the leaves of the tree is the first, or primary, consumer. The bird that gets its energy by feeding on the caterpillar is a secondary consumer.

Decomposers

Also important to the maintenance of an ecosystem are decomposers, a group of organisms that often go unseen. **Decomposers** are organisms that break down dead plant and animal matter into simpler compounds. In a forest, consumers such as deer and insects eat only a tiny fraction of the leaves on trees and shrubs. The leaves that are left on the forest floor, as well as dead roots and branches, are eventually digested by **fungi** and **bacteria** living in the soil, a pinch of which may contain almost half a million fungi and billions of bacteria. Decomposers are the organisms that release the last bit of energy from once-living matter. Decomposers also return matter to soil or water where it may be used again and again.

Models of energy flow

There are numerous ways to depict the flow of energy in an ecosystem. One is by a **food chain,** a model which describes the feeding relationship between a producer and a single chain of consumers in an ecosystem. Another is a **food web,** a model of the feeding relationships between many different consumers and producers in an ecosystem. It is like a spider web, with many overlapping and interconnected food chains and a better model for the complex feeding relationships in an ecosystem. Finally, an **energy pyramid** is a model that shows the amount of energy available at each feeding level of an ecosystem. The first level includes the producers, the second level the primary consumers, and so on. Because usable energy decreases as it moves from producers to consumers, the bottom level is the largest, and the available energy gets smaller and smaller the farther up the pyramid you go. The energy within an ecosystem gets used up as it flows from organism to organism.

Key Concept Words

bacteria – (n.) small one-celled organisms

consumers – (n.) organisms that get their energy by eating other organisms

decomposers – (n.) organisms that break down dead plant/animal matter

ecosystem – (n.) plants, animals, and microorganisms and their environment

energy pyramid – (n.) model that shows energy available at levels of ecosystem

food chain – (n.) model that describes the relationship between a producer and chain of consumers

food web – (n.) model of feeding relationships between many consumers and producers

fungi – (n.) class of living things that feed on living or dead plant/animal matter

organism – (n.) living thing such as a plant or animal

photosynthesis – (n.) process plants use to change water and carbon dioxide into food

producer – (n.) organism that captures energy and stores it in food

Glossed Words

a pinch of soil – (n.) a small amount of dirt or earth; **depict** – (v.) to represent or show; **fraction** – (n.) a part of something; **hike** – (n.) a long walk on foot; **maintenance** – (n.) supporting the existence of; **matter** – (n.) anything with mass or volume; **meadow** – (n.) an open area of grassy land; **scavenger** – (n.) an animal that feeds on dead/decaying plant/animal matter; **shrub** – (n.) a bush; plant that is smaller than a tree; **tertiary** – (adj.) third; **vital** – (adj.) important or necessary for life

Summarizing

Share What You Read

A. Go back to Reading 2 and mark the text. Mark the main ideas and key words. Mark the topic sentence in each paragraph. Use abbreviations and symbols for definitions and examples. Make comments in the margins.

B. Use two or three sentences to tell your partner what you thought the reading was about. Then listen to your partner's sentences. Next, read the following statements and circle the number of the statement that best summarizes the reading.

1. An important biological process is how energy flows through the ecosystem to all living things.

2. Energy from the Sun is captured by organisms called producers and then moved through the ecosystem by consumers and producers in a continuous process.

3. The energy within an ecosystem gets used up as it moves from producers to consumers, as depicted in the energy pyramid.

Check Your Comprehension

Each sentence contains a factual error. Find and correct each error.

1. There is only one way to depict the flow of energy in an ecosystem.

2. Animals and other photosynthetic organisms take water and carbon dioxide from their environment and use energy from the Sun to produce sugars.

3. Leaves that are left on the forest floor are eventually eaten by fungi and bacteria, which are also called consumers.

4. Producers produce food for themselves and not for the rest of the ecosystem.

5. A food chain shows the feeding relationship between many different consumers and producers in an ecosystem.

6. In a meadow ecosystem, grasshoppers that feed on grasses are secondary consumers.

7. Decomposers return once-living matter to the soil or water where it is never used again.

8. To use the Earth's energy, living things must first capture that energy and store it in some usable form.

9. A food web, with its overlapping and interconnected food chains, is a better model for the simple feeding relationships in an ecosystem.

10. Studying feeding relationships helps us to more easily understand how energy is transferred from a producer to a decomposer as it flows through an ecosystem.

Academic Word List

ACTIVITY **14**

Scan and Define

A. Look at the ten words listed below. Scan the reading and underline the words from the list. Write the definition for the words you know. Do not use a dictionary. Their first one has been done for you.

1. available _accessible, usable, ready to use_ _____

2. complex (adj.) _____

3. compounds (n.) _____

4. energy _____

5. eventually _____

6. overlapping (adj.) _____

7. primary (adj.) _____

8. release (v.) _____

9. transfer (v.) _____

10. via _____

B. Share your definition with a partner and then with the rest of your classmates. As a group, try to complete the definitions for all ten words. Use a dictionary to check the definitions if you are unsure about them. Then complete the vocabulary activity.

ACTIVITY **15**

Vocabulary Challenge

A. Using your dictionary, work with a partner to find the missing word forms and complete the chart. If no form exists, draw a line in the space. The first one has been done for you.

Noun	Verb	Adjective	Adverb
1. availability	avail	available	---------
2.		complex	
3. compound			
4. energy			
5.			eventually
6.		overlapping	
7.		primary	
8.	release		
9.	transfer		

B. Read the definitions of the words below. Then decide which meaning is the one used in the sentence. Put the definition number next to the sentence. The first one has been done for you.

1. **compound** *noun* **1.** something consisting of a combination of two or more parts or ingredients; **2.** a substance formed by chemical combination of two or more elements in definite proportions by weight

   ___1___ Decomposers are organisms that break down dead plant and animal matter into similar **compounds**.

2. **release** *verb* **1.** to free something from somebody or something that fastens or holds back; let go; **2.** to make something available to the public

   _____ The chemical energy stored in sugars can be **released** when sugars are broken down.

3. **primary** *adjective* **1.** basic or fundamental; **2.** first in order or importance

   _____ An antelope is a **primary** consumer because it is the first link between the producers and the rest of the consumers in the ecosystem.

4. **transfer** *verb* **1.** to move or cause somebody or something to pass from one place, person, or thing to another; **2.** to shift the ownership of property to another

   _____ Studying feeding relationships helps us to more easily understand how energy is **transferred** from a producer to a consumer as it flows through the ecosystem.

5. **via** *preposition* **1.** by way of (a place); **2.** by means of (a method)

   _____ Energy, **via** photosynthesis, enters the ecosystem through a tree, which is a producer.

Using Context to Guess Meaning—*Surrounding Sentences*

You can often guess the meaning of an unfamiliar word by using other words or clues in the sentence. In cases where you cannot guess, look to the surrounding sentences for help. They may provide definitions, descriptions, or examples which will clarify the meaning of the unfamiliar word.

Read the sentences and explanation below to see how surrounding sentences help define the word *homeostasis.*

*The human body is a complex system and must maintain **homeostasis** to survive. An excess of carbon dioxide signals the lungs to increase activity in order to expel more of the gas. Too much glucose in the blood triggers insulin production in the pancreas. A higher-than-normal body temperature causes the skin to sweat or perspire. In bright sunlight, the eyes' pupils shrink to limit the amount of light entering the retina. Thus, any change in the body's internal balance will effect a response in the body.*

The first sentence of the paragraph does not provide many clues to the meaning of the word *homeostasis.* The word *survive,* however, suggests that *homeostasis* is something important. The next four sentences all offer examples of the body's reaction to excess. These four examples suggest that the body somehow regulates itself. This, along with your knowledge that too much carbon dioxide will lead to death, as will too much glucose in the blood or overheating of the body, leads to the conclusion that *homeostasis* means stable levels or balance within the body's systems. The last sentence of the paragraph confirms the meaning.

 ACTIVITY 16

Guess Meaning from Context

Read the sentences below. Use the information in the surrounding sentences and your background knowledge to determine the meaning of the word in bold. On the line, write the definition of the word. Share your definitions with a partner and explain how you guessed the meaning.

1. Many **abiotic** factors affect an ecosystem. Abiotic factors include the air that supplies oxygen and carbon dioxide, the soil that provides nutrients, the water in a pond, and the sunlight that plants and other biotic factors need to grow.

   abiotic = _____

2. Across Earth, there are large geographic areas that are similar in climate and that have similar types of plants and animals. There are six major land **biomes** on Earth. Land biomes include the taiga and tundra, deserts and grasslands, and temperate and tropical forests. In addition, there are aquatic biomes: freshwater and saltwater.

   biome = _____

3. Pollution endangers **biodiversity.** As pollution becomes common in an ecosystem, living things may be threatened. Plant and animal populations may decrease and biodiversity may decline. Healthy ecosystems support a variety of species. An ecosystem with a variety of organisms can recover more easily from disturbances than an ecosystem that has fewer species.

   biodiversity = _____

4. Some farmers are practicing **sustainable** methods that protect land and provide nutritious food. Nearly one-third of U.S. farms practice conservation tillage, a method that involves planting seeds without plowing the soil. This technique can cut soil erosion by more than 90 percent. Energy companies are also promoting sustainability by developing alternative energy sources that do not come from fossil fuels.

   sustainable = _____

5. **Commensal** relationships are very common in ocean ecosystems. Small fish called remoras use a type of built-in suction cup to stick to a shark's skin and hitch a ride. When the shark makes a kill, the remora eats the scraps. The shark makes no attempt to attack the remora. The remora benefits greatly from this commensal relationship; the shark is barely affected.

   commensal = _____

In this section, you will learn some skills and strategies associated with the writing process. This section addresses adverb clauses, a grammatical structure used in the readings, as well as writing complex sentences with subordinating conjunctions. You will practice different steps in the writing process and will write a paragraph of process.

The Grammar of Adverb Clauses

Adverb clauses are dependent clauses and, as such, need to be connected to independent clauses. Subordinating conjunctions introduce adverb clauses, which can come before or after the main clause. If an adverb clause comes before the main clause, at the beginning of the sentence, a comma follows the adverb clause. Study the subordinating conjunctions and their meanings in the chart below.

> Example: *After energy is captured by producers, it moves through the ecosystem by consumers.*
>
> *Energy moves through the ecosystem by consumers after it is captured by producers.*

Subordinating Conjunction	Meaning
although, even though, though	concession
if, even if, unless, only if	condition
although, even though, though, while, whereas	contrast and opposition
as, because, since	reason or cause
in order that, so that, so + adj./adv. + that, such + noun + that	result or purpose
after, as, as soon as, before, by the time, once, until, when, whenever, while	time

ACTIVITY 17

Identify Adverb Clauses

Read the sentences below and underline the adverb clause. Circle the subordinating conjunction.

1. (Because) energy is continuously used by the activities of living things, it must be continuously replaced in the ecosystem.

2. The muscles draw the ribs outward and expand the lungs so that air can flow into the lungs.

3. Once the oxygen gets into the bloodstream, it is picked up by the hemoglobin.

4. The energy within an ecosystem gets used up as it flows from organism to organism.

5. The chemical energy stored in sugar can be released when sugars are broken down.

6. Before the air moves down the throat toward the trachea, the nasal cavity warms the air slightly.

Use Adverb Clauses

Connect the two clauses with an appropriate subordinating conjunction from the chart to form a complex sentence with an adverb clause. You may have to change some words. Be sure to place the subordinating conjunction with the correct clause. The first one has been done for you.

1. The body is unable to store very much oxygen. The body relies on the respiratory system to get oxygen from the environment. (Reason/Cause)
    The body relies on the respiratory system to get oxygen from the environment _____
    __because__ it is unable to store very much oxygen. _____

2. Oxygen is in the tissues. The oxygen moves from the hemoglobin in the capillaries into the body's cells. (Time) _____
    _____

3. Decomposers are important to the maintenance of an ecosystem. Decomposers often go unseen. (Concession) _____
    _____

4. We cannot produce our own food. We get our energy by eating, or consuming, other organisms. (Reason/Cause) _____
    _____

5. Air is taken in through the nose. The process of inhalation begins. (Time) _____
    _____

6. Usable energy decreases as it moves from producers to consumers. The bottom level is the largest, and the available energy gets smaller and smaller the farther up you go. (Reason/Cause) _____
    _____

7. A tree, which gets energy via photosynthesis, is a producer. A caterpillar which gets its energy by feeding on the leaves of the tree is a consumer. (Opposition) _____
    _____

8. The epiglottis covers the opening of the windpipe (trachea). Air cannot enter the stomach. (Result) _____
    _____

9. Carbon dioxide is in the lungs. Carbon dioxide passes into the alveoli to be exhaled. (Time) _____
    _____

10. Carbon dioxide is not removed from the human body. The human body will die. (Condition) _____
    _____

Sentence Essentials

Complex Sentences

Complex sentences are formed by using a subordinating conjunction to join a dependent clause, such as an adverb clause, to an independent clause.

Complex Sentences with Adverb Clauses

Choose the Correct Subordinating Conjunction

Read each pair of sentences and determine their relationship to one another. Use words from the chart on page 148. Choose an appropriate subordinating conjunction and create a complex sentence. The first one has been done for you.

1. Oxygen is necessary to sustain life. Your body cannot store very much. <u>Contrast.</u>
   <u>Although oxygen is necessary to sustain life, your body cannot store very much of it.</u>

2. It is important that you exhale carbon dioxide. High levels of it will damage cells. _____

   _____

3. Levels of oxygen and carbon dioxide change in your body. Your nervous system tells your body to breathe faster or slower. _____

   _____

4. The ribcage expands during inhalation. Your lungs have room to fill with air.

   _____

   _____

5. Air enters the mouth and nose and travels to the lungs. Air enters the alveoli.

   _____

   _____

6. We breathe hundreds of times per day. We don't even think about it. _____

   _____

Add a Clause to Complete the Sentence

Read each clause. Add an adverb clause to create a complex sentence. The first one has been done for you.

1. An animal is a primary consumer <u>if it is the first link between the producers and</u>
   <u>consumers in an ecosystem.</u>

2. Plants and trees are important to the ecosystem. (because) _____

   _____

3. A consumer must obtain its energy by eating other organisms. (if) _____

   _____

4. Energy is used in the ecosystem. (as soon as) _____

   _____

5. Create a food web for your presentation. (so that) _____

   _____

6. We rarely see decomposers. (even though) _____

   _____

Create Complex Sentences with Adverb Clauses

Use the subordinating conjunction in the parentheses to create a sentence with an adverb clause. Your sentence can be about any topic.

1. (although – concession) *The patient agreed to take the medication although he hated the side effects.*

2. (unless) _____

3. (whereas – opposition) _____

4. (since) _____

5. (in order that) _____

6. (after) _____

7. (by the time) _____

 ACTIVITY **22**

Correct the Sentence Errors

Each sentence below contains an error. Identify each type of error and correct it. Errors include punctuation, incorrect conjunctions, subject-verb agreement, fragments, and comma splices. The first one has been done for you.

1. Most of the organisms alive on Earth ~~is~~ *are* made up of a single cell.

   Error: *subject-verb agreement*

2. A blood cell can deliver oxygen to your muscles since it cannot cause your body to move as a muscle cell can.

   Error: _____

3. Because a tissue is a group of similar cells that do a specific job.

   Error: _____

4. A complex organism has trillions of cells, for a simple organism has only a few types of cells.

   Error: _____

5. Mitochondria are the parts of cells that use oxygen to get energy from food?

   Error: _____

6. Blood flows to the tissues from the arteries, oxygen moves into the body's cells.

   Error: _____

7. An antelope is a primary consumer in a meadow ecosystem because the antelope is the first link between the grass producers and other animal consumers like lions.

   Error: _____

Making the Connection

Readers use unity to quickly identify the main idea—the topic which all of the sentences address. They use the logical order of the sentences, coherence, to understand how the details support the main idea. Similarly, writers focus on one idea in each paragraph and present their ideas in a logical order. Unity and coherence in writing ensure that the reader will understand the views the writer is trying express.

Get Ready to Write

Use Unity and Coherence in Writing

Good writing is more than putting grammatically correct sentences together. An accomplished writer will use other techniques to ensure that the reader easily understands the intended message. Unity and coherence make writing clear and orderly for the reader.

Unity—*One Topic Per Paragraph*

In order for a paragraph to have unity, only one main idea should be discussed. The idea to be discussed is the one stated in the topic sentence. For example, if your paragraph is about the advantages of living in the city, do not discuss any disadvantages. If you are writing a paragraph about water pollution caused by pesticides, do not discuss water pollution caused by sewage. Read the paragraph below and decide whether it discusses one main idea or more than one.

> Unlike other organisms, fungi reproduce themselves in more than one way. Many fungi reproduce by releasing spores, or single reproductive cells capable of growing into new organisms. Fungi can also reproduce asexually, when hyphae break off and form new mycelium. Yeasts, which are single-celled fungi, can reproduce by simple cell division or by releasing spores. This variability makes fungi unique in nature. As decomposers of nature, fungi can be helpful or harmful. Fungi can be helpful, for instance, when they decompose dead trees, releasing nutrients back into the soil. They can be harmful, however, when they attack tissues of living trees. Fungi are multifaceted organisms.

The previous paragraph does not have unity because it discusses more than one main idea. Although all of the sentences talk about fungi, the stated main idea is *the ways fungi reproduce*. This paragraph should be split into two at the sentence, *As decomposers of nature, fungi can be helpful or harmful.* This is a topic sentence for a paragraph about the positive or negative effects fungi can have.

No Irrelevant Sentences

Unity in a paragraph also means that all of the sentences discuss, explain or support the main idea stated in the topic sentence. Sentences that do not support the topic sentence are called *irrelevant*. Read the paragraph below and find the irrelevant sentence, the sentence which does not support the main idea.

> Unlike other organisms, fungi reproduce themselves in more than one way. Many fungi reproduce by releasing spores, or single reproductive cells capable of growing into new organisms. Fungi can also reproduce asexually, when hyphae break off and form new mycelium. Yeasts, which are single-celled fungi, can reproduce by simple cell division or by releasing spores. Yeast is used to make most kinds of bread. This variability makes fungi unique in nature.

This paragraph does not have unity because it contains an irrelevant sentence: *Yeast is used to make most kinds of bread.* Although it is a true statement and yeast is a fungus, this sentence does not explain the main idea: *the ways fungi reproduce.*

Recognize Unity

Read paragraphs A and B and complete the following steps.

1. Underline the topic sentence of the main paragraph.

2. Decide whether the paragraph should be divided into two or more paragraphs. If so, underline the additional topic sentence(s).

3. Cross out any irrelevant sentences.

A. All plants derive energy from a process called photosynthesis. There are many varieties of plants. A plant begins the process by taking in carbon dioxide from the air and water from the soil. Then, the carbon dioxide and water enter the plants cells, which contain chlorophyll. The chlorophyll, which captures energy from the sun, changes the carbon dioxide and water into oxygen and glucose. Finally, the oxygen is released into the air and the glucose is used for energy. Humans also use glucose in their bodies. Plants do not immediately use all of the glucose they produce. Some of it is combined together to make starch. The plant then stores the starch until energy is needed. This process of photosynthesis allows plants to gain food energy from the light of the sun.

B. The invention of the microscope led to the discovery of cells. In the 1660s, Robert Hooke began using a microscope to look at all sorts of materials. A man named Anton van Leeuwanhoek did similar work in the 1670s using pond water. While looking at a sample of cork, Hooke saw a group of similarly shaped compartments that looked like tiny rooms, or cells. Cork comes from oak trees. Hooke used the term *cell* to name his discovery.

Coherence—*Transitions*

In a paragraph with coherence, all of the sentences hold or stick together. Like links in a chain, they will flow from one to the next. They should not jump or suddenly change direction. Transitions are words or phrases that connect sentences and guide the reader through any changes in direction.

Read paragraphs 1 and 2. Which is easier to understand? How do the italicized words help you?

Paragraph 1

In cellular respiration, cells use oxygen to release energy stored in sugars like glucose. Glucose is broken down into smaller molecules, releasing a small amount of energy. The molecules enter the cell's mitochondria. Oxygen enters the cell and travels to the mitochondria. The molecules are broken down further, releasing hydrogen and allowing the cell to capture energy. The energy is transferred to other molecules that carry it where it is needed.

Paragraph 2

In cellular respiration, cells use oxygen to release energy stored in sugars like glucose. *The process begins* when glucose is broken down into smaller molecules, releasing a small amount of energy. *Then*, the molecules enter the cell's mitochondria. *At the same time*, oxygen enters the cell and travels to the mitochondria. *As* the molecules are broken down further, hydrogen is released, allowing the cell to capture energy. *Finally*, the energy is transferred to other molecules that carry it where it is needed.

The italicized words in paragraph 2 are all transitions. They direct the reader through the steps of cell respiration in chronological order, the order used in process paragraphs and essays.

The process begins lets the reader know what the first step is.

Then is a transition used for the next step.

At the same time makes it clear that the steps are happening simultaneously.

As is also used to show simultaneous steps.

Finally signals the end of the process.

Other transitions commonly used in process writing include:

after	during	later
as	eventually	meanwhile
at first, at last,	finally	next
at the same time	first, second, etc.	then
before	in/at the beginning	while

Transitions can link sentences in many ways. There are transitions to introduce additional information, contrasting information, examples, results, and conclusions. A chart showing these transitions can be found in Appendix 3 on page 198.

Recognize Coherence

A. Read the paragraph and circle all transitional words or phrases.

The process of mitosis is essential in cell division. Although mitosis is a continuous process, scientists divide the events of mitosis into four phases. The first phase of mitosis is prophase. During prophase, the DNA in the cell nucleus condenses. The membrane around the nucleus then disappears. The second phase in mitosis is metaphase. In metaphase, the chromosomes line up in the middle of the cell. During anaphase, the third phase, chromatids split, resulting in two identical chromosomes. The chromosomes are pulled to opposite sides of the cell. The fourth phase is telophase. During telophase, a new nuclear membrane forms around each group of chromosomes. Finally, mitosis is finished and the cell divides completely in two.

B. Fill in the blank with appropriate transitional words or phrases from the chart above. Look for clues in the sentences which come before and after the transitions.

Digestion is the process of breaking down food into useable materials and energy your body can use. (1) _____ is mechanical digestion. During this phase, your teeth break food down into pieces small enough to swallow. (2) _____, chemical digestion also begins. Saliva works while you are chewing to soften food and produce a chemical change. (3) _____ you swallow, the food travels down the esophagus into the stomach. (4) _____ the food is in the stomach, it is mixed and mashed by strong muscles. (5) _____ the stomach produces strong acids to break down food. (6) _____, the partially digested food moves into the small intestine. (7) _____, chemicals released by the liver, pancreas, and gall bladder break down nutrients. Most of the nutrients broken down during digestion are absorbed in the small intestine. In the large intestine, water and some other nutrients are absorbed. (8) _____, the material is compacted and stored until elimination.

How Did They Do That?

ACTIVITY 25

Follow the Steps

Read the following process paragraph about respiration. Then review *Writing 1B: The Process* on pages 24-32 in Chapter 1, which outlines the steps the writer took to develop the paragraph, to complete the activity.

The Process of Respiration

We breathe in and out thousands of times every day, giving our bodies the oxygen needed to function. Because we don't even think about breathing, we might think it is a simple process. But respiration is actually made up of several steps. The first stage of respiration is inhalation. During inhalation, the diaphragm contracts, pulling air into the nose or mouth and down the trachea to the lungs. Once in the lungs, the air then continues through the bronchial tubes to the air sacs, or alveoli. Next, oxygen passes through the thin walls of the alveoli into the bloodstream to be used in the body. In the next phase of respiration, exhalation, carbon dioxide passes through the same thin alveolar walls and into the air sacs. The diaphragm then relaxes, sending the carbon dioxide through the bronchial tubes, up the trachea and out through the nose or mouth. The automatic act of breathing seems very simple, but without the respiratory process we would not be able to survive.

1. Circle the idea the writer brainstormed and used in the paragraph.

2. Underline the narrowed topic in the paragraph.

3. Draw two lines under the details, major and/or minor, in the paragraph.

4. List some key words which identify the text structure. _____
   _____

5. Write the topic sentence here. _____
   _____

6. Write the concluding sentence here. _____
   _____

Paragraph of Process

Write Your Paragraph

Choose a process from your field of study that interests you. Examples of processes are *conducting a research survey, writing an essay,* and *conducting a lab experiment.* Follow the steps below to write a process paragraph. Your audience is your instructor and your classmates. After you finish writing your paragraph, complete the two final activities, *Revising* and *Editing and Proofreading*.

Steps:

1. Brainstorm the topic.
2. Narrow the topic.
3. Brainstorm and narrow the details.
4. Choose the text structure (process).
5. Organize the details.
6. Write the topic sentence.
7. Write an outline.

Process Paragraph

Topic Sentence: _____

_____

    A. Step/Phase One

       1.

       2.

       3.

    B. Step/Phase Two

       1.

       2.

       3.

    C. Step/Phase Three

       1.

       2.

       3.

Concluding Sentence: _____

_____

8. Change outline phrases into sentences.

9. Write concluding sentence (restate topic sentence).

10. Put in paragraph format.

Revising

Follow the Steps

A. Follow the steps outlined below to revise the paragraph of process.

Revising Checklist

1. Assignment

   ☐ Follows the assignment to write a paragraph of process for subjects from your field of study or area of interest

   ☐ Addresses your instructor and classmates as your audience

   ☐ Follows the ten steps listed in the assignment

2. Topic sentence

   ☐ Is limited to a specific topic

   ☐ Includes the topic

   ☐ Includes what the reader needs to know about the topic

   ☐ Gives a clue to the text structure

3. Details

   ☐ Relate to the topic

   ☐ Are organized in a logical order

   ☐ Follow the outline

   ☐ Enough in number (not too many, not too few)

4. Concluding sentence

   ☐ Restates the topic sentence

   ☐ Alerts the reader to the end of the paragraph

   ☐ Summarizes the key points in the paragraph, makes a prediction, or poses a question

5. Unity

   ☐ Discusses one main idea in the paragraph

   ☐ Relates all sentences to the main idea

6. Coherence

   ☐ Uses correct text structure

   ☐ Uses appropriate transitions

B. Share your paragraph with a classmate. Ask your classmate to use the Revising Checklist to check your paragraph and give you some feedback. Make any changes to your paragraph that you feel are necessary. The changes you make should improve your paragraph.

Editing and Proofreading

The Final Steps

A. Follow the steps outlined below to edit and proofread the paragraph of process you wrote for the *On Your Own* section.

Editing and Proofreading Checklist

1. Grammar

   ☐ Verb tenses are correct.

   ☐ Each subject agrees with its verb (singular/plural).

   ☐ Prepositions are correct.

   ☐ Pronouns are correct (agree in number/gender).

   ☐ Articles are correct (a, an, the).

2. Spelling

   ☐ All words are spelled correctly.

   ☐ Abbreviations, if any, are used correctly.

   ☐ First word of each sentence begins with a capital letter.

3. Punctuation

   ☐ All sentences end with a punctuation mark.

   ☐ Periods are after statements, and question marks are after questions.

   ☐ Commas are used with independent clauses joined by coordinating conjunctions.

   ☐ Semicolons and commas are used with independent clauses joined by conjunctive adverbs.

4. Sentences

   ☐ All sentences are complete.

   ☐ Each sentence has a subject and a verb.

   ☐ There are no fragments.

5. Format

   ☐ Paragraph has a title.

   ☐ First line is indented.

   ☐ All sentences are in paragraph format (not listed or numbered).

   ☐ Writer's name is on the paper.

   ☐ Paper is neat, clean, and legible (easily read).

B. Share your paragraph with a classmate. Ask your classmate to use the Editing and Proofreading Checklist to check your paragraph and mark any errors in grammar, spelling, punctuation, sentences, or paragraph format.

C. Fix any mistakes your paragraph contained. Proofread your paragraph one more time. Turn in your final draft to your instructor.

A Hindu temple in Madurai, India

6 From the Social Sciences: Philosophy

The study of philosophy concerns itself with the nature of human existence and all that surrounds it. Classes in philosophy explore a variety of topics and might include, for example, man's capacity to think creatively or the use of logical reasoning to examine one's beliefs and values. Philosophy courses explore assumptions and analyze arguments.

The following quotes are from Buddha and Confucius, two well-known philosophers. Discuss the quotes and their meanings with a partner or in a small group.

- "He is able who thinks he is able." —Buddha
- "Three things cannot be long hidden: the sun, the moon, and the truth." —Buddha
- "Before you embark on a journey of revenge, dig two graves." —Confucius
- "Study the past if you would [want to] define the future." —Confucius

This chapter will help you understand some of the **key concepts** of Eastern religion and philosophy such as:

- Hinduism
- Buddhism
- Confucianism
- Daoism

Get Ready to Read

Agree or Disagree

Read the following statements and decide whether you agree or disagree with each. Circle your choice. Discuss your answers and your reasons for them with a partner.

1. Studying philosophy can help you in everyday life.   AGREE   DISAGREE

2. Studying philosophy improves a person's critical thinking.   AGREE   DISAGREE

3. It is important to study both Eastern and Western philosophy.   AGREE   DISAGREE

4. Philosophical thought influences science, social science, and humanities.   AGREE   DISAGREE

Surveying and Predicting

Survey and Predict

A. Follow the steps below to survey Reading 1 on pages 161-162.

1. Read the title. Write it here. _____

2. Read the first paragraph. Write one or two words which tell the topic or what the paragraph is about. _____

3. Write the main idea here. _____

4. Read the headings, the titles of the sections in the reading. Write them here.

_____

5. Look for any graphic or visual aids in the reading. Graphic aids are charts, graphs, pictures, maps, diagrams, etc. Describe them here. _____

_____

6. Look for key (important) terms related to the topic. They are usually in bold. List them here. _____

7. Read the last paragraph. It is a summary of the entire reading.

B. Share your survey answers with a partner and discuss what you think the reading will be about. Then circle the number of the statement below which matches your prediction.

1. The passage will compare and contrast two religions: Hinduism in India and Buddhism in China and Japan.

2. The passage will present an overview of the main points of Eastern religion and philosophy in India, China, and Japan.

3. The passage will define four Eastern religions or philosophies: Hinduism, Buddhism, Confucianism, and Daoism.

C. Now read the passage to see if your prediction is correct. Try to read as quickly as you can. Do not stop to look up words in your dictionary.

Reading 1

Eastern Religion and Philosophy

India gave birth to two of the world's great religions, **Hinduism** and **Buddhism**. Because the group of Hindu gods and the body of doctrines are so large, it is difficult to speak of a Hindu theology. Nonetheless, the fact is that there are some fundamental principles of Hinduism. One principle is **dharma**, one's role in life. Another principle is **reincarnation.** Followers of Hindu believe that the soul progresses through a cycle of deaths and rebirths until it ultimately attains peace in **nirvana**. A third principle is **karma**, the accumulated record of many lives. In addition, Hinduism recommends the practice of **yoga**, a word that means the bond or yoke between body and spirit. Although yoga has many different forms, it basically involves the disciplining of the body in order to enhance concentration and meditation. Yoga that emphasizes physical conditioning is called hatha yoga. Hatha yoga is now commonly practiced in the West.

Gautama Buddha

The founder of Buddhism was Gautama Buddha. He began his life as a devout Hindu and carried these beliefs and practices into the new religion. He sought to simplify the caste system, an important part of the Hindu culture. The Buddha also developed a body of ethical teachings. These teachings were based on the notion of compassion that resembles the teachings of Jesus in many ways. In Mahayana Buddhism, he emphasized that suffering can be stopped through the attainment of nirvana. This emphasis was interpreted as a form of salvation similar to the Christian belief in heaven.

Confucianism and Daoism

Mahayana Buddhism played a less important role in India than in China, which did not develop a great world religion of its own. The two important Chinese systems of thought are Confucianism and **Daoism**. They both emphasize life in this world rather than in the next. The mystical element of Daoism, however, may also be considered religious. **Confucius** taught by asking questions and making paradoxical (contradictory) statements. He used this method to stimulate discussion.

Historians note that the "Confucian" system had a profound impact on Chinese society. For example, in this system, bureaucrats were chosen through competitive examinations, not through class privilege. Confucians sought the best way to live in this world. They advocated honesty, loyalty, and integrity. Daoism appears to contrast with Confucianism in that its followers seek "the way" through the abandonment of the self to the natural rhythms of the universe rather than through rational thought. Yet in practice, the two are often blended. Buddhism, Confucianism, and Daoism all had a profound impact on Chinese artistic expression.

Buddhism in Japan

Native religious practices in Japan before the introduction of Buddhism went under the name of **Shinto**, or "way of the gods." Some of these are still practiced in Japan today. These practices include reverence for and communication with the spirits of departed ancestors. Buddhism had an important impact on Japanese art and architecture, *tanka* poetry, and the Noh theater. Examples are the emphasis on impermanence and change in poetry and the theater. They fit with the Buddhist belief in the instability of worldly things and the source of human suffering in our attachment to them. Sometimes even today, Shintoism and Buddhism are mixed together in traditional rituals.

In sum, there is obvious continuity of tradition in the Asian civilizations of India, China, and Japan. In addition, each stresses harmony or reconciliation. It must be noted, however, that vast differences exist not only among the ancient civilizations of India, China, and Japan, but within each civilization as well.

Key Concept Words

Buddhism – (n.) a religion founded in India; teaches leading a life which will allow the soul to attain nirvana

Confucius – (n.) Chinese philosopher and teacher (551–479 B.C.)

Daoism – (n.) "the way"; giving oneself over to the natural rhythms of the universe and living simply

dharma – (n.) a person's role in life

Hinduism – (n.) the religion and social system of India; viewed as a way of life rather than as a set of doctrines to follow

karma – (n.) the accumulated record of many lives

nirvana – (n.) supreme happiness resulting from the final freeing of the soul

reincarnation – (n.) the progress of a soul through a cycle of deaths and rebirths

Shinto – (n.) a Japanese religion; teaches reverence for the spirits of natural forces and one's ancestors

yoga – (n.) the bond or connection between body and spirit

Glossed Words

blended – (adj.) mixed or combined; **caste system** – (n.) social class (inherited) based on wealth, rank, or occupation; **class privilege** – (n.) advantage or right received due to one's social status; **departed ancestor** – (n.) relative who died long ago; **devout** – (adj.) devoted or dedicated, especially to a religion; **doctrine** – (n.) a teaching or belief; **impermanence** – (n.) the temporary nature of something; **mystical** – (adj.) spiritual; **profound** – (adj.) deep or intense; **reverence** – (n.) a mixture of honor, respect and devotion; **rituals** – (n.) ceremonies, especially religious, that involve specific steps or procedures; **seek** – (v.) to look for or search; **suffering** – (n.) pain, hardship, misery; **theology** – (n.) study of religion or religious ideas and beliefs

Summarizing

Share What You Read

A. Use two or three sentences to tell your partner what you thought the reading was about. Then listen to your partner's sentences. Next, read the following statements and circle the number of the statement that best summarizes the reading.

1. Hinduism and Buddhism, practiced in India, focus on life in the next world; Confucianism and Daoism, practiced in China, focus on life in this world; Shinto, practiced in Japan, focuses on reverence for and worship of one's ancestors.

2. Whereas Hinduism has basic principles including dharma, reincarnation, and karma, Buddhism emphasizes that suffering can be stopped through attainment of nirvana, and Confucianism emphasizes life in this world.

3. India, China, and Japan all have religions and philosophies, but Buddhism influenced religions and was practiced in all three countries.

B. Did you choose statement 1? If you chose a different answer, go back and review your survey answers. Try to determine why they lead to summary statement 1.

Check Your Comprehension

Read the following statements and put an X in front of those which describe the religion or philosophy.

a. Hinduism

_____ 1. focus on life in this world

_____ 2. birthplace is India

_____ 3. dharma, reincarnation, nirvana

_____ 4. emphasis on stopping of suffering through attainment of nirvana

b. Buddhism

_____ 1. founded by a devout Hindu

_____ 2. emphasizes physical conditioning called yoga

_____ 3. teachings based on compassion

_____ 4. played a larger role in China than India

c. Confucianism

_____ 1. karma, yoga, and *tanka* poetry

_____ 2. deep impact on Chinese society

_____ 3. focus is on life in the next world

_____ 4. discussion stimulated by asking questions

d. Daoism

_____ 1. abandon self to natural rhythms of universe

_____ 2. followers seek "the way"

_____ 3. practiced widely in Japan

_____ 4. focus is on life in this world

e. Shintoism

_____ 1. means "the way of the gods"

_____ 2. sometimes mixed with Hinduism in rituals

_____ 3. practices include communication with spirits of ancestors

_____ 4. practiced in Japan before Buddhism introduced

Academic Word List

Scan and Define

A. Look at the ten words listed below. Scan the reading and underline the words from the list. Write the definitions for the words you know. Do not use a dictionary. The first one has been done for you.

1. abandonment *the act of letting go, surrendering, or giving something up*

2. accumulated (adj.) _____

3. emphasis _____

4. enhance _____

5. founder _____

6. impact (n.) _____

7. instability _____

8. principles _____

9. role _____

10. ultimately _____

B. Share your definition with a partner and then with the rest of your classmates. As a group, try to complete the definitions for all ten words. Use a dictionary to check the definitions if you are unsure about them. Then complete the vocabulary activity.

ACTIVITY **6**

Vocabulary Challenge

A. Read each sentence and the definitions that follow. Circle the letter of the definition that more closely matches the meaning of the underlined word. The first one has been done for you.

1. The <u>principles</u> of Hinduism include dharma, reincarnation, and karma.
   - (a.) a basic or fundamental belief
   - b. a rule or standard, especially of good behavior

2. The <u>emphasis</u> on life in the next world distinguishes Buddhism from Confucianism.
   - a. the importance or focus given to something
   - b. the stress given to a syllable, word, or phrase

3. Buddhism played a more important <u>role</u> in China than it did in India.
   - a. a character in a performance
   - b. a function in an organization

4. The <u>founder</u> of Buddhism was Gautama Buddha.
   - a. a person who establishes something
   - b. a person who casts metal

5. The Confucian system had an <u>impact</u> on Chinese society.
   - a. a collision
   - b. an effect

6. The <u>abandonment</u> of the self to the natural rhythms of the universe is indicative of Daoism.
   - a. going away; desertion
   - b. surrendering; letting go

7. The <u>instability</u> of worldly things is indicative of Buddhist belief.
   - a. unsteadiness; shakiness
   - b. impermanence

8. Karma is the <u>accumulated</u> record of many lives.
   a. collected   b. increased

9. The soul cycles through births and deaths until it <u>ultimately</u> attains peace in nirvana.
   a. finally; at last   b. fundamentally

B. Read the statements and answer the questions. Sometimes more than one answer is possible. Discuss the reasons for your choice(s) with a partner.

1. One of the fundamental <u>principles</u> of Hinduism is dharma, one's role in life. Which of the following is also a principle?
   a. the law of gravity
   b. the belief in reincarnation
   c. the theory of supply and demand

2. The Confucian system had a profound <u>impact</u> on Chinese society. Which of the following might be a person's response to a religious impact?
   a. becoming a Buddhist
   b. becoming an educator
   c. becoming an environmentalist

3. The <u>founder</u> of Buddhism was Gautama Buddha. Who among the following is also a founder?
   a. Prime Minister Harper of Canada
   b. Queen Elizabeth of England
   c. Bill Gates of Microsoft

4. Yoga <u>enhances</u> concentration and meditation. Which of the following cannot be enhanced?
   a. a computer image
   b. a ten-dollar bill
   c. a person's reputation

5. *Karma* is defined as the <u>accumulated</u> record of many lives. Which of the following cannot be accumulated?
   a. time
   b. money
   c. junk

6. Daoism seeks "the way" through the <u>abandonment</u> of the self to the natural rhythms of the universe. Which of the following is an example of abandonment of the self?
   a. experiencing the joy of walking in the woods during the spring
   b. changing your behavior and diet in order to lose twenty pounds
   c. quitting your job without giving two weeks' notice

7. Buddhism played a less important <u>role</u> in India than it did in China. Which of the following can play a role in a person's life?
   a. religion
   b. education
   c. birthplace

8. Buddhists believe in the <u>instability</u> of worldly things and the source of human suffering in our attachment to them. Which of the following worldly things could have instability?
   a. feelings of hate and jealousy
   b. a house and its furnishings
   c. a plate of pasta

9. The <u>emphasis</u> of both Confucianism and Daoism is on life in this world rather than in the next. Which of the following is something that can receive emphasis?
   a. an interstate highway
   b. a political agenda
   c. an educational method

10. In nirvana, a soul <u>ultimately</u> attains peace. Which of the following is an example of an event that can ultimately happen?
   a. a soccer team wins the World Cup
   b. a person buys groceries
   c. a country experiences a natural disaster

Tools for Interactive Reading

In Chapter 5, you learned that interactive reading uses highlighting, underlining, and commenting as ways to mark a text. Another way readers interact with a text is through note-taking. There are three ways to take notes on a text: paraphrasing, summarizing, and outlining.

Paraphrasing Ideas and Details

Paraphrasing means using your own words to explain what the passage or text is about. When you paraphrase a passage or section of a text, you paraphrase all of the information in the text. As a result, a paraphrase of a section will be almost as long as the original passage.

Summarizing Main Ideas and Important Points

Paraphrasing only the main ideas or most important points of a passage is another option. This shorter paraphrase is actually a summary of the passage and does not include many of the specific details contained in a paraphrase. Thus, a summary is shorter than the original paragraph. Readers sometimes summarize passages in the margins of the text itself instead of in a notebook.

Outlining

Instead of paraphrasing or summarizing a text, it is sometimes easier to outline it. Your outline can be formal or informal, i.e., it can contain Roman numerals, numbers, and letters, or it can simply list the ideas in the text. Informal outlines typically indicate how ideas are related by aligning main points and indenting details, for example, or by placing stars next to important ideas.

The chart below lists the steps for paraphrasing, summarizing, and outlining. Notice that, with the exception of step 2 in summarizing, the steps for paraphrasing and summarizing are the same.

Paraphrasing	Summarizing	Outlining
In order to paraphrase a text you are reading, follow these steps:	In order to summarize a text you are reading, follow these steps:	In order to outline a text you are reading, follow these steps:
1. Be sure you understand the section you have read. Look up any words that are unfamiliar or that you do not understand.	1. Be sure you understand the section you have read. Look up any words that are unfamiliar or that you do not understand.	1. Begin with the title of the text or the heading/subheading of the section. Titles and headings often indicate the topic or main idea of the passage.
2. List, in your own words, the ideas and details presented in the section.	2. Identify the main ideas and most important points in the section.	2. Write down the thesis statement (of a long section) or topic sentence (of a short section).
3. Convert the ideas and details into sentences.	3. List, in your own words, the ideas and important points in the section.	3. Write down the major details of the section. Details which support the thesis statement or topic sentence should be indented under the thesis statement/topic sentence. Do not include minor details or other support unless they are needed to understand the major details.
4. Read your paraphrase to make sure there has been no change in meaning.	4. Convert the ideas and important points into sentences.	
5. If you write your paraphrase in a notebook, identify the source of the paraphrase.	5. Read your summary to make sure there has been no change in meaning.	4. Be consistent with the format you use for indenting and for the symbols you use as well. Follow the same format for all sections of the passage; this makes it easy to identify all the main ideas of the passage.
	6. If you write your summary in a notebook, identify the source of the summary.	

Study the sample paraphrase, summary, and outline of the introductory paragraph from Reading 1.

Original

India gave birth to two of the world's great religions, Hinduism and Buddhism. Because the group of Hindu gods and the body of doctrines are so large, it is difficult to speak of a Hindu theology. Nonetheless, the fact is that there are some fundamental principles of Hinduism. One principle is dharma, one's role in life. Another principle is reincarnation. Followers of Hindu believe that the soul progresses through a cycle of deaths and rebirths until it ultimately attains peace in nirvana. A third principle is karma, the accumulated record of many lives. In addition, Hinduism recommends the practice of yoga, a word that means the bond or yoke between body and spirit. Although yoga has many different forms, it basically involves the disciplining of the body in order to enhance concentration and meditation. Yoga that emphasizes physical conditioning is called hatha yoga. Hatha yoga is now commonly practiced in the West.

Paraphrase

Ideas:

- Hinduism and Buddhism from India
- many Hindu gods and principles; no one system of belief
- basic beliefs: dharma (purpose/duty), reincarnation (dying/reborn), nirvana (highest level), karma (person's many lives)
- yoga: practiced by Hindus and now popular in the western hemisphere, too; improves meditation and focus; promotes connection of body and mind; called hatha yoga here and focus is more on physical.

Sentences:

The religions of Hinduism and Buddhism were both founded in India. The religion of Hinduism has many gods as well as many principles. As a result, there is no one specific belief system associated with Hinduism. Hinduism does have some basic principles, however. The basic principles include dharma, reincarnation, nirvana, and karma. Dharma is a person's purpose or role in life; reincarnation is the continual dying and being reborn a person experiences; nirvana is the highest level one reaches—a state similar to the Christian belief of heaven; and karma is the many lives a person has. Hinduism also promotes yoga. Yoga is an exercise which focuses on the connection between the mind and body. Practicing yoga improves a person's concentration and meditation. Yoga is practiced by Hindus and is also popular in the western hemisphere. Hatha yoga is practiced in the West and focuses more on physical aspects.

Summary

Ideas (same as above)

Sentences:

Hinduism and Buddhism were both founded in India. There is no one specific system of beliefs, but there is belief in the principles of dharma, reincarnation, nirvana, and karma. Hinduism promotes yoga as a way to connect the body with the mind. Hatha yoga is practiced in the West and targets a person's physical condition more than the mind's condition.

<u>**Outline**</u>

Title: Eastern Religions and Philosophy

Topic Sentence: Hinduism and Buddhism founded in India

               *Hinduism→ many gods, many principles, no one belief system

               *Basic principles

                    1. dharma

                    2. reincarnation

                    3. nirvana

                    4. karma

               *Yoga→ promoted by Hinduism

                    1. different forms

                    2. mind ↔ body connection

                    3. hatha yoga: focus on physical, popular in West

Paraphrasing, Summarizing, Outlining

Using the guidelines above, on a separate piece of paper, paraphrase, summarize, or outline the following paragraph from Reading 1. When you are finished, compare your results with those of a partner.

Gautama Buddha

The founder of Buddhism was Gautama Buddha. He began his life as a devout Hindu and carried these beliefs and practices into the new religion. He sought to simplify the caste system, an important part of the Hindu culture. The Buddha also developed a body of ethical teachings. These teachings were based on the notion of compassion that resembles the teachings of Jesus in many ways. In Mahayana Buddhism, he emphasized that suffering can be stopped through the attainment of nirvana. This emphasis was interpreted as a form of salvation similar to the Christian belief in heaven.

Identifying Text Structure—*Summary*

As noted in the previous section, a summary typically consists of the main ideas of a longer reading passage. Summaries, because they focus on the main ideas, generally do not contain a lot of details.

In this chapter, the title of Reading 1, "Eastern Religions and Philosophy," along with the length of the reading, is a clue to the fact that the passage is a general overview or summary of the topic. Six paragraphs would never be enough to adequately discuss such a large topic.

The first paragraph introduces Hinduism and Buddhism but confines its discussion to Hinduism. The second paragraph introduces Buddha and gives a brief overview of his life and his view of religion, known as Buddhism. In the third and fourth paragraphs, the writer introduces a new country, China, and two additional religions: Confucianism and Daoism. The fifth paragraph covers Japan and its religion, Shintoism, identifying its general principles. The last paragraph is a short summary statement noting that while there are similarities among the civilizations of India, China, and Japan, there are also great differences. It does not go into detail by explaining what they are.

Key Words—*Summary*

Because summary focuses on the main concepts of a topic, key words and phrases tend to be general as well. Some of the key words associated with the pattern of summary include:

based on	many
basically	overall
in general	some
generally	usually

Recognize Key Words

Read the sentences below and underline the key words associated with the pattern of summary.

1. Buddhism is <u>based on</u> the teachings of its founder, Gautama Buddha.

2. Hinduism is generally thought to be the oldest major religion in the world.

3. Shintoism has many characteristics of Buddhism and Daoism.

4. Attachment to feelings or perceptions as one of the causes of human dissatisfaction with life is part of the overall philosophy of Buddhism.

5. Generally, the followers of Buddhism and Hinduism regard nirvana as liberation from the cycle of reincarnation.

6. Hatha yoga is based on the Hindu practice of yoga but emphasizes physical conditioning.

Use Key Words

Summarize the main ideas in the following sentences. Include the key word in parentheses in your sentence.

1. Hindu gods include Devi and Vishnu. Shiva and Krishna are two other Hindu gods. (some) *Some Hindu gods include Devi, Vishnu, Shiva, and Krishna.*

2. Buddhism teaches followers to perform good and wholesome actions. Followers of Buddhism try to avoid bad and harmful actions. Buddhist followers attempt to purify and train the mind. (generally) _____

_____

3. Dharma has been defined in different ways. It means the principles or body of teachings expounded by Buddha in Buddhism; it means "way of life" in Hinduism. (basically) _____

_____

4. Yoga is both a philosophy and a practice. It is a philosophy concerned with the connection between the body and soul. It is a practice that involves disciplining the body. (based on) _____

_____

5. The concept of yin and yang is from ancient Chinese philosophy. Although it is part of Confucianism, it figures prominently in and is associated with Daoism. (usually) _____

_____

6. Religions that have one life with a beginning and an end, and which have a judgment day at the end, are called linear religions. Those religions which are cyclic have the idea of birth, death and rebirth, and reincarnation. Hinduism and Buddhism are cyclic religions. (in general) _____

_____

READING 2   ● On Your Own

In the first section of this chapter, you were introduced to the skills of and strategies for paraphrasing, summarizing, and outlining, and to identifying the text structure of *summary*. In this section you will review the strategies you learned for guessing meaning from context.

Get Ready to Read

True or False

Read the following statements and decide whether they are true or false. Circle your choice. Discuss your answers and your reasons for them with a partner.

1. Buddha was a real person and considered a holy man.   TRUE   FALSE

2. Some aspects of Buddhism come from Hinduism.   TRUE   FALSE

3. Buddhism spread from India to China and even to Korea and Japan.   TRUE   FALSE

Surveying and Predicting

Survey and Predict

A. Survey Reading 2 and predict what information you will find.

1. Read the title. Write it here. _____

2. Read the first paragraph. Write one or two words which tell the topic or what the paragraph is about. _____

3. Write the main idea here. _____

4. Write the headings here. _____

5. Describe any graphic or visual aids in the reading here. _____

_____

6. List any key (important) terms related to the topic here. _____

_____

7. Read the last paragraph.

B. Share your survey answers with a partner and discuss what you think the reading will be about. Then circle the number of the statement on the following page which matches your prediction.

1. The passage will give an overview of Buddha, his teachings, and the growth of Buddhism.

2. The passage will explain the different versions of Buddhism as practiced in central and Southeast Asia.

3. The passage will define Buddhism and explain the process of achieving nirvana through Buddha's teachings.

C. Now read the passage to see if your prediction is correct. Try to read as quickly as you can. Do not stop to look up words in your dictionary.

Reading 2

An Eastern Philosopher

Siddhartha Gautama (c. 563-486 B.C.), known as Buddha ("one who has awakened"), was a member of a Ksatriya (warrior) caste, probably from what is now Nepal. Buddha came from within the Hindu tradition, and in some ways can be regarded as a Hindu **guru** (holy man). He revolted against certain aspects of Hinduism, especially caste and the Brahman pretensions of divinity. However, he retained other aspects, notably karma, reincarnation, yoga, and nirvana. Buddha himself did not claim that he was a god or that he had founded "a religion."

Foundation of Buddhism

As a young aristocrat, he left his wife and son and went into the wilderness, where he engaged in the deep, extended meditation known as *yoga,* a word that refers to the link or yoke between body and soul. He concluded that existence was a great wheel. Life consists of suffering (or sorrow). Suffering is based on desire. Since desire cannot be fulfilled, the only way to stop suffering is to stop desiring. And the only way to do that is through yoga. By means of such concentration, a person can even ignore pain to the point that it no longer exists and can even rise above the endless cycle of rebirths (perpetual suffering) and achieve nirvana (the absence of suffering).

Buddha's Teachings

Through his teachings, Buddha sought to provide the guidance or law necessary for governing the wheel of existence. The wheel of existence would now become the wheel of the law that would help his followers to attain the contemplative state. For Buddha, contemplation was an end in itself, the stopping of suffering. However, it is not hard to see how, in time, the stopping of suffering (nirvana) could be interpreted as salvation, or heaven. By the first century A.D., if not earlier, one strain of Buddhism arrived at just this interpretation.

Mahayana Buddhism

This version of Buddhism acknowledged that Buddha was the **incarnation** of the eternal heavenly Buddha. It also developed a whole series of deities or gods. These deities were the **bodhisattvas,** or various manifestations of Buddha, to whom worshipers could pray for their salvation. This version of Buddhism was known as Mahayana. **Mahayana Buddhism** was rivaled by **Hinayana Buddhism**. This older version of the faith claimed to remain loyal to Buddha's own conception of himself as a teacher and of nirvana as a state of mind limited to this life.

Spread of Buddhism

Gautama Buddha and his successors, whether Hinayana or Mahayana Buddhists, institutionalized their religion in monasteries. There, monks (and sometimes nuns) practiced the contemplative life. Scattered along the trade routes, these monasteries became the vehicle for extending Buddhism into central Asia, Tibet, and China. Eventually, Buddhism reached Southeast Asia, Korea, and Japan. But in India itself, Buddha's attack on the vested interests of the **Brahmans** naturally raised their anger. Consequently, by the seventh century A.D., Buddhism could no longer be counted as a major religion of the Indian subcontinent. Under the **Mauryan dynasty**, Buddhism had thrived for centuries, especially in the second and third centuries B.C. Buddhism continued to grow, however, in several regions of the south and east until the fourteenth century.

Key Concept Words

bodhisattvas – (n.) deities or gods; "enlightened ones"

Brahmans – (n.) the priests, the highest of the four castes

guru – (n.) holy man, teacher

Hinayana Buddhism – (n.) version of Buddhism which demands that its followers lead a monk's life and give up all possessions

incarnation – (n.) taking human form, personification

Mahayana Buddhism – (n.) version of Buddhism which believes that everyone can attain enlightenment

Mauryan dynasty – (n.) ruled the first unified empire of India from 322 B.C. to 183 B.C.

Glossed Words

contemplative state – (n.) a condition of deep meditation; **interpretation** – (n.) explanation or meaning; **monasteries** – (n.) residence of members of religious groups, especially monks; **monks** and **nuns** – (n.) men and women who join religious orders and live under a set of rules; **pretensions of divinity** – (n.) claims or statements of high virtue or excellence; **region** – (n.) area; **revolt against** – (v.) to oppose; **was rivaled by** – (v.) competed with; **scatter** – (v.) distribute over a wide area; **strain** – (n.) kind; **thrive** – (v.) to be successful, to grow; **vehicle** – (n.) method, way, or means to express ideas; **version** – (n.) particular form or variation; **vested interests** – (n.) strong reasons for not wanting change; **wilderness** – (n.) uninhabited area; **worshipers** – (n.) those who honor and respect a god or idol

Summarizing

Share What You Read

A. Go back to Reading 2 and mark the text. Mark the main ideas and key words. Mark the topic sentence in each paragraph. Use abbreviations and symbols for definitions and examples. Make comments in the margins.

B. Use two or three sentences to tell your partner what you thought the reading was about. Then listen to your partner's sentences. Next, read the following statements and circle the number of the statement that best summarizes the reading.

1. Buddha rejected some aspects of Hinduism as he helped his followers attain a contemplative state called nirvana. Buddhism then spread throughout central and southeast Asia as a major religion until the fourteenth century.

2. Buddhism contains some of the same beliefs as Hinduism, including karma, yoga, reincarnation, and nirvana. Various kinds of Buddhism exist today, and the religion/philosophy continues to grow to this day.

3. Buddha invented the wheel of existence, which helped his followers attain nirvana. In monasteries throughout India, Buddhism grew and was accepted by the Brahmans until the seventh century A.D.

ACTIVITY 13

Check Your Comprehension

Read each sentence and circle the correct answer.

1. Buddha himself did not claim that he was *a god / an aristocrat.*

2. Leaving his wife and young son, Buddha went into the *monastery / wilderness.*

3. The way to stop suffering is to stop desiring, which can be done through *yoga / nirvana.*

4. Buddha's own beliefs were best modeled by *Mahayana / Hinayana* Buddhism.

5. By the first century A.D., one strain of Buddhism arrived at the interpretation that nirvana was *suffering / heaven.*

6. The monasteries, which helped spread Buddhism, were scattered *along trade routes / among the wilderness.*

7. Buddhism ceased to be a major religion in the Indian subcontinent due to the *Brahmans' / monks' and nuns'* anger at Buddha's attack on their vested interests.

8. The wheel of *existence / the law* would help Buddha's followers to attain a contemplative state.

9. Buddha came from within the *Hindu / Confucian* system.

10. Buddha and his successors institutionalized their religion in *temples / monasteries.*

Academic Word List

ACTIVITY 14

Scan and Define

A. Look at the ten words listed below. Scan the reading and underline the words from the list. Write the definition for the words you know. Do not use a dictionary. The first one has been done for you.

1. achieve <u>to accomplish or acquire something</u>

2. acknowledge _____

3. attain _____

4. consequently _____

5. cycle (n.) _____

6. ignore _____

7. link (n.) _____

8. major (adj.) _____

9. retained _____

10. tradition _____

B. Share your definitions with a partner and then with the rest of your classmates. As a group, try to complete the definitions for all ten words. Use a dictionary to check the definitions if you are unsure about them. Then complete the vocabulary activity.

ACTIVITY **15**   *Vocabulary Challenge*

A. Circle the word that does not belong. The first one has been done for you.

1. **achieve**	complete	accomplish	(fail)	realize
2. **link**	knot	yoke	connection	bond
3. **major**	primary	popular	main	dominant
4. **acknowledge**	admit	accept	refute	recognize
5. **consequently**	because	hence	thus	therefore
6. **attain**	purchase	gain	reach	achieve
7. **tradition**	belief	culture	custom	fable
8. **ignore**	overlook	include	omit	disregard
9. **cycle**	sequence	recurrence	list	repetition
10. **retain**	preserve	keep	continue	forget

B. Read the definition of the words below. Then decide which meaning is the one used in the sentence. Put the definition number next to the sentence. The first one has been done for you.

1. **cycle** *noun* **1.** a series of events that is periodically repeated; **2.** a bicycle, motorcycle, or similar vehicle

    __1__ A person can even rise above the endless **cycle** of rebirths and achieve nirvana.

2. **link** *noun* **1.** one of a series of connected units; **2.** something that joins or connects

    _____ *Yoga* is a word that refers to the **link** or yoke between body and soul.

3. **acknowledge** *verb* **1.** to admit or accept something as true; **2.** to recognize the authority of somebody

    _____ This version of Buddhism **acknowledged** that Buddha was the incarnation of the eternal heavenly Buddha.

4. **attain** *verb* **1.** to achieve or accomplish something over a period of time; **2.** to obtain or possess something

    _____ The wheel of existence would now become the wheel of the law that would help his followers to **attain** the contemplative state.

5. **major** *adjective* **1.** relating to a musical scale; **2.** greater or more important than others

    _____ By the seventh century A.D., Buddhism could no longer be counted as a **major** religion of the Indian subcontinent.

6. **retain** *verb* **1.** to continue to have; **2.** to hold something

    _____ However, he **retained** other aspects, notably karma, reincarnation, yoga, and nirvana.

7. **tradition** *noun* **1.** long-practiced, unwritten doctrines or teachings handed down; **2.** a custom or usage handed down, especially orally

_____ Buddha came from within the Hindu **tradition,** and in some ways can be regarded as a Hindu guru.

Using Context to Guess Meaning—*Review*

In each chapter of *Key Concepts* you have practiced strategies for guessing meaning from context. These strategies have included using definitions and punctuation, examples, inferences, synonyms and antonyms, and surrounding sentences to determine the meaning of a word or phrase. In this chapter, you will review them all.

ACTIVITY **16**

Guess Meaning from Context

Read the short passages below. Use the strategies you have learned to determine the meaning of the words in bold. Next to each word, write its meaning and describe the strategy you used (definition, punctuation, example, inference, synonym, antonym, or surrounding sentences) to determine it. The first one has been done for you.

1. India gave birth to two of the world's great religions, Hinduism and Buddhism. Because the group of Hindu gods and the body of **doctrines,** the principles which are taught, are so large, it is difficult to speak of a Hindu **theology** or religious doctrine. Nonetheless, there are some **fundamental** principles of Hinduism. These basic principles form the foundation of Hinduism.
   a. doctrines <u>principles which are taught; the commas signal the meaning of the word</u>
   b. theology _____
   c. fundamental _____

2. The two important Chinese systems of thought are Confucianism and Daoism. They both **emphasize** life in this world rather than in the next. For example, Daoism focuses on health, beauty, and balance in this world. This focus, however, reflects the non-mystical part of the religion. The mystical **element** of Daoism may also be considered religious. Confucius taught by asking questions and making **paradoxical** (contradictory) statements. He used this method to stimulate discussion.
   a. emphasize _____
   b. element _____
   c. paradoxical _____

3. As a young **aristocrat,** Buddha left his wife and son, along with his life of luxury and future title of "prince," and went into the wilderness. There he sought answers to the reason for man's existence. He **engaged** in the deep, extended meditation known as *yoga,* a word that refers to the **link** or yoke between body and soul. Through his practice of yoga he came to the conclusion that existence was a great wheel.
   a. aristocrat _____
   b. engaged _____
   c. yoga _____
   d. link _____

In this section, you will learn some skills and strategies associated with the writing process. This section addresses noun clauses, a grammatical structure used in the readings, as well as variety in writing through the use of simple, compound, and complex sentences. You will practice different steps in the writing process and will write a paragraph of summary.

The Grammar of Noun Clauses

Noun clauses are dependent clauses and, as with all dependent clauses, need to be connected to an independent clause. Noun clauses are introduced by relative pronouns or adverbs including *what, that, who, whom, which, when, where, whatever, wherever, whomever,* or *however.* In a sentence, a noun clause may function as the subject, the object of a verb, the object of a preposition, or a complement. Noun clauses are commonly used to report what someone else has said and are used in embedded questions.

Examples: *Historians reported <u>that Buddhism was institutionalized in monasteries.</u>*
Does anyone know <u>where Buddha first began to share his teachings?</u>

Subject	Verb	Object/Complement
When Buddha first practiced yoga	remains	a mystery.
Many of Buddha's followers	believed	**that they could achieve nirvana.**
Millions of people	were	interested in **what Buddha had to say.**
It	is	clear **that Eastern religions spread to the West.**

ACTIVITY **17**

Identify Noun Clauses

Read the sentences below and underline the noun clause. Then identify its function in the sentence. The first one has been done for you.

1. ___subject___ <u>That Confucius had an impact on Chinese society</u> is worth noting.

2. _____ Historians believed that Confucius had an impact on Chinese society.

3. _____ It is true that Buddha left his wife and child to go into the wilderness to meditate.

4. _____ The belief is that Buddha was the incarnation of the eternal heavenly Buddha.

5. _____ The fact that Hinduism has no single theology makes it unique among religions.

6. _____ What followers of Confucianism and Daoism have in common includes emphasis on life in this world rather than in the next.

7. _____ Today people are still trying to figure out which religion best fits their personal needs and beliefs.

8. _____ According to what Hindus believe, one has to be reincarnated many times before attaining peace in nirvana.

9. _____ However one approaches Eastern religions and philosophies, the fact is that they have played a major role in the history of world religions.

10. _____ It seems that up until the fourteenth century, Buddhism continued to grow in southern and eastern India.

Use Noun Clauses

Complete the following sentences with noun clauses. A relative pronoun or adverb has already been given. Be sure to include both a subject and a verb in your noun clause. The first one has been done for you.

1. I know that _we will have a test on this tomorrow_____.

2. That _____ cannot be changed.

3. Do you believe that _____?

4. It's a fact that _____.

5. Is it true that _____?

6. It is important to know how _____.

7. I don't know where _____.

8. What _____ just cannot be true!

Sentence Essentials

Sentence Review

In each chapter of *Key Concepts* you have practiced identifying and writing different sentence types. These types include simple, compound, and complex sentences. In this section you will review them all.

Identify the Sentence Type

Read each sentence and label its type: *S* for simple, *CP* for compound or *CX* for complex.

_____ 1. Gautama Buddha wanted to simplify the Hindu caste system.

_____ 2. Because there are so many Hindu gods, it is difficult to speak of just one Hindu theology.

_____ 3. It is not hard to see that nirvana could be interpreted as salvation.

_____ 4. Buddha himself did not claim to be a god.

_____ 5. Gautama Buddha was born an aristocrat.

_____ 6. Although yoga has many forms, it basically involves the disciplining of the body to enhance concentration.

_____ 7. Confucianism and Daoism emphasize life in this world, but Daoism also includes a mystical element.

_____ 8. Buddha was a devout Hindu before he developed his own body of teachings.

_____ 9. Daoism and Confucianism differ in many ways, yet the two are often blended in practice.

ACTIVITY 20 *Complete the Sentences*

Connect the clauses with the appropriate coordinating conjunction to form compound sentences. Use *for, and, nor, but, or, yet,* or *so.* The first one has been done for you.

1. Gautama Buddha established monasteries, ___and___ he was joined there by monks and nuns.

2. Gautama Buddha did not like the Hindu caste system, _____ did he believe the Brahmans were divine.

3. Buddhism was founded on the Indian subcontinent, _____ it did not remain a major religion there.

4. He needed to meditate deeply, _____ he left his wife and son.

5. Mahayana Buddhists believe Buddha was the incarnation of the eternal heavenly Buddha, _____ Buddha himself did not consider himself a god.

6. In Japan you can see many Shinto shrines, _____ you can visit Buddhist temples.

ACTIVITY 21 *Identify the Subordinate Clause*

Underline the subordinate clause, and identify it as an adjective clause (ADJ), adverb clause (ADV), or noun clause (N). The first one has been done for you.

___ADV___ 1. <u>Because many aspects of Buddhism contradicted traditional culture in China,</u> conflict was inevitable.

_____ 2. Siddhartha Gautama, who is known as the Buddha, was a member of the warrior caste.

_____ 3. Buddha taught that the only way to stop suffering is to stop desiring.

_____ 4. Travelers came upon Buddhist monasteries as they traveled the Silk Road.

_____ 5. Buddhism began to gain popularity in China because it promised an afterlife.

_____ 6. Daoist teachings state that followers should seek "the way" by abandoning the self to the natural rhythms of the universe.

ACTIVITY 22 *Write Sentences of Your Own*

Write a sentence of your own about any topic for each sentence type.

1. Simple _____

_____

2. Compound with a coordinating conjunction _____

_____

3. Complex with an adjective clause _____

_____

4. Complex with an adverb clause _____

_____

5. Complex with a noun clause _____

_____

Use Sentence Variation in Writing

By now you have learned how to write simple, compound, and complex sentences. These different sentence types add variety to your writing. A paragraph with only simple sentences would be boring and choppy, while a paragraph with only complex sentences might seem unclear or long-winded. It is best to mix sentence types in your writing.

Rewrite the Paragraphs

The paragraphs below lack sentence variation. Rewrite the paragraphs on a separate sheet of paper using a variety of sentence types.

A. There are three architectural forms established by Buddhists. They were used to create retreats for pilgrims. The pilgrims would come there to contemplate. The first is the *vihara*. It is a monastic cell group. The second is the *chaitya*. That is the hall of worship. The last is the *stupa*. It is a burial mound.

B. Many Buddhist retreats were carved into mountains. Some were in caves. The route into the hall was ritually prescribed. The route around the stupa was also prescribed. The walls and columns were carved. They were decorated. The scenes were from Buddha's life. The journey into the hall and stupa was planned to stimulate contemplation.

Making the Connection

Evaluating a writer's support is part of the reading process. Readers must rely on the writer's details to decide whether to accept what the writer says as true. Paying attention to in-text citations the writer uses or sources the writer quotes assists in evaluating the writer's support. Writers, in order to convince the reader to accept evidence presented in a passage, rely on outside sources for facts, statistics, and other kinds of support. Good writers include these sources in their writing in the form of direct and indirect quotes, paraphrases, and summaries. They give credit to their sources through in-text citations, footnotes, and/or a bibliography or "works cited" page.

WRITING 1B ● The Process

Get Ready to Write

Avoid Plagiarism

Plagiarism is a serious academic offense—it is a form of theft. Plagiarism happens if you present someone else's words or ideas as if they were your own. It is absolutely necessary to give credit to the people whose ideas and words you use. There are serious consequences for plagiarism—a student can be expelled, or thrown out of school. Using quotations, citing your sources, and using your own words are the ways to avoid academic stealing.

Use Quotations

Quotations are the written or spoken words of someone else. They are often used in academic writing, including summaries, because they add authority or interest to your writing. Quotations can come from experts in the field or from the person you are writing about. For example, if you were writing about nonviolence, it would be effective to include the words of Martin Luther King, Jr. or Mahatma Gandhi. In this case, you would use quotations. Using quotes can enhance your writing, but they must be used correctly.

- Do not overuse quotes or use very long quotes. Your reader will think you have nothing to say yourself.
- Use correct punctuation to make the quote clear to your reader.
- The source of the quote must always be acknowledged.

Quotations are used with reporting verbs or phrases such as *claim, declare, maintain, say, state,* and *write.*

There are two kinds of quotations:

Direct: *Buddha said, "Three things cannot long be hidden: the sun, the moon, and the truth."*
Indirect: *Buddha said that three things cannot be long hidden: the sun, the moon, and the truth.*

Direct Quotations

A direct quote contains the words of someone *exactly* as they were written or spoken. The actual quotation may come at the beginning, in the middle, or at the end of a sentence. It can also be split by the reporting phrase.

> *Confucius suggested, "Forget injuries, never forget kindnesses."*
>
> *"Forget injuries," Confucius suggested, "never forget kindnesses."*
>
> *"Forget injuries, never forget kindnesses," Confucius suggested.*

Punctuating Direct Quotations

Read the following direct quotations, paying attention to the punctuation.

> *"Those who are free from resentful thoughts surely find peace," said Buddha.*
>
> *Confucius stated, "Before you embark on a journey of revenge, dig two graves."*
>
> *"It does not matter how slowly you go," Confucius said, "so long as you do not stop."*

- A comma separates the quotation from the reporting phrase.
- The exact quote is surrounded by quotation marks.
- The first word of the quotation is capitalized even if it is not the first word in the sentence.
- If a quotation is split by the reporting phrase, surround both parts in quotation marks and separate them with commas. Only the first word of a split quotation should be capitalized.

Identify and Punctuate Quotations

The following sentences are actually quotes. Follow the steps to identify the parts of the quote and punctuate it correctly: underline the reporting phrase, place quotation marks around the quote, and punctuate the entire sentence. The first one has been done for you.

1. Martha Washington <u>wrote,</u> **"**I have learned that the greater part of our happiness or misery depends on our dispositions and not upon our circumstances.**"**

2. People say that beauty is in the eye of the beholder says Salma Hayek and I say that the most liberating thing about beauty is that you are the beholder

3. Abraham Lincoln maintained Character is like a tree and reputation like its shadow. The shadow is what we think of it; the tree is the real thing

4. Nearly all men can stand adversity wrote Abraham Lincoln but if you want to test a man's character, give him power

5. If you want others to be happy, practice compassion. If you want to be happy, practice compassion suggests the Dalai Lama

6. Dwight D. Eisenhower declared I like to believe that people in the long run are going to do more to promote peace than our governments. Indeed, I think that people want peace so much that one of these days our governments had better get out of the way and let them have it

Indirect Quotations

Indirect quotations are written or spoken statements that are reported indirectly. They are introduced by reporting verbs with the word *that*, forming a noun clause, but they are not enclosed in quotation marks. Sometimes *that* is omitted from an indirect quotation.

Sometimes, when changing direct quotations to indirect ones, there is a shift in verb tense. If the reporting verb is in past tense, the verb in the noun clause will also be in the past. When the indirect quotation is a fact or statement of truth, it is often left in the present tense.

> Direct: *Confucius said, "It does not matter how slowly you go, so long as you do not stop."*
> Indirect: *Confucius said that it did not matter how slowly you went, so long as you did not stop.*
> *Confucius said that it does not matter how slowly you go, so long as you do not stop.*

ACTIVITY **25**

Writing Direct and Indirect Quotes

On a separate sheet of paper write each of the quotes below as a direct and an indirect quotation. You may use any reporting verb (*claim, declare, maintain, say, state, write*). The first one has been done for you.

1. Buddha: Happiness never decreases by being shared.

   Direct: "Happiness never decreases by being shared," maintained Buddha.

   Indirect: Buddha maintained that happiness never decreases by being shared.

2. Buddha: Virtue is more persecuted by the wicked than it is loved by the good.

3. Buddha: Chaos is inherent in all compound things.

4. Buddha: He who envies others does not obtain peace of mind.

5. Confucius: Everything has its beauty but not everyone sees it.

6. Confucius: Men's natures are alike. It is their habits that carry them far apart.

7. Confucius: The superior man is modest in his speech but exceeds in his actions.

A statue of Confucius

Use Your Own Words

Earlier you read that paraphrasing and summarizing are useful tools for note-taking. They are also useful skills in academic writing. You may be asked to paraphrase an essay or summarize a chapter as a class assignment. You will also be expected to discuss general ideas or well-known concepts. These skills are exercised in your own words. This means that you *do not* copy directly out of a text or take words directly from speech.

> "Returning violence for violence multiplies violence, adding deeper darkness to a night already devoid of stars." —Martin Luther King, Jr.

> "An eye for an eye leaves the whole world blind." —Mahatma Gandhi

Both of the quotes above express the idea that violence results only in more violence. The quotes also express King's and Gandhi's belief in nonviolence even as a response to violence. It would be plagiarism, however, if you used these quotes in your own paragraph about nonviolence without citation, unless you made your own statement with your own words.

> *Using violence to stop violence does not work; the violence only continues to spread.*

The above statement expresses a similar opinion on the topic of nonviolence without plagiarizing the words of King or Gandhi.

Use Your Own Words

Below are quotes from individuals on similar topics. Read the quotes and write your own version of the idea being expressed. See the example above.

1. "The wisest mind has something yet to learn." —George Santayana

   "The fool doth think he is wise, but the wise man knows himself to be a fool." —William Shakespeare

   "To be conscious that you are ignorant is the first step towards knowledge." —Benjamin Disraeli

   _____

2. "The hatred you're carrying is like a live coal in your heart—far more damaging to yourself than to them." —Lawana Blackwell

   "Holding on to anger is like grasping a hot coal with the intention of throwing it at someone else; you are the one who gets burned." —Buddha

   "Forgiveness is almost a selfish act because of its immense benefits to the one who forgives." —Lawana Blackwell

   _____

3. "Hate cannot drive out hate—only love can do that." —Martin Luther King, Jr.

   "Hatred does not cease by hatred; but only by love. This is the eternal rule." —Buddha

   _____

4. "Actions speak louder than words." —Unknown

   "I have long since come to believe that people never mean half of what they say, and that it is best to disregard their talk and judge only their actions." —Dorothy Day

   _____

526.29 MARTIN LUTHER KING, Jr (1929-1968).
Credit: The Granger Collection, New York

Dr. Martin Luther King, Jr.

5. "Courage is doing what you are afraid to do. There can be no courage unless you're scared." —Eddie Rickenbacker

   "Courage is being scared to death—and saddling up anyway." —John Wayne

   "Courage is resistance to fear, mastery of fear—not absence of fear." —Mark Twain

---

Citing Sources

In academic work you will be expected to use information from lectures, textbooks, and research in your writing. You must give the lecturer, author, or researcher credit in order to avoid plagiarism.

When to Cite Sources

- if you use information from or the ideas of someone else in your writing by quoting, paraphrasing, or summarizing
- if someone else's information or ideas contribute to or influence your ideas, even if you do not quote directly

When Citation is Unnecessary

- if you use a familiar proverb
- if you use a famous quote (Note: The person who made the quote must be acknowledged, but you do not need to cite the book or Web site where you found the quote)
- if you use common knowledge, or things generally known to be true

How to Cite Sources—Style

There is more than one style of citing a source. The most commonly used styles are from the APA (American Psychological Association) and MLA (Modern Language Association). It is important to know which style to use because some professors and fields have preferences. For example, MLA style is used for writing in the humanities or liberal arts, while APA style is used in the social sciences. Handbooks are available for each style at libraries and in bookstores.

In this chapter, we will practice APA style. Guidelines for MLA style are in Appendix 6 on page 206. Pay close attention to punctuation, capitalization, and the use of italics.

Basic APA Format—Books

A. Author, A. (Year of Publication). *Title of book: Capital letter for a subtitle.* Location: Publisher.
Andrea, A., & Overfield, J. (2005). *The human record: Sources of global history.* Boston: Houghton Mifflin.

B. Edited Book—No Author
Editor, A., & Editor, B. (Eds.). (Year of Publication). *Title of book: Capital letter for a subtitle.* Location: Publisher.
Lauter, P. (Ed.). (2004). *The Heath anthology of American literature: Concise edition.* Boston: Houghton Mifflin.

C. Edited Book—With Author

Author, A. (Year of Publication). *Title of book: Capital letter for a subtitle* (A. Editor, Ed.). Location: Publisher.

Shakespeare, W. (2006). *The complete works of Shakespeare* (D. Bevington, Ed.). New York: Longman.

Electronic Sources

D. Web Page

Author, A. (Date of Publication). *Title.* Retrieved month day, year, from http://Web address.

Lorentz, M. (2007). *Life of the Buddha* [Online]. Retrieved September 1, 2008, from http://www.mnsu.edu/emuseum/cultural/religion/buddhism/history.html.

Placement of Citations

In Text

An in-text citation comes immediately after a paraphrase or summary of someone else's idea, but before the period. Include the author's name and the year the book was published. If a direct quote is used, include the page number and enclose the citation in parentheses.

Examples:

> There cannot be too much charity (Bacon, 1625).

> "There is no clear determination of when Hinduism began in India. Although the religious rites of today's India greatly differ from those of the Indus civilization, it is not possible to identify a time when India was not Hindu" (Witt et al., 2005, p.429).

Further information about your source is given in a footnote, references cited page, or bibliography.

Footnotes and References/Works Cited Pages

A footnote is a reference found at the bottom of a page, below the text. The number of a footnote corresponds with the number placed in a text. See the bottom of this page for the footnote for the following example.

Example: There is no clear determination of when Hinduism began in India. Although the religious rites of today's India greatly differ from those of the Indus civilization, it is not possible locate a time period when India was not Hindu.[1]

In APA style, it is customary to list footnotes/endnotes on a separate page which follows the References page. A References page is one (or more) pages at the end of your paper that lists all of the references in your text alphabetically by the authors' last names.

A bibliography is a list of all the sources you consult. It contains more sources than those you will list on your References page.

---

[1] Witt, et al. (2005). *The Humanities: Volume 1* (7th ed.). Boston: Houghton Mifflin.

ACTIVITY 27

Write References

Use the information in the chart to write citations in your notebook or on a separate sheet of paper.

Publisher	Year	Title	Author	Location
1. University Press	1962	A History of Greek Philosophy	Editor: W. K. Guthrie	Cambridge
2. Cambridge University Press	2003	The Cambridge Companion to Greek and Roman Philosophy	Editor: D. Sedley	New York
3. Oxford University Press	1999	Plate Vo. 2: Ethics, Politics, Religion and the Soul	Editor: Gail Fine	Oxford
4. Baylor University Press	1987	Contemporary Essays on Greek Ideas	Editor: R. Baird et al.	Waco, TX
5. Humanities Press	1964	Doctrine and Argument in Indian Philosophy	Ninian Smart	London

How Did They Do That?

ACTIVITY 28

Follow the Steps

Read the excerpt from Reading 2, "An Eastern Philosopher," and review the steps for summarizing from Tools for Interactive Reading in this chapter. Then read the summary paragraph and complete the activity.

Excerpt:

Foundation of Buddhism

As a young aristocrat, Buddha left his wife and son and went into the wilderness, where he engaged in the deep, extended meditation known as *yoga,* a word that refers to the link or yoke between body and soul. He concluded that existence was a great wheel. Life consists of suffering (or sorrow). Suffering is based on desire. Since desire cannot be fulfilled, the only way to stop suffering is to stop desiring. And the only way to do that is through yoga. By means of such concentration, a person can even ignore pain to the point that it no longer exists and can even rise above the endless cycle of rebirths (perpetual suffering) and achieve nirvana (the absence of suffering).

Buddha's Teachings

Through his teachings, Buddha sought to provide the guidance or law necessary for governing the wheel of existence. The wheel of existence would now become the wheel of the law that would help his followers to attain the contemplative state. For Buddha, contemplation was an end in itself, the stopping of suffering. However, it is not hard to see how, in time, the stopping of suffering (nirvana) could be interpreted as salvation, or heaven. By the first century A.D., if not earlier, one strain of Buddhism arrived at just this interpretation.

Mahayana Buddhism

This version of Buddhism acknowledged that Buddha was the **incarnation** of the eternal heavenly Buddha. It also developed a whole series of deities or gods. These deities were the **bodhisattvas,** or various manifestations of Buddha, to whom worshipers could pray for their salvation. This version of Buddhism was known as Mahayana. **Mahayana Buddhism** was rivaled by **Hinayana Buddhism**. This older version of the faith claimed to remain loyal to Buddha's own conception of himself as a teacher and of nirvana as a state of mind limited to this life.

Steps for Summarizing

1. Be sure you understand the section you have read. Look up any words that are unfamiliar or that you do not understand.

2. Identify the main ideas and most important points in the section.

3. List, in your own words, the ideas and important points in the section.

4. Convert the ideas and important points into sentences.

5. Read your summary to make sure there has been no change in meaning.

6. If you write your summary in a notebook, identify the source of the summary.

Summary:

Buddha basically believed that life consists of suffering, which comes from desire. Based on his beliefs, Buddha taught that the only way to stop suffering was to stop desiring. He also taught that yoga was the means to stop desiring. According to Buddha, when a person stops suffering, he or she has reached nirvana, which is sometimes described as salvation. Generally, the followers of Buddha are split into two groups. The Mahayana Buddhists believe that Buddha was actually the incarnation of the heavenly Buddha and, thus, divine. Hinayana Buddhists stayed with Buddha's own view of himself as a teacher. (Reading 2: "An Eastern Philosopher")

1. Circle the main idea from each section that the writer included in the summary.

2. Underline any additional important points the writer included.

3. Compare the original and the summary. Is the summary in the writer's own words? _____

4. Does the summary accurately reflect the original passage? Has there been any change in meaning? _____

   _____

5. Does the writer list the source of the summary? _____

   _____

6. List any key words the writer used which identify the text structure as *summary*.

   _____

Paragraph of Summary

Write Your Paragraph

Choose a short reading (two to three paragraphs) from your field of study or an area in which you are interested and summarize it. Examples of subjects to summarize are *natural disasters, the history of a political party, Impressionist art,* or *the music of Ancient Greece.* Follow the steps below to write a paragraph of summary. Your audience is your instructor and your classmates. After you finish writing your paragraph, complete the two final activities, *Revising* and *Editing and Proofreading.*

Steps:

1. Be sure you understand what you have read. Look up any words that are unfamiliar or that you do not understand.

2. Identify the main ideas and most important points in each section. (Highlight or underline them.)

3. List, in your own words, the ideas and important points in each section.

4. Choose the text structure (summary).

5. Write a topic sentence to introduce the summary.

6. Organize the ideas and important points. Make an outline.

Topic Sentence: _____

A. Point One
1.
2.
B. Point Two
1.
2.
C. Point Three
1.
2.

Concluding Sentence _____

7. Convert the ideas and important points into sentences.

8. Write a concluding sentence to end the summary.

9. Put in paragraph format.

10. Read your summary to make sure there has been no change in meaning.

11. Identify the source of the summary.

Revising

Follow the Steps

A. Follow the steps outlined below to revise the paragraph of summary.

Revising Checklist

1. Assignment
   - ☐ Follows the assignment to write a paragraph of summary for subjects from your field of study or area of interest
   - ☐ Addresses your instructor and classmates as your audience
   - ☐ Follows the eleven steps listed in the assignment

2. Topic sentence
   - ☐ Is limited to a specific topic
   - ☐ Includes the topic
   - ☐ Includes what the reader needs to know about the topic
   - ☐ Gives a clue to the text structure

3. Details
   - ☐ Relate to the topic
   - ☐ Are organized in a logical order
   - ☐ Follow the outline
   - ☐ Enough in number (not too many, not too few)

4. Concluding sentence
   - ☐ Restates the topic sentence
   - ☐ Alerts the reader to the end of the paragraph
   - ☐ Summarizes the key points in the paragraph

B. Share your paragraph with a classmate. Ask your classmate to use the Revising Checklist to check your paragraph and give you some feedback. Make any changes to your paragraph that you feel are necessary. The changes you make should improve your paragraph.

Editing and Proofreading

ACTIVITY 31

The Final Steps

A. Follow the steps outlined below to edit and proofread the paragraph of summary you wrote for the *On Your Own* section.

Editing and Proofreading Checklist

1. Grammar

   ☐ Verb tenses are correct.

   ☐ Each subject agrees with its verb (singular/plural).

   ☐ Prepositions are correct.

   ☐ Pronouns are correct (agree in number/gender).

   ☐ Articles are correct (a, an, the).

2. Spelling

   ☐ All words are spelled correctly.

   ☐ Abbreviations, if any, are used correctly.

   ☐ First word of each sentence begins with a capital letter.

3. Punctuation

   ☐ All sentences end with a punctuation mark.

   ☐ Periods are after statements, and question marks are after questions.

   ☐ Commas are used with independent clauses joined by coordinating conjunctions.

   ☐ Semicolons and commas are used with independent clauses joined by conjunctive adverbs.

   ☐ Quotation marks and parentheses are used for quotes and citations respectively.

4. Sentences

   ☐ All sentences are complete.

   ☐ Each sentence has a subject and a verb.

   ☐ There are no fragments.

5. Format

   ☐ Paragraph has a title.

   ☐ First line is indented.

   ☐ All sentences are in paragraph format (not listed or numbered).

   ☐ Writer's name is on the paper.

   ☐ Paper is neat, clean, and legible (easily read).

B. Share your paragraph with a classmate. Ask your classmate to use the Editing and Proofreading Checklist to check your paragraph and mark any errors in grammar, spelling, punctuation, sentences, or paragraph format.

C. Fix any mistakes your paragraph contained. Proofread your paragraph one more time. Turn in your final draft to your instructor.

APPENDIX 1 • Academic Word List

Chapter 1

Reading 1

appropriate*	identify
authority*	illogical*
automatically	intelligently
aware*	involve*
challenge	logical
conclusion	mental
creative thinking	priority*
critical*	process*
define/definition	psychologist
evaluation	research*
focus*	

Reading 2

adequate*	prior
analyze	reject*
author*	reliable
convince*	reveal*
evaluate	selection
evidence	source*
expert*	sufficient
issue*	techniques
methods*	text
objective	valid*

Chapter 2

Reading 1

apparently	individuals
approach	initial*
commit*	involved
communicated	issue
computing	items*
conformity	labor
consist*	methods
contrast (in)*	norms
deny*	obtains
experts	occur*
granting	potential*
procedure	strategist*
process	substitutes
psychologists	technique*
purchase	

Reading 2

accompany	labels
analysis	link
apparent*	major
approach*	methods
components	normal
conclusions/conclude	precede*
consistently*	precisely
contemporary	psychologist
cultural	reliable*
dimensions	researcher/research
display*	reveal
dominate	similarities
economic	specific
emergence*	stable/stability
equivalent	structure
evidence	technique
factor*	theorist/theorist
focus	traced
identification	uniqueness
individual*	variations
internal	version*
investigates	

*Used in vocabulary exercise

Chapter 3

Reading 1		Reading 2	
beneficiaries	licensing	advocates*	issue
benefit	major	alternative	justified
consumers	physical	ambiguity	labor
creates	promotion	analysis	legal
declines*	qualitative*	approach	minimal
domestic*	range*	codes*	nevertheless
export*	regulations	community	norms*
generate*	requirements	constitute*	objective
global*	restrictions*	convinced	obvious
identified	revenues	culture	occurred
impose*	technological	debate*	ongoing*
inevitable	thereby	economy	perspectives*
labeling	transit*	emerge	physical
legislation	virtually	emphasis	policies
liberalization	visible	ethics*	potential
		eventually	principles
		global	security
		guidelines	similar
		impact	strategy
		implement	transition
		implication	unique
		interpreted*	violate
		investments	widespread*

Chapter 4

Reading 1		Reading 2	
acquire*	liberal*	analysis*	injured*
ambiguities*	military	attached	investigation
civil	policy*	civil*	investigative
clarify*	reaction	committed	involve
conduct*	regulation	concept*	legal
create	reliance	conducted	maintain
definition	restoration	defined	major
economic/economy	revolution	distinction	procedural
emphasis	role	enormous*	pursue*
enforcement*	significant*	ensure*	require
goals	similarly	evidence	resolution*
guaranteeing	welfare*	expert	role
individual		federal	seek*
intervene*		fees	specific
involving		financial	techniques
issues		impose	violations*
labor		individual	

*Used in vocabulary exercise

Chapter 5

Reading 1		Reading 2	
automatically*	relax*	available*	interaction
contract*	rely*	chemical	link
eliminate*	remove*	complex*	maintenance
environment*	reverse*	compounds*	overlapping*
expand*	structure*	consumers	primary*
process		energy*	process
		environment	release*
		eventually*	sources
		finally	transfer*
		instance	via*

Chapter 6

Reading 1		Reading 2	
abandonment*	impact*	achieve*	institutionalized
accumulated*	instability*	acknowledge*	interpreted
attain/attainment	integrity	aspects	link*
bond	interpreted	attain*	major*
communication	involves	concentration	regions
concentration	nonetheless	conception	retained*
contrast	notion	conclude	routes
culture	physical	consequently*	series
cycle	principles*	consist	sought
element	rational	cycle*	successors
emphasis*	role*	eventually	tradition*
enhance*	sought/seek	founded	vehicle
ethical	source	ignore*	version
founder*	traditional		
fundamental	ultimately*		

*Used in vocabulary exercise

APPENDIX 2 ● Brainstorming Methods

Brainstorming means generating a list of ideas for topics and/or support. During brainstorming, the writer lists all of the ideas that come to his/her mind when thinking about a topic. It is the first step in writing. Without ideas, you have nothing to write about.

Points to remember about brainstorming

1. Brainstorming takes more than one or two minutes. The more time you devote to brainstorming, the more ideas you will generate.

2. Brainstorming does not include evaluating your ideas. If you stop to evaluate your ideas before writing them down, you are not brainstorming.

3. Brainstorming is not the same as writing your paragraph or essay. It is the first step in the process. You will not use all of the ideas that you brainstormed in your paragraph or essay.

4. After you brainstorm topics, you go back and evaluate them, choosing those ideas that might be suitable for your writing. All of the other ideas, the ones you don't use, are discarded.

5. Sometimes, while you are brainstorming, you will generate ideas that will later become support or details for your writing. As you evaluate your ideas, note which ones might be good details to include in your writing.

Types of brainstorming

There are many ways to generate ideas, and the best way is the one that helps you generate the most and/or the best ideas. Below are some examples of different types of brainstorming.

1. Generating a list—this is the most common type of brainstorming. You simply write down everything that comes into your mind and generate a list of ideas. Later you go back and evaluate the items on your list, choosing those that are the best.

Brainstormed list for the topic *Success in College*

good reading skills	keeping up with work
know how to take notes	using the library
study for an exam	choosing a major
good teachers	getting a tutor if I need one
classes not too big	good grades
have a good computer	asking teacher for help
don't waste time	study groups
attending class every day	schedule for studying
doing assignments	time management

2. Creating a web or cluster—this is another common type of brainstorming. Place your topic in the center of the web/cluster and then generate your ideas, connecting related ideas to one another.

Brainstormed web/cluster for the topic *Success in College*

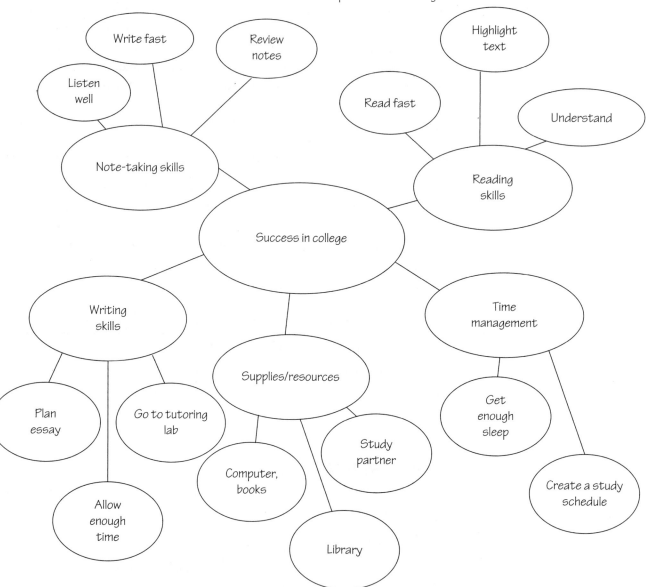

3. Free writing—this type of brainstorming is sometimes mistaken for the actual writing of a paragraph or essay. However, it is brainstorming: generating your ideas. In free writing, you write almost as if you are writing in a journal, i.e., you write your ideas in sentences and write whatever comes to mind about your topic. Later, during the evaluation process, you go back and search for ideas in what you have written.

I am really nervous about going to college. I'm so afraid that I won't know what to do or how to study. What if I get bad grades on all my tests? I'll be so depressed and humiliated. I can feel the stress already. I wonder if anyone else feels this way. Well, I'll just have to make sure that I'm prepared. I have good reading skills. When I read, I can always figure out what the main idea is. I just have to make sure that I am prepared for class by reading the chapter or assignment before class meets. I'm not really worried about writing. I always get pretty good grades in writing. The thing is, writing takes time, so I have to make sure I don't wait till the last minute to start my writing. I'm strong in math, so that shouldn't be a problem for me. The good thing about math is that the homework doesn't seem so time-consuming as maybe a reading class would be. I think that if I'm going to succeed, I'll really have to manage my time. Everything kind of keeps coming back to that.

4. Questioning—this type of brainstorming does not work for every topic and so is not used as often as the other types of techniques. As with most questions, you will generate more ideas if you use *wh-* questions (who, what, where, when, how, why) instead of yes/no questions. After you brainstorm your list of questions, you answer them. Your answers will contain the ideas you evaluate and eventually write about.

Brainstormed questions for the topic of *Success in College*

What does it mean to be successful in college?

Why are some people successful and others not?

Who is successful in college?

What types of students succeed in college?

Do only smart people succeed?

What kind of skills do people need to do well?

How good do your reading skills have to be in college?

Do you do a lot of reading in college?

How much reading do you have to do?

Is there a lot of writing in college?

How much writing do you have to do?

What kinds of writing do you have to do?

Who can help you get those skills if you don't have them or if they aren't very good?

Where can you learn about the skills you will need to succeed in college?

Where can you go for help if you need it?

When do most people decide to go to college?

When do most students study at college – during the day or at night?

Does it make a difference what time of day you study?

How long do students usually study for tests?

What do I do with my brainstorming results?

Once you have finished brainstorming, you begin to evaluate your ideas. You go over your list of ideas and cross out any which seem unrelated to the topic. Cross out ideas which are boring or too difficult to write about. Also cross out ideas which are too narrow to develop into a paragraph. The chances are that one of your ideas will appeal to you more than the others will. This is the idea you want to develop into a topic sentence for your paragraph or into a thesis statement for your essay. Be sure to scan your list of brainstormed ideas for details that might help support your topic sentence. Next, organize your ideas and, if necessary, brainstorm additional details. Once you have your topic sentence and supporting details organized, start writing your first draft.

Additional Brainstorming Techniques

If you are brainstorming ideas for a specific type or pattern of writing, for example, comparison/contrast, there are graphic organizers you can use. See the examples below.

1. This Venn diagram graphic organizer is good for brainstorming and organizing comparison/contrast writing. In one circle you list all the ideas that apply only to Topic A. In the other circle, you list all the ideas that apply only to Topic B. In the center, where the circles overlap, you list the ideas that Topic A and Topic B have in common.

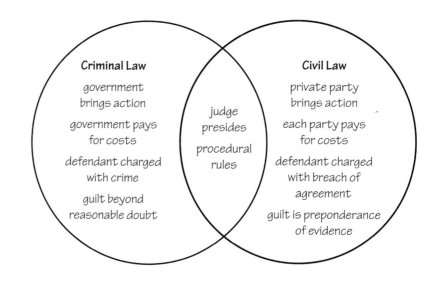

2. In this T-structure, all the points related to Topic A are listed on the left, and those related to Topic B are listed on the right. Similarities and differences can then easily be compared, and the focus of the paragraph or essay can highlight whichever predominates, the similarities or differences.

Criminal Law	Civil Law
government brings action	private party brings action
government pays for costs	each party pays for costs
defendant charged with crime	defendant charged with breach of agreement
guilt beyond a reasonable doubt	guilt is preponderance of evidence
judge presides	judge presides
follow procedural rules	follow procedural rules

3. In this flow chart, the topic is heart disease. The causes of heart disease are listed on the left; the effects of heart disease are listed on the right. It is possible to have different configurations for cause/effect essays: one cause and one effect, one cause and multiple effects, multiple causes and one effect, and multiple causes and multiple effects.

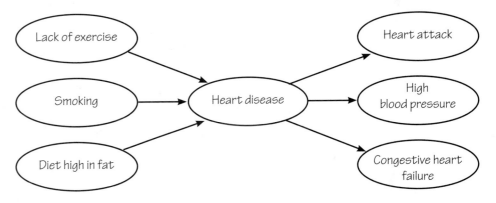

• **Conjunctions, Transitions, and Key Words**

Conjunctions

Conjunctions join or connect words, phrases, and clauses. See the following charts for the different types of conjunctions.

Coordinating Conjunctions

Coordinating conjunctions connect words, phrases, or clauses that are equal in importance.

Coordinating Conjunction	Use and Meaning
for	introduces reason (more formal than *because*)
and	introduces another idea or more information
nor	introduces another idea or more information (negative)
but	introduces contrast
or	introduces an alternative
yet	introduces contrast
so	introduces the result

Example sentences

1. People listened when he spoke, **for** he was the authority on the subject.

2. There are many ways to brainstorm ideas, **and** all of them are effective.

3. I don't have the time to help her with her math today, **nor** do I have the energy.

4. Most people are making an effort to conserve energy, **but** we still have a long way to go.

5. We can travel by train to California next month, **or** we can get there by plane.

6. She's explained this economic principle to me several times, **yet** I still don't understand it.

7. He's always been great at math, **so** he decided to major in accounting in college.

Subordinating Conjunctions

Subordinating conjunctions connect dependent and independent clauses and show the relationship between the two; the conjunction introduces the dependent clause.

Subordinating Conjunction	Use and Meaning
although even though though	concession
if even if unless only if	condition
although even though though whereas while	contrast
as because since	reason or cause
in order that so that so + adjective/adverb + that such + noun + that	result or purpose
after once as until as soon as when before whenever by the time while	time

Example sentences

1. **Although** the new academic advisor is not very friendly, she's not rude.

2. We aren't going to make our flight **unless** the security line is short.

3. **Whereas** I prefer to vacation at the beach, my family prefers to go to the mountains.

4. **Since** it was too early to go to the mall, we stopped at a restaurant and had breakfast.

5. He left himself a voicemail message **in order that** he would remember to bring the latest version of his report with him the next day.

6. They formed a study group for their business class **so that** they could divide up the work and meet to review for tests.

7. **As soon as** the snow starts melting, people start smiling and feeling better, knowing that winter is almost over.

8. I listen to the classical music station **whenever** I have the chance.

Conjunctive Adverbs / Transitional Words

Conjunctive adverbs are words or phrases which connect independent clauses or which introduce an independent clause. Because they show the relationship between ideas, sentences, and paragraphs, and add coherence to one's writing, many conjunctive adverbs are used as transitional devices.

Conjunctive Adverb / Transition	Use and Meaning
also besides furthermore in addition moreover	introduces another idea or more information
in that case otherwise	introduces a condition
however in contrast instead nevertheless nonetheless on the contrary on the other hand	introduces a contrast or concession
for example for instance in fact in other words that is (i.e.) to illustrate	introduces an explanation or example
accordingly as a result consequently for that reason hence therefore thus	introduces a result
afterward finally first last meanwhile next second then	introduces a sequence
also likewise similarly	introduces a similarity

Example sentences

1. I really didn't like the characters in the latest novel I read; **furthermore**, the plot made absolutely no sense.

2. She practices yoga for its health benefits; **moreover**, she says it's also a way for her to meet new people with whom she has something in common.

3. Please let me know if you plan to use your ticket for the concert; **otherwise**, I'll give it to someone else.

4. Lillian wants to live out in the country, away from the city; **however**, her husband prefers to live in the city because of his interest in art and the theater.

5. We hadn't planned to buy a new car until next year; **nevertheless**, when our old one broke down again last week, we bought a new one.

6. For some reason, Ella thinks her supervisor doesn't like her; **on the contrary**, her supervisor admires her and speaks highly of her.

7. I'm thinking about going back to school to study medicine because it's what I want to do; **on the other hand**, I don't know if I want to spend the next seven years of my life in med school.

8. Jason was let go from his job. **In other words,** he was fired.

9. He waited too long before he made a plane reservation; **consequently**, he couldn't get a flight to the conference.

10. I have to work late every night this week and on the weekend as well; **thus**, I won't be able to see you as planned.

11. Samantha practiced the piano for years. **Finally,** her perseverance was rewarded with a music scholarship to a four-year university.

12. Anita's brothers all worked for the family business; **likewise,** Anita expected to join the family team after she finished college.

Key Words

Key words act as signals: they give the reader an indication of the way a writer has organized a paragraph or essay. The key words listed below are commonly used with the text structure noted.

Key Word			Text Structure
against argue con for / pro should / should not	in favor of in fact oppose support	disagree must / must not ought to	argument
because / because of cause for since result	as a result of reason thus consequence	therefore due to effect as	cause / effect
category classify comprise consist of	divided into division sort part	type of kind group	classification / division
alike also and compared to differ from	in contrast to instead likewise same similar	too unlike versus whereas while	comparison / contrast
mean refer to	such as be defined as	is / are	definition
as an example as an illustration consider for example (e.g.)	for instance imagine that in the case of specifically	such as to demonstrate to illustrate	exemplification
impact on influence issue	option recommend warrant	answer benefit solution	problem / solution
how to method phase procedure process stage step after for X amount of time	beginning with during eventually finally first second before	third last meanwhile next once X happens starting with at the same time then	process / sequence
based on basically in general	generally many overall	some usually	summary

Chapter 1 – Definition

- a specific object (a piano, a computer, a microwave)
- an abstract concept (courage, love, friendship, fear)
- a field of study (nursing, marine biology, law, medicine)
- a political philosophy (communism, socialism, democracy, republic)
- a specific occupation (radiologist, peer coach, concert pianist)
- an environmental term or concept (global warming, fossil fuel, red tide)

Chapter 2 – Classification / Division

- people: types of students, teachers, friends
- specializations in a field: types of law, medicine, mechanics, pilots
- movies, books, music: different types or genres
- results of major events: types of effect (economic/political/social/psychological)
- problems: types of behavior, environmental, political, health

Chapter 3 – Problem / Solution

- computers: online safety, privacy, scams
- identity theft
- addictions: alcohol, tobacco, gambling, computer
- terrorism
- environmental: global warming, pollution, deforestation

Chapter 4 – Comparison / Contrast

- two wars: causes, how they were fought, outcomes
- two types of computers
- two careers
- two authors or film directors or actors
- two pieces of art or musical compositions
- two people

Chapter 5 – Process

- physics: how gravity works, how energy is transferred, how rain clouds form
- government: how a president is elected, how a bill becomes law
- culture: how to adapt to a new culture
- how to become a citizen
- how to prepare for an interview
- how to study for a test
- how hurricanes, tornadoes, or earthquakes occur

Chapter 6 – Summary

- literature: a short story or novel
- history: a historical period (the Industrial Revolution, the Gold Rush, the 1920s)
- debate of an issue
- political platforms of a specific political party
- business: the history of a company
- the culture of a specific country or group of people

Academic Word List: a list of words that will help prepare students for study at a college or university

analysis: a study of a specific topic and the components of which it is made

antonym: a word that means the opposite of another word

appositive: a word or phrase that describes or gives more information about a topic

audience: the readers of a piece of writing

body: the main part of a paragraph or essay, it contains the support for the topic sentence or thesis statement

brainstorming: generating ideas for topics and/or support by listing all the ideas that come to mind when thinking about a topic

cited works: a list of sources the writer has referred to or used in his/her work

classification: a style of writing in which items are first grouped or categorized according to their common or shared characteristics or traits and then analyzed

clustering: grouping similar items or ideas

coherence: used to describe writing that is clear and logical; writing that follows a logical order

compare/contrast: a style of writing in which two or more items are shown to be similar or different

controlling idea: indicates what the writer will address when discussing the main idea; the specific aspects of the main idea that will be addressed in the writing

definition: a style of writing in which the meaning of a term or concept is explained

detail: support or evidence for the statements the writer makes; major details support the topic sentence, and minor details provide more information and may include facts, statistics, or examples

draft: a piece of writing that is still in progress and that is not yet final or ready to be submitted

drawing a conclusion: using all the information presented in a piece of writing in order to make a judgment about a topic or viewpoint that has been presented

edit: to correct errors or rewrite unclear statements in a piece of writing

emphatic order: the order in which ideas are presented: smallest to largest, most well-known to least well-known, most important to least important, etc.

fact: a piece of information known to be true and which can be proved

free writing: a brainstorming technique in which the writer puts down, in sentence form, ideas as they occur in his/her mind

graphic aid: a visual image such as a chart, graph, diagram, or picture that accompanies a piece of writing

heading: a group of words which summarizes a section of writing; usually in bold font

inference: drawing a conclusion from indirect evidence or support the writer offers

listing: a brainstorming technique in which the writer puts down, in list form, ideas as they occur in his/her mind

main idea: the topic of a piece of writing; an implied main idea is not stated or directly written

opinion: the writer's personal view or feelings about a subject based on his/her knowledge or interpretation of the facts on a subject

outline: an organized list which summarizes the main ideas of a piece of writing

paraphrase: to restate a writer's ideas in your own words

pattern of organization: rhetorical or academic style, or text structure; a specific way of writing to show cause and effect, compare and contrast, definition, narration, etc.

predict: to anticipate what comes next in a piece of writing

problem/solution: a style of writing in which a problem is stated and possible solutions are offered; a preferred solution is often suggested in the conclusion

process: a style of writing in which the steps to a procedure or method of doing something are outlined

proofread: to look for errors in grammar, spelling, punctuation, and format in a piece of writing

purpose: the reason for writing: to persuade, inform, or entertain

revise: to make changes or corrections in or rewrite a piece of work

rewrite: to revise, to make changes or corrections in a piece of work

spatial order: presenting information according to place or area; for example, *on the left, on the right, above, below*

summary: a style of writing in which only the most important pieces of information are presented

survey: to look over something in order to get a general view or idea

synonym: a word that means the same as another word

text structure: pattern of organization or method of development writers use to express their ideas; examples include cause/effect, comparison/contrast, definition, narration, etc.

thesis statement: in an essay, the sentence or statement which contains the main and controlling ideas that will be presented

time order: presenting information chronologically, in the order in which events occur

tone: the attitude the writer has about the subject: serious, optimistic, critical, informative, etc.

topic: the general or main idea a piece of writing will discuss or focus on

topic sentence: in a paragraph, the sentence or statement which contains the main and controlling ideas that will be presented; for example, in the sentence "Thinking is a purposeful mental activity," the main idea is "thinking" and the controlling idea is "a purposeful and mental activity."

transition: a word or phrase that connects ideas, sentences, or paragraphs, resulting in a smooth flow of ideas between them

unity: used to describe writing that contains ideas which are all related to the topic; typically, each paragraph contains ideas related to one topic

APPENDIX 6 • MLA Style

In Chapter 6, guidelines and examples for citing sources using the APA style were used. Below are examples for citing the same sources using the MLA style.

Basic MLA Format—Books

A. Book—Author

Last name, First name. <u>Title</u>. Location: Publisher, Year of Publication.

Andrea, Alfred H., and James H. Overfield. <u>The Human Record: Sources of Global History</u>. Boston: Houghton Mifflin, 2005.

B. Edited Book—No Author

Last name, First name, ed. <u>Title</u>. Location: Publisher, Year of Publication.

Lauter, Paul, ed. <u>The Heath Anthology of American Literature: Concise Edition</u>. Boston: Houghton Mifflin, 2004.

C. Edited Book—With Author

Last name, First name. <u>Title</u>. Ed. First name Last name. Location: Publisher, Year of Publication.

Shakespeare, William. <u>The Complete Works of Shakespeare</u>. Ed. David Bevington. New York: Longman, 2006.

Electronic Sources

D. Web page

Author. "Title of Web Page." <u>Title of the Site</u>. Editor. Date and/or Version Number. Name of Sponsoring Institution. Date of Access <URL>.

Lorentz, M. "Life of the Buddha." <u>Emuseum @Minnesota State University, Mankato</u>. 2007. Minnesota State University, Mankato. 1 Sept. 2008 <http://www.mnsu.edu/emuseum/cultural/religion/buddhism/history.html>.

Text Credits

Chapter 1

Reading 1, pp. 3–4: Adapted from RUGGIERO. *BECOMING A CRITICAL THINKER. 4/E STUDENT TEXT*, 4E. © 2002 Wadsworth, a part of Cengage Learning, Inc. Reproduced by permission. www.cengage.com/permissions; *Reading 2, pp. 13–14:* Adapted from HMCO. *HOUGHTON MIFFLIN READING SERIES: MIDDLE*, 1E. © 2003 Heinle/Arts & Sciences, a part of Cengage Learning, Inc. Reproduced by permission. www.cengage.com/permissions; Adapted from RUGGIERO. *BECOMING A CRITICAL THINKER. 4/E STUDENT TEXT*, 4E. © 2002 Wadsworth, a part of Cengage Learning, Inc. Reproduced by permission. www.cengage.com/permissions.

Chapter 2

Reading 1, p. 37, Reading 2, pp. 46–47: Adapted from BERNSTEIN. *ESSENTIALS OF PSYCHOLOGY. 2/ETXT*, 2E. © 2002 Wadsworth, a part of Cengage Learning, Inc. Reproduced by permission. www.cengage.com/permissions; *Paragraph #1, chart, and paragraph #2, pp. 41–42; Paragraph from Activity 19, p. 57; Charts from Activity 22, p. 60:* Adapted from NEVID. *PSYCHOLOGY*, 1E. © 2003 Wadsworth, a part of Cengage Learning, Inc. Reproduced by permission. www.cengage.com/permissions.

Chapter 3

Reading 1, pp. 67–68; Activity 17, Part A, p. 83: Adapted from JEANNET. *GLOBAL MARKETING, 5E*, 5E. © 2001 South-Western, a part of Cengage Learning, Inc. Reproduced by permission. www.cengage.com/permissions; www.wto.org; *Reading 2, pp. 76–77; Parts B and C:* Adapted from MCFARLIN. *INTERNATIONAL MANAGEMENT. 2E*, 2E. © 2003 South-Western, a part of Cengage Learning, Inc. Reproduced by permission. www.cengage.com/permissions; *Summarize your paragraph, p. 89:* Adapted from PRIDE. *Business*, 8E. © 2005 South-Western, a part of Cengage Learning, Inc. Reproduced by permission. www.cengage.com/permissions.

Chapter 4

Reading 1, pp. 97–98: Adapted from WILSON. *AMERICAN GOVERNMENT: ESSENTIALS, 9E*, 9E. © 2004 Wadsworth, a part of Cengage Learning, Inc. Reproduced by permission. www.cengage.com/permissions; *Activity 7, Part A, p. 104:* Adapted from JANDA/BERRY/GOLDMAN/HULA. *The Challenge of Democracy*, 6E. © 2006 Wadsworth, a part of Cengage Learning, Inc. Reproduced by permission. www.cengage.com/permissions; *Activity 7, Part B, p. 104:* Reprinted with permission from *The Washington Monthly*. Copyright by Washington Monthly Publishing, LLC, 5471 Wisconsin Avenue, Suite 300, Chevy Chase, MD 20815. (240) 497-0321. Web site: www.washingtonmonthly.com; *Reading 2, pp. 110-111:* Adapted from SCHUBERT. *Introduction to Law and the Legal System*, 8E. © 2004 Wadsworth, a part of Cengage Learning, Inc. Reproduced by permission. www.cengage.com/permissions.

Chapter 5

Reading 1, p. 133; Activity 9, paragraph, p. 141; Reading 2, pp. 142–143; Activity 16, five paragraphs, p. 147; Unity, two paragraphs, p. 152; Activity 23, Parts A and B, p. 153; Activity 24, Parts A and B, pp. 154-155: Adapted from McDougal Littell

Chapter 6

Reading 1, pp. 161-162; Reading 2, pp. 171–172; Activity 23, Parts A and B, p. 179; Footnote example, p. 184; Adapted from WITT. *The Humanities, Volume I,* 7E. © 2005 Wadsworth, a part of Cengage Learning, Inc. Reproduced by permission. www.cengage.com/permissions.

Photo Credits

Chapter 1

Page 1, Vanni/Art Resource, NY
Page 24, Alexander Motrenko/Used under license from Shutterstock

Chapter 2

Page 37, Andersen Ross/Getty Images
Page 37, Jacob Wackerhausen/istockphoto.com
Page 37, Jose Luis Pelaez/Getty Images
Page 37, Catherine Jones/Used under license from Shutterstock

Chapter 3

Page 65, Anyka/Used under license from Shutterstock
Page 83, Getty Images

Chapter 4

Page 95, Emmanuel Dunand/Getty Images
Page 106, Library of Congress, Prints and Photographs Division Washington, D.C. [LC-USZ62-8278R]
Page 126, ColorBlind Images/Digital Railroad

Chapter 5

Page 131, Alinari/Art Resource, Inc.
Page 131, Alan and Sandy Carey/Getty Images
Page 131, Andreas Gradin/istockphoto.com
Page 131, Used under license from Shutterstock
Page 131, Gerry Ellis/Getty Images
Page 131, Galyna Andrushko/Used under license from Shutterstock
Page 152, Christopher Elwell/Used under license from Shutterstock

Chapter 6

Page 159, Resource Foto/Digital Railroad
Page 171, Amy Nichole Harris/Used under license from Shutterstock
Page 181, Craig Hanson/Used under license from Shutterstock
Page 182, The Granger Collection